Bamboo & Barbed Wire

Eight years as a volunteer
in a refugee camp

another goodbook

Bamboo and Barbed Wire
ISBN: 1 876 575 38 7

Margot Grant
72 Dunsborough Lakes Drive
DUNSBOROUGH
W Australia 6281

Email: margot@netserv.net.au
Website: http://www.geocities.com/pictim/index.html

Photographs © Margot Grant, Tim Grant & Bruce Horgan.
Cover Design by Tim Grant.
Cover Photo by Margot Grant.
Edited by Geoff Fortune

Published and produced in Western Australia by:

db Publishing
MANDURAH
WA 6210

0500 502 639
040 744 1147

Printed by:

Smallprint
7 Hampton St, MANDURAH
WA 6210
Ph: 9581 7946 e-mail: smallprint@tik.com.a

What started out as a bit of an adventure, or a chance to do 'something different', for a 56-year-old suburban housewife, turned into an overwhelming emotional and spiritual experience – one which lasted eight years and changed her life forever.

Far from the tranquillity of Western Australia, Margot Grant found herself surrounded by politics and war and she takes the reader with her into this climate. Her account of this unusual experience takes you behind the barbed-wire fence of a refugee camp. The camp, Site 2, on the Thai/Cambodian border, was home to more than 200,000 Cambodian displaced persons forced from their homes by years of war.

This story, told with humour and compassion ...

... tells of her ordeal when taken hostage by Khmer Rouge soldiers while participating in a Peace Walk, and her illegal forays into Cambodia by motorbike, boat, and on foot.

... depicts the fear, despair, resilience and courage shown by the camp people, their amazing will to survive at all costs, and how they lived from day to day while experiencing shelling, grenade and bandit attacks, and abuse by their Thai guards.

... describes daily life and camp life for the 350-odd foreign workers who entered the camp each morning to dispense medicine, treat the ill, teach, and care for the orphans, the elderly, the poor and the destitute.

... gives an insight into what drives workers to travel halfway round the world to work in dangerous and remote areas, and how they cope under daily pressure

... offers light-hearted accounts of the humorous moments, and explains the rewards gained from doing such worthwhile work while surrounded by ...

Bamboo and Barbed Wire

Acknowledgements

I would like to thank my family and many friends, who, through their never-ending support and encouragement, made this book possible.

Those who read the manuscript or part thereof, making useful suggestions: My sons, Chris, Tim and Roger, Beryl Yeomans, Aud Glaskin. Anna Marchesani, Phil Pope, the late Gerry Glaskin, Leo van der Pas, Tom Luongo, Therese Caouette, Agnes Bingham, Val Coventry, Malcolm Ramsay and Terri Bouquet.

Special thanks to Annie de Monchaux for her useful comments and criticism. Also to my son, Tim for his tireless work preparing the photographs.

All these people and others, gave me the encouragement I needed to keep going, when I was ready to toss it all in, because it was just too hard.

But most of all I would like to thank Ken Bingham, without whom this book would never have been attempted. He gave me the inspiration to get going and along the way supplied unending support and encouragement telling me, 'Of course, you can do it!'

This book is dedicated to my sons:
Chris, Tim and Roger
and to the memory of Russ,
who would have been so proud.

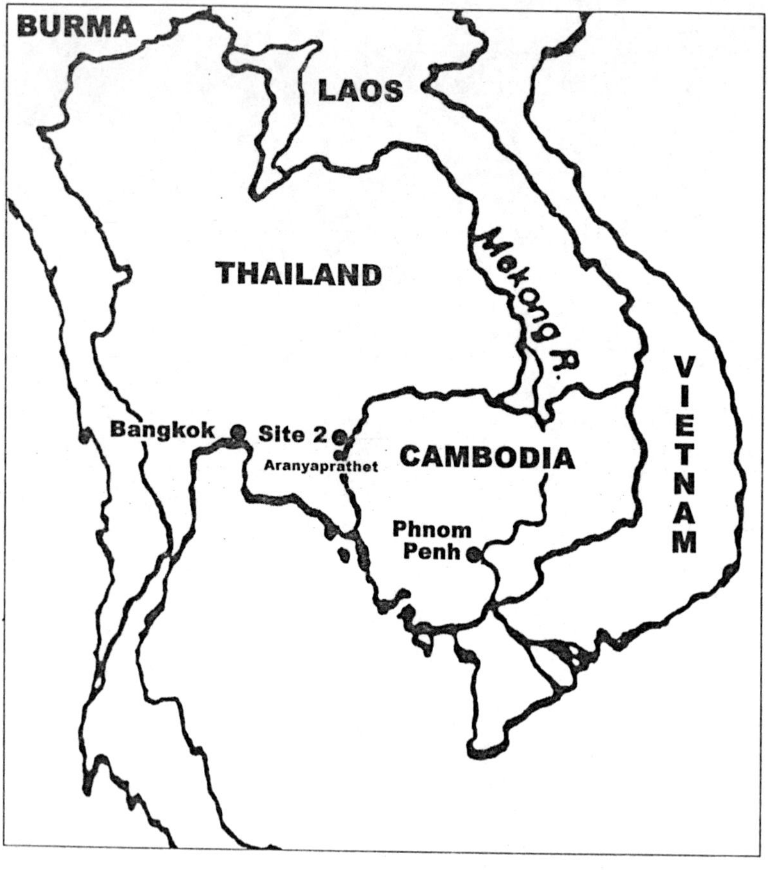
BURMA
LAOS
THAILAND
Mekong R.
VIETNAM
Bangkok
Site 2
Aranyaprathet
CAMBODIA
Phnom
Penh

SITE 2
NORTH
RESERVOIR
D.P.R.U.
CHECKPOINT
D.P.P.U
PRIMARY SCHOOL
HIGH SCHOOL
SITE 2
SOUTH

Security is mostly a superstition.
It does not exist in nature,
nor do the children of men as a whole experience it.
Avoiding danger is no safer in the long run than outright exposure.
Life is either a daring adventure, or nothing.
To keep our faces toward change and
behave like free spirits in the presence of fate is strength undefeatable.

-Helen Keller
Let Us Have Faith (1940)

Bamboo & Barbed Wire

CHAPTER 1

It sounded like all hell had broken loose. Gunshots, rockets screaming and exploding, soldiers shouting, moans of the injured, muttered prayers and gasping breaths from the young monk lying next to me on the ground. Could it have been only a short time ago I had been walking along a bush track in this remote area of Cambodia, enjoying the rare sight of a flock of white birds flying overhead, while relishing the peacefulness of the scene? Now I lay face down on the hard ground along with scores of others. I lifted my head slightly and looked around. Next to me lay my son, Tim, camera clutched in his hand, still taking photos even though danger threatened. I reached out to touch his hand and was rewarded with a wry smile. I gave a small prayer of thanks that we were together at this time.

Around us could be seen the bright orange robes of the monks and the white gowns of the Buddhist nuns, all spread-eagled on the ground, burying themselves as far into the dirt as possible to avoid flying missiles from the crossfire. On one side of us Khmer Rouge soldiers armed with AK 47s and RPG rocket-launchers, waged their guerilla war against the 'enemy', the soldiers loyal to the Cambodian Government. Our Peace Walk had stumbled on this battle and was now caught in the middle.

How had I got myself into this? It all started with a newspaper article I read back in Australia. 'Helpers Pitch in for Khmers' was the heading that caught my eye as I sat on my front verandah, drinking my morning coffee on a warm December day in 1984.

The following story of a local man, Max Francis, who had volunteered to work in a refugee camp on the border of Thailand and Cambodia, really caught my interest. The article described the wonderful work being undertaken there by dedicated workers, who willingly devoted their time to assist in these border camps. Try as I might, I could not get this article out of my mind. Surely I could give some of my time to help these unfortunate people, after all, what was I doing with my life that was useful? Nothing really! I always liked to do something different and this work sounded challenging and worthwhile.

I took stock. Here I was, a 56-year-old woman with plenty of energy, just whiling my life away in Perth. I had recently separated from my husband and my four adult sons were all busy with their lives. Chris was in Melbourne, Russ in the North-West, Tim in Sydney and Roger living in Belgium. For the last few years, I had split my time between teaching swimming to schoolchildren during summer months and working in the tax office, so there was absolutely nothing to keep me here.

Next morning I contacted Maria, the local woman, who had been named in this article, and made an appointment to meet with her to learn more about the situation. The following day, on arrival at her house, to my surprise, I was greeted by a woman around my own age, who ushered me into her living room where I met her husband, Neil, who had also visited the camps. Both seemed pleased to hear of my interest and desire to help these unfortunate people and they proceeded to give me a rundown on the situation.

Maria had been a constant visitor to the camps since they were first formed four years earlier, and had a good insight into the most pressing needs of the camp residents. The hours flew by, as we talked about the plight of the people flocking to the border and the very involved political situation. Finally, we discussed work possibilities and how my skills could best be utilized.

I learnt something of the history of the country. From 1975 to 1979, Cambodia had been under the control of the Khmer Rouge (Red Khmer), led by the notorious Pol Pot. Determined to transform the country into an agrarian, communist utopia, the Khmer Rouge xenophobic leaders closed the country's borders, abolished all currency, ordered all major cities emptied and established rice-growing collectives, which were planned to make the country self-sufficient. Instead, these rice crops failed, plunging Cambodia into desperate famine. During this period, Khmer Rouge extremists turned Cambodia into a vast killing field, responsible for the deaths of up to two million of the population from torture, execution, starvation and disease.

An invading Vietnamese army drove the Khmer Rouge from power in 1979, but by this time, the country's social infrastructure was in shambles. Although freed from Khmer Rouge domination, the Cambodian people held an age-old distrust of the Vietnamese and still feared for their lives. For years, they had dreaded a Vietnamese takeover, which had been likened by Prince Sihanouk to 'a starving boa constrictor leaping on an innocent animal'. This fear of the Vietnamese prompted many Cambodians to flee to Thailand, where they sought refuge in camps set up along the border by UNHCR (United Nations High Commissioner for Refugees).

Initially, all of these border camps were controlled by UNHCR with the assistance of the Thai Government, but as thousands more Cambodians fled and additional camps were set up, a new subsidiary UN (United Nations) group, UNBRO (United Nations Border Relief Organization) was formed in 1982. This group took over responsibility for all but one of these border camps, which became both refugee and resistance camps. Three resistance groups were formed by different factions, with members recruited from the border camps.

They were:

1. ANS (Armée Nationale Sihanoukiste) controlled by Prince Sihanouk and his family.
2. KPNLF (Khmer Peoples National Liberation Front) under the leadership of former Prime Minister, Son Sann.
3. KR (Khmer Rouge) reformed with remaining Khmer Rouge soldiers, who had fled to the border after the Vietnamese invasion.

A constant guerilla war was waged by these groups against the Vietnamese and Cambodian troops. Vietnamese were ranked as the most hated of Cambodia's enemies and always referred to as 'yuon', a derogatory term literally meaning 'savage'.

Each of the resistance factions was thoroughly engaged in its own military effort to throw the Vietnamese out of their country. Over the years, these groups would sometimes fight together against their common enemy, sometimes alone and many times against each other!

I Have a Go

I had recently returned to studies, gaining a mature age matriculation, which I followed up with a Diploma in Health Education. Maria was of the opinion that this last qualification could be put to good use in the camp and suggested that I write to COERR (Catholic Office for Emergency Relief and Refugees), the Thai organization with which she had been involved, to offer my services.

I duly despatched this letter to their head office in Bangkok, offering to work voluntarily for six months, then waited anxiously for a reply. Maria promised to follow it up.

By this time, I had made up my mind that this type of work was what I really wanted to do.

When I first read the article about the Cambodian refugee camps, I had only a vague idea where this country was situated. I recalled being horrified on seeing a '60 Minutes' show about Cambodia, featuring piles of human bones and skulls and realizing that these remains were once people. Somehow, I wanted to help.

On searching world maps to find where Cambodia was located, I was surprised to find a tiny country not much bigger than our state of Victoria. I felt quite ignorant and haunted the library, to locate as much literature as I could, to familiarize myself with the country's history.

A couple of months of anxious waiting went by and still I had not received a reply from COERR. In desperation, I rang Maria.

"Haven't you booked your air ticket to Thailand yet?" she asked in surprise.

Hardly daring to hope, I asked, "Does that mean I have the job?"

"Yes, you can go any time," was her laughing reply.

Full of excitement, I set about making plans to leave. My sons had already heard of my tentative plan.

"Go for it, Mum," was their encouraging answer. Now I could tell my friends.

Most people thought I was crazy. Their knowledge of Cambodia was about the same as mine had been, and they were concerned that I would be going into a dangerous war zone. How right they were!

I began to make my plans to leave. First, I had to tie up all business matters, find someone to look after my house, somewhere to leave my car and then book an air ticket. I had no idea what the living conditions would be, what clothes would be suitable, or if there would be access to shops, and by this time, Maria had left for Bangkok, so I had no one to ask. I packed everything I thought might come in handy, which eventually turned out to be far too much.

Teaching swimming would finish at the end of March, so I decided to leave as soon as possible after that. I was told all seats on the planes were booked for the next two months, but fortunately I secured a cancellation on a Thai bound plane for April 5th. As the time approached, I was getting most excited at the prospect of this new venture.

About two weeks before my departure date, I received a letter from Bangkok, in a COERR envelope. Expecting a 'welcome to the team' invitation, I tore it open only to be shocked to read the following:

Madam,

I wish to acknowledge the receipt of your letter dated the 15th January, 1985 offering your services to the COERR.

I sincerely appreciate your wonderful spirit but regret very much to inform you that at the moment there is no vacancy left in our organization.

Yours faithfully,

Rev. Fr Bunlert Tharachatr
Executive Director

I nearly hit the floor, I was so shattered! What would I do now? I had already made plans, tied up loose ends and was almost on the plane.

I rang Bangkok office to find what was going on. After telling my story, and of my disappointment at receiving the letter when I already thought I had the job, I was told, "Just come, anyway."

Relieved, but somewhat sceptical, I wondered what sort of organization this was, to which I was committing for the next six months. I could not envisage then that my involvement with COERR and the border camps, would last for the next eight years.

By the time I landed in Thailand, word had preceded my arrival at the COERR office and my employment had already been discussed. I was promptly ushered into the office of the Executive Director, Fr Bunlert, who never mentioned the letter of refusal, but greeted me warmly and welcomed me to the team.

Fr Bunlert, a Thai Catholic priest, with a serene face and kindly manner was a man in his late fifties, who I would have a lot to do with over the following years. During this time, I came to admire the compassion, generosity and humility shown by this kind and gentle man. He explained that I would be working in a newly formed KPNLF faction camp, situated seventy kilometres from the border town of Aranyaprathet, and that I would live in this town and travel along the border to Site 2 each day, as overnight stays in the camp were considered too dangerous for workers.

COERR was originally created by the Catholic bishops of Thailand, to provide emergency assistance to victims of natural disasters throughout the country. Later, it was extended to meet the needs of Thai villagers along the border, who had been affected by the war and to give assistance to Cambodian refugees who were pouring into Thailand. This agency operated on funds donated by Catholic charities from around the globe, their staff members being volunteers who only received a minimal living allowance.

I was taken to the operations office to meet other members of the staff and negotiate terms of my contract. Here I met the Thai accountant, Mr Manui, whom I found to be a brusque, grumpy old man, apparently uncomfortable with foreigners. The terms of my contract were that I would work for a period of six months on the social service programme in Site 2, for which I would receive a monthly stipend of 3,000 baht (approx AUD$150). I was required to cover the cost of my own fare, visa renewal, accommodation and food, which he told me, was standard procedure for volunteer workers. Mr Manui informed me it would take a week or two for my pass into the camp to be processed, as this task was undertaken by the Supreme Command of the Thai Military. Then he abruptly dismissed me, with instructions to return when it was ready.

My next step was to book into the YMCA near the office and familiarize myself with the large, sprawling city of Bangkok. It was an interesting and exciting metropolis with its beautiful pagodas, department stores, markets, street stalls, restaurants, modern hotels - many next to squalid buildings - and its very own Chinatown, complete with 'thieves' market. At night, the city completely changed its personality. Bright lights lit up the streets and vendors came from nowhere with their carts full of wares to be sold along the footpath. Formica-topped tables and rickety stools appeared as if by magic, together with carts displaying a variety of local foods to tempt the palate. The quiet daytime business area off Silom Road transformed into a red-light district with neon lights flashing, touts endeavouring to lure tourists into their sex shows and scantily clad girls arrayed on stools outside. The street so full of stalls selling an assortment of cheap goods that it was difficult to get through.

There was a variety of transport in this city. You could choose to sit on the pillion of a motorbike, which was the fastest, (but the most frightening), a minibus, bus, regular taxi, or a tuktuk, a converted motorbike with a covered seat for two at the back. I chose the two baht (five cents) bus, for my main mode of transport, for the service was excellent. I soon learnt to push my way on like everyone else; no standing back here, or you would find yourself left on the kerb. I became adept at keeping on my feet, as drivers careered through the unbelievably heavy traffic, twisting, turning and slamming on brakes. The bus map of Bangkok was invaluable, enabling me to find my way out whenever I considered myself hopelessly lost. This happened a number of times, until I became familiar with the city.

I found Thai people friendly and courteous, always ready with a smile for the foreigners. The girls on their way to work impressed me with their well-groomed appearance, beautifully dressed, as if on their way to a wedding, with never a hair out of place, despite being crushed into the overcrowded buses. How come they didn't sweat like we foreigners, in these unbelievably hot and humid conditions?

Over the next two weeks, I kept myself busy sightseeing, shopping in the markets and at street stalls, where goods could be bought for a fraction of the price, learning the art of bartering; most likely paying much more than locals, but happy with my 'bargains'. I visited pagodas, travelled up the klongs by boat, watched Thai dancing, ate Thai food and generally acclimatized myself to this new culture. Along the way, I learned about many of the cultural taboos. This knowledge would stand me in good stead over the years ahead. During this time, I kept in constant touch with the COERR office to check on the progress of my camp pass. Two weeks later I was advised it had finally come through.

Now I was almost on my way!

I wasted no time in making arrangements to leave for my new destination, as I was most anxious to start my new job. A COERR car arrived next morning to take me to the bus station, from where I would embark on the 350-kilometre journey to Aranyaprathet. After purchasing my ticket and leaving my cases to be stowed in the luggage compartment, I boarded the bus, settled in a seat at the back and looked around me, only to find I was the sole foreigner aboard. No sooner had we left the city than all heads around me were nodding. Not for me though; I did not intend to sleep, as I was afraid I would miss something.

The journey took us through a couple of larger towns, many small villages and kilometres of farmland. The fields were full of brown stubble from the previous season's rice crop, contrasted here and there with the bright green of rice seedlings ready for transplanting. Mango trees and coconut palms lined the roads that ran alongside small ponds filled with pink and mauve lotus blossoms, all combining to make a colourful display. It was siesta time and the only movement on the farms was the occasional buffalo constantly swishing its tail to keep off flies, or a lone dog moving to a shadier spot as the sun beat relentlessly down.

In contrast, the towns at which we stopped were hives of activity. Marketplaces were thriving; hordes of traders, their goods displayed in front of them on stands or on the ground, vied with each other for sales. Women in their brightly coloured sarongs, many with baskets balanced on their heads, bargained noisily for the best price. As the bus approached the villages, motorbike taxi riders playfully jostled each other for front position, hoping to secure the first passenger. I was enjoying this new scene, all so different to anything back home.

Finally, after a four-and-a-half-hour journey, we arrived in Aranyaprathet. I realized that we must be there, as all passengers had alighted and the bus driver was motioning for me to do the same. Following directions given by Mr Manui, I retrieved my luggage and struggled up the street with the heavy bags to the COERR office, which was situated only three hundred metres from the bus terminus.

I had learnt by now that you were on your own in this country, so I found my way to the office of the administrator, Father Sawaeng, a Thai priest. After introducing myself, I was relieved to find that he had been advised of my impending arrival. Although his English was very poor and I had to struggle to make sense of what he was telling me, I eventually caught the gist of it all. Essentially, he was telling me there was no designated job for me at present, but that I should go to the camp the next day, look around at the different services and see where I could make myself useful. This seemed a strange format to follow, for a big organization like COERR and even though I was disappointed, I would go along with it; after all, I had no choice. Later I was able to see the value of this exercise as it did allow me to get my bearings, see how the people lived and develop an insight into the conditions under which I would work.

Ning, a friendly Thai nurse, offered to show me to my quarters, situated above the office. Together we hoisted my heavy bags up the stairs, where she directed me to my new home. I could see four doors opening off a passageway, three of which, Ning told me were occupied by Thai nurses, the fourth, I was to share with a Burmese nurse, Maureen. This room, barely three metres square, contained two single iron beds, each with a wooden base, covered by a four-centimetre thick, hard kapok mattress, desk and chair, cloth collapsible wardrobe and a fan on a stand. The afternoon sun was beating in through the bare window and it was like walking into an oven. Now, looking around me in dismay at this hot, tiny, sparsely furnished room, I wondered how I would cope.

Seeing the look of apprehension on my face, Ning hastily guided me downstairs to familiarize me with the remainder of the facilities for the residents. There was a small kitchen with a refrigerator, coffee bar for workers, a table and four chairs. Three doors led off this room into separate bathrooms, where I received my biggest shock. In one corner was a bricked-in tub of water with plastic dipper, which, I was told was the 'shower'. This method of showering entailed standing on the floor, wetting yourself with dippers of water, soaping down your body, then rinsing off with more dipperfuls of cold water. I was aghast at the thought of having to shower in such a primitive manner. However, over the years, I came to find this an excellent way of cooling off after coming in dirty and sweaty from a day in the camp, even preferring it to the conventional shower, which was installed in some of the houses I later occupied.

Still more surprises were to come. In the other corner of the room at floor level, was a squat toilet with its own small tub of water with dipper for flushing. I realized that there would be no relaxing on the toilet with a good book here, for these were not made for comfort.

So, gone would be the soft bed, hot water, sit-down toilet, shower, television, telephone, washing machine and labour-saving devices to which I was accustomed. This would be my new life for the next six months. Though basic, I knew I could adjust and I was determined to make the best of it.

After unpacking a few immediate essentials and leaving the rest of my clothes in the case, mainly because there was nowhere else for them, I made my way downstairs for my first shower, Thai style. Feeling refreshed, I then ventured out to meet my colleagues. Workers were now arriving back tired, dusty and dishevelled after their day's work in the hot, humid conditions at the camp and as each member came in, I was introduced. They were divided into two teams - social services, to which I would be attached, and medical. The social service team consisted of a French priest, Father Pierre Ceyrac, Father John Bingham from USA, Annie Van Zoggel from Holland, an American Jesuit brother, Tom

Williams and Rasi, an Australian/Cambodian, who had come back to help his people. Over the years, this team would expand to include education and comprise over forty members, but at this time, there were only six. The medical team that staffed two hospitals in Site 2, consisted of thirteen people. Max, a medical technician from my home town, two doctors from Burma and one each from Thailand and Holland, plus eight Thai and Burmese nurses. I would travel into the camp daily in the medical van with this group, as there was no available social service transport.

That evening, I was taken on a tour of the town by Maureen, and two of the Thai nurses. Aranyaprathet was quite a large town, situated only four kilometres from the border. Before 1975, it had been a flourishing trading post for merchants coming in from Cambodia, but the war had put an end to the trading, now this crisis had transformed it, once again, to a boom town. Aid workers from all corners of the globe set up residence here, causing rentals to rise rapidly. As a result, shopkeepers were kept busy supplying equipment for camp programmes, traders shuttled goods across the border and journalists flocked to this, the closest town to Cambodia, anxious to secure the latest scoop on the war.

The roads were busy with agency vehicles, trucks, cars, buses, motorbikes, bicycles and pedicabs and there were many streets full of shops. My guides took me to the large market in the centre of the town, where I was amazed to see the variety of goods on sale in the stalls - clothes, hats, bags, shoes, kitchen utensils, baskets, flowers, cooked food, vegetables, fruit, meat - all available in one place. I realized that I need not have worried about bringing stocks of toiletries with me from home, as I could buy them much cheaper here. As we approached the centre of the building, we were assailed by this offensive odour I could not identify, but it was not long before I discovered the source of this smell. We had arrived in the meat market. Under the dome of the building, scores of benches were set up, each one displaying different chunks of meat with the animal hide still on them. Above the benches hung more meat samples, plus chickens and ducks complete with heads and big basins of water with live fish swimming in circles. Around and all over the meat were thousands of flies. Sellers sat gossiping with other stallholders and peremptorily flicking their homemade flyswats - a piece of bamboo with a plastic bag tied on the end - over their wares. There was no refrigeration and I wondered just how they managed to keep the meat from rotting in this heat, or did they? I was to see these meat markets many times over the years but never acclimatized to the repulsive odour of unrefrigerated raw meat.

When we arrived back at the office, Max was waiting for me. He had been working here for almost six months, so was familiar with the area and offered to take me out for dinner to introduce me to the eating places around the town. He pointed out many venues, from one quite modern restaurant to small cafes to open-air stalls with seats outside and a range of cooked food on display. We chose Ploens, an up-to-date restaurant, which sold both Western and Thai meals and was a popular meeting place for the expatriate community. The food was very tasty and quite cheap.

After a delicious Thai meal, Max took me around the corner to a small cafe called Khim Khim's. This place was especially popular on Sunday, when many of the foreigners congregated to chat and partake of pancakes and ice-cream; the only shop that sold these delicacies in this remote town. Their ice-creams were delicious and came in many flavours, including durian (a strongly flavoured local fruit) and corn. After enjoying a strawberry sundae, it was time to head back to my quarters and retire to bed, tired out after a long but interesting day.

Heading In - to what!

I rose early next morning, quite excited at the prospect of my first day in the camp. Many of the drivers, office staff and fellow camp workers were already downstairs crowded around the coffee bar, having the last cup before heading off to work. At 7am sharp, all workers boarded their respective vehicles bound for the camp and I joined the medical team in their van for the two-hour drive.

We were stopped at the first military checkpoint about ten kilometres from Aranyaprathet. Soldiers approached the driver of the van to check our camp passes that had already been collected and sent forward. These passes were thoroughly scrutinized and followed by a headcount before we were waved on our way. Back on the road, we joined a steady stream of cars, vans and trucks from United Nations and other agencies, all heading in the same direction.

Along the way we passed the first of the camps, KID (Khao-i-dang). Behind a high bamboo fence surrounding the camp, I could just make out rows and rows of bamboo huts. Max explained to me that this was a holding camp, the only border camp still under the control of UNHCR. Here were housed the people, who had passed the first criteria for resettlement in a 'third' country - one that could offer them a safe haven. They would still have another two or three interviews and several more processes to complete before they could be deemed eligible. The successful ones would then be transferred to Phanat Nikhom, another camp closer to Bangkok. Here, they would learn the language of their new country and attend orientation classes to equip them for the transfer into their new culture.

However, only a very small percentage of Cambodians made it legally into Khao-i-dang and even fewer to a third country. Over the years, hundreds of people from other camps would enter illegally at night, with the hope that they would be accepted for interviews and eventually resettlement. Some did make it, but hundreds of not so lucky ones languished in this camp for years without a food ration, before being returned to other camps or finally back to Cambodia. A few hundred metres from KID we passed another settlement, Site 7 or Ban Phu. This camp was surrounded by a high barbed wire fence with strategically placed boxes on stilts, all containing guards with guns, poised ready to deter any escape attempt into KID camp.

After an hour's driving, we pulled up at the COERR store the small village of Tapraya. Here, the nursing staff went through the daily ritual of filling iceboxes with medical needs from the refrigerator, as there was no electricity in Site 2. Next stop was the town market, where everyone alighted to select their breakfast and food to take to camp for lunch. The market, set in the centre of the village, was similar to its counterpart in Aranyaprathet but on a smaller scale. Stalls set up around the outside, sold a variety of piping hot food cooked on small claypot stoves that were on the ground, positioned next to the stall. The main purchases by our group were the rice porridge (a favourite breakfast dish for Thai staff), a variety of rice dishes, and rice cakes, which were delicious and enjoyed by foreigners and Thais alike, as well as many varieties of fresh tropical fruit. Then it was off for the last leg of the journey into Site 2.

We had left the sealed road and were now on a narrow dirt track heading towards the camp. Clouds of dust, stirred up by countless vehicles, enveloped our van and I wondered how the driver could possibly see the road ahead. Along the way, we passed through four villages containing clusters of small, weathered wooden houses on stilts. These were occupied by poor farming families classified as 'affected Thais', because of their close proximity to the border. The soil was of very poor quality, thus, the farmers waged a constant battle for survival.

In addition, their lives were punctuated by regular identity checks, intermittent evacuations due to shelling and the ever-present fear of death or maiming from the thousands of landmines dotting the landscape. Next to many houses were large cement water containers with 'UN' emblazoned on them, donated to the villagers by the United Nations.

The Thai Government decreed that owing to the disruption in their lives, the UN must provide assistance and be responsible for the maintenance of the roads passing through their settlements. These formerly isolated settlements, now had a daily flow of heavy traffic cutting through their farmland, causing noise, danger and clouds of red dust that hung in the air, coating houses, trees and crops. This only added to the rigour of their lives. Eventually, the UN supplied villagers with a communal well, but at present they made do with rainwater or water carried in buckets from the town dam.

There was no slowing down on the part of our Thai driver as we made our way towards the camp. He went full pelt along narrow, potholed roads and through villages, not even reducing speed to manoeuvre the sharp bends, which were invariably taken on the wrong side of the road. It took all his skill to avoid the bicycles, carts, chickens, ducks, pigs, dogs and sometimes buffalo, sharing the road with us. As I sat with my fingers gripping the seat in front, I wondered if I would ever get out of this country alive! While home on leave a few months later I was not surprised to hear that one of the COERR cars was involved in a rollover on the way to the camp. Sadly, a young American volunteer, who had just finished her medical training, was left a paraplegic as a result of this accident.

The countryside around us had now deteriorated to nothing more than sun-scorched scrubland, with no farms or animals in sight on the approach to our destination. As I looked around, the bare fields gave way to a conglomeration of makeshift buildings and I experienced my first glimpse of Site 2 camp. Alongside the road stood a two-metre high fence strung with barbed wire, behind which, could be seen endless rows of bamboo and thatch huts set about two metres apart. Here and there were makeshift canopies of bright blue plastic, housing families who had not yet built their homes.

As we stopped at the entrance, armed soldiers appeared from their enclosure and camp passes were thoroughly examined before a sign-in board was produced for all team members to sign. On departure, we were required to sign out in the box provided next to our earlier signature. This board was checked by UNBRO security before the camp could be closed each night, to ensure that no one was left behind. I realized there would be no chance of entering this camp without the required pass, for this was our fourth checking by soldiers along the way. What could possibly lay ahead that would require such tight security?

We drove in through the gates and I craned my neck to see as much as possible of this whole new scene, but nothing could have prepared me for the sight that met my eyes. People were everywhere, stirring up clouds of red dust; men in their T-shirts and long pants, chequered krama (Cambodian scarf) around their necks; women and girls in light-coloured tops and patterned sarongs; little naked boys running around, handicapped on crutches and in wheelchairs; people on bicycles; others pushing handmade carts, mothers carrying babies on their backs, held there with kramas tied over the shoulder - and the noise! Shouts, babies crying, cocks crowing, children squabbling, workmen hammering and the constant babble of voices were overwhelming and I wondered just how I would adjust to this life and would I ever get used to this noise?

The roads were crowded with human traffic, as we wended our way through along the dusty, dirt track leading to the hospital run by COERR. I couldn't believe this was the hospital when the van pulled up and passengers alighted. I guess I had expected to see a typical white building with a red cross painted on top; instead, I saw a long bamboo structure with thatch roof, the sides comprised of shards of bamboo, woven into a lattice-like pattern and erected up to waist height, then open to the roof. Next to this, an open-air construction of thick bamboo uprights supporting a thatch roof was used as an 'outpatients clinic', where hundreds of sick men, women and children received medical attention each day. Now it was filled with queues of people waiting patiently for the medical staff to arrive and administer to their needs. As we left the van, we were immediately surrounded by people clamouring for attention; staff, patients, children, all talking, shouting and clutching at our clothes. It took a few minutes before order was restored and the medical staff could get on with their work.

Before consultations could begin, tables had to be set up and medical supplies arranged on the back of the supply truck, for dispensation. As soon as these tasks were completed, the nurses turned their attention to the stream of outpatients and the doctor on duty, with two of his Cambodian medics, commenced his rounds.

The hospital held about thirty wooden-based beds on which the patients lay, without any mattress or covering over them. Suspended between the beds, at intervals, were hammocks that many of the patients had brought with them, preferring them to the uncomfortable hospital beds. In the centre of the building stood a blackboard. On this was chalked bed numbers and a description of each patient's complaint, showing patients with malaria, chronic infections, tuberculosis, pneumonia, bullet wounds and numerous ailments. Three beds together at the end of the ward, held women with small babies. One mother, realizing I was a new worker, beckoned me over and handed me her baby to nurse. I could not keep the tears back as I looked down at this wafer-thin baby girl in my arms, with skin pulled tight over her bones, arms and legs no thicker than my thumb and a massively protruding belly. The medic told me that this child was suffering from heart problems and malnutrition and would most likely only live a few more days. Although only the size of a newborn baby, I was told she was six months old. I requested permission from the mothers to take photos of them with their children, promising that I would bring the photographs as soon as they were developed. As I left, I could not help but think of our healthy, well-nourished babies at home and how privileged we are to have medical services so readily available.

The obstetric ward at the end of the building was closed off from this open ward by a wall of plastic sheeting. Immediately after giving birth, the mother and new baby were taken into the main ward with other patients. Beds containing new mothers could be easily identified by the coal fire burning beneath, the woman wrapped in blankets and lying in a bath of perspiration. When I asked the medic the purpose of this procedure, I was told that this was traditional treatment to correct the imbalance of hot and cold within the body. This remedy seemed so out of place in this hot and humid climate but the people really believed in it. After the birth, mother and baby stayed in the hospital for a day before being taken home by their husbands, sometimes walking or more often riding sidesaddle on the back seat of a bicycle with the baby in their arms. Surprisingly, only a small percentage of camp babies were born at the hospital, as the mothers were still unsure about Western medicine, trusting themselves instead to the services of one of the many traditional midwives operating in the camp. The birth rate in Site 2 was among the highest in the world, estimated at 65-75 per 1,000 population, resulting in almost 50% of the camp population being under the age of fourteen.

Small children, chickens and dogs roamed the dirt floor of the hospital making it difficult for medical staff to attend to their patients. Whole families gathered around the bed of family members, sometimes with the claypot stove on the floor next to it, cooking their rice. Toilets situated only three metres from the building, comprised a hessian-covered frame around a hole in the ground, with the smell emanating from these facilities attracting hordes of flies. When I saw an IV bottle hooked over the top of the frame, while its user was occupied in the toilet, I wondered how anyone could possibly recover from an illness under these unhygienic conditions!

As I walked down the ward, I noticed a crowd had formed beside one of the beds. Here Dr Rob was performing a spinal tap on a patient with suspected TB meningitis, while a host of interested onlookers gathered, including a US press cameraman taking photos of the procedure. No anaesthetic was administered and it took four men to hold the patient down while the doctor struggled to complete the task. I was told that the extracted fluid would be taken to KID hospital to be tested, with the results being sent back at a later date.

Meantime, at the outside clinic, wounds were being dressed, throats and ears checked, medicines dispensed, abscesses lanced, cuts stitched; all with audiences of curious onlookers pushing in to get a closer look. I was amazed that the nurses were not at all fazed to be working under these seemingly intolerable conditions. There appeared to be an endless stream of sick and ailing people requiring attention, for as fast as the queues diminished, more patients replaced them. As I was watching the nurses treating their patients, two men hurried in with a sick patient lying in a hammock suspended from a pole, which was carried on their shoulders. This was the only means of transporting ill or injured patients or women in labour, to the hospital. If a patient needed surgery or advanced medical treatment they were taken by 'ambulance' to KID hospital, where an operating theatre run by ICRC (International Committee of Red Cross), was connected to electricity. The ambulance used to transport them was a utility with a rear canopy, under which, patients were placed on a thin mattress on the floor for an extremely uncomfortable one-hour ride over very rough roads to KID hospital.

After what seemed an age, the morning patients had been attended to and the Cambodian staff adjourned to their homes for a two-hour lunchbreak. Hammocks could be seen swinging outside the huts as people partook of this siesta time all over the camp. In the outdoor clinic, chairs and tables were pulled together and staff gathered around for lunch. I was amazed at the food that was brought out by the Thai staff and wondered how such little people could eat so much. They invited me to share in their feast, as more and more rice and noodle dishes were spread out on the table.

No sooner had we sat down and commenced to eat, than small children appeared and gathered around. It was very unnerving, attempting to eat under the soulful gaze of all those eyes and I could not help but pass some tidbits behind to the children. These were gratefully taken, held on to until lunch was over, when all the children gathered together to divide their spoils. It was very touching to see these youngsters, who had so little but were willing to share with others.

When lunch was over, I decided to walk around, to get my bearings and have a look at some of the programmes operating in the camp. No sooner had I taken off than a retinue of small children formed at my back, where they stayed two steps behind me all afternoon, giggling every time I looked at or spoke to them. Cambodian children are most appealing, with big brown eyes and beautiful smiles. Their favourite cry when they saw a foreigner was, "Okay, bye, bye" and I was followed by this chant on my way around. I was amazed at the children, who seemed forever happy, never appearing to be affected by the problems all around them. Whether playing games with thongs, rubber bands, or marbles made of dried mud, they always managed to find enjoyment and laughed, giggled and squealed with delight, as they played in the dust and mud.

I found my way to the workshop for the handicapped, which was a COERR project run by an American Jesuit brother, Tom. It was sad to see so many handicapped people, mostly landmine victims. Some were blind, others who had lost a limb, and double amputees were confined to homemade wooden chairs. Tom told me that most of the handicapped were young men, who had been soldiers, but he also had among his students a woman amputee, who stepped on a landmine while collecting wood, and a small boy who lost a leg tending buffalo inside Cambodia.

One of the handicapped men, who spoke some English, was anxious to show me around, as he was very proud of the workshop and his co-worker's achievements. First he took me to the zinc shop where metal bowls, cups and buckets were being cut and welded. COERR supplied a generator that was in full use every day in this workroom, with special permission being granted by the Thai military to bring in fuel to keep it operational. The workshop was quite big and full of men, some on crutches, others in wheelchairs, still others with only one arm, but all hard at work. They stopped what they were doing when I entered, greeting me with big smiles and the traditional Cambodian greeting of clasped hands to the forehead. I spent quite some time here, watching them at work and answering numerous questions fired at me about my nationality, age and family.

We finally dragged ourselves away and headed for the next stop, the blacksmith shop, where axes and tools were made and repairs carried out. The men working here were covered in sweat from the intense heat of the huge fire but were only too pleased to stop work to greet their visitor and show me their finished products. After some time, bombarded with the same questions, we ventured on to the carpentry shop. One group of men was busy making bamboo and wooden furniture, another group was attending a woodcarving class in another part of the room. I was amazed at the quality of goods being produced; workmanship in all areas being top class, considering the workers were all handicapped in some way, the primitive tools being used, and the conditions under which they worked. It was good to see these skills being learned and applied, as they should hold them in good stead when they returned to their country. It was mid-afternoon when I stepped outside the building, to be greeted with whoops of delight by my little followers, who had waited patiently for me. Next day, I decided, I would bring a bag of sweets for the camp children.

I still had an hour or so to spare, as camp closing time was 5pm and I would need to be back at the hospital, fifteen minutes before. As I wandered the streets, I was greeted along the way by smiles and clasped hands. Women came up to me and rubbed their hands up my arms, then laughed delightedly. I couldn't make this out, until I was told later that Cambodians do not have hairs on their arms and they thought it hilarious that we had and loved to feel them. Along the road, I saw a makeshift shelter of bamboo and plastic, which I soon realized was a dental clinic. A woman sat in the chair while the Cambodian dentist performed a tooth extraction, making not a sound, as the operation took place without anaesthetic. However, I could see her whitened knuckles as she gripped tightly to the sides of the bamboo chair. After the extraction, she jumped out to make way for the next patient, then walked off spitting blood.

Spitting was something I realized I would have to get used to, as everywhere I went I could see people spitting on the ground. There were red spots from betel nut chewers, and many other disgusting dobs that I don't want to go into. Sometimes you would admire a beautiful, well-dressed young woman, then she would spit and spoil the whole image.

Overall, there was an air of poverty in the camp, with many people in virtual rags, or shirts and sarongs badly in need of laundering because these were their only clothes. As I looked around, it was obvious that so many of these people were in dire straits, but this did not take the smile off their faces. I wondered how they could live under such terrible conditions and still be able to smile!

Water tankers could be seen all over the camp, disgorging their contents into metal tanks set at intervals along the roads. Every day, chlorinated water was trucked in from dams nearby, for there was no natural water supply in the camp. Muddy water from camp reservoirs was unsuitable for consumption but in the hot, dry season when there was a dire shortage, many people used this water for bathing or washing clothes. Residents knew the approximate time of the tanker's arrival and would be waiting patiently in line with their buckets or cans, sometimes waiting in the hot sun for hours, until the tankers turned up with their precious supplies. Each person received an allowance of seventeen litres of water per day. This was never enough for cooking, drinking, bathing and washing clothes, and certainly contributed to the high incidence of skin infections suffered in the camp. In the hot months, this ration was often reduced when dams inside Thailand, the main source of supply, dried up. Ideally, water is recommended at 100 litres, per person, a day.

As these converted petrol carriers commenced filling the tanks, cans were pushed under the connections to catch escaping drops, babies were washed under leaking hoses and little boys took advantage of the mud pools made by escaping water. Many water carriers were small children, a bamboo pole strung across their small shoulders with a bucket of water balancing at each end. Their little legs would almost collapse under the heavy weight, as they waddled along so as not to spill a precious drop.

Along the tracks between the huts, I could see small bamboo and hessian-covered structures near some of the houses. I soon realized what they were when I got close, as the smell from these makeshift toilets was overpowering. A number of families shared each toilet that consisted of a cement slab with a slit in the middle, which had been placed over a hole in the ground with a can of water beside it to use for flushing.

I received many invitations to come inside as I wandered through the housing area. I accepted a couple of times and as I entered, a place was cleared for me on the bamboo bed and a glass of water offered. I was touched by the warmth of the people's hospitality. Communication was difficult, for not many people spoke English, but I soon discovered that I could make myself known with universal sign language.

It was getting late when I arrived back at the hospital and nurses were busily packing up the medical supplies, which were taken out of the camp every night. A roster of Cambodian medics stayed on duty, to see to the needs of patients until morning. However, this was not always necessary, as most of the beds were emptied when families took their sick members home. This was due to the fear of a shelling attack and they wanted all the family together should this occur. Patients were all back in their beds next morning when medical staff arrived.

Finally, the packing was done and I took my place in the van with the medical staff for the two-hour journey back to Aranyaprathet. As I thought back over my day's activities, I was excited at the prospect of working with these people and I promised myself that I would do my best to make a better life for them.

A huge rainstorm hit that night, contributing to extremely high humidity, while the one oscillating fan in our bedroom did little to alleviate the heat. My roommate, Maureen, was a devout Christian and I had no choice but to listen, as she knelt in the middle of the floor and loudly said her prayers. I lay awake for hours, thinking about the camp, my mind ticking over with a myriad ideas about where my efforts could best be used. I could not help but ponder on the plight of the camp people, running from Vietnamese invaders after all they had been through during Pol Pot's reign; it just did not seem fair. I made a mental vow not to get too attached to anyone in camp, as it would be too hard when the time came to leave. Hours later, I drifted into fitful sleep, dreaming of children grabbing food from my hands, stashing it under hospital beds where it caught alight, patients screaming and fleeing.

It's Called - 'Site 2'

THE CAMP

The people in Site Two
Are too full of sadness,
Some husbands are dead
And there are poor families
Visages are dreary,
Black visages,
Unhappy
Sorrow in their lives
Having no money
Can make our hard worry
Haven't someone who can be near
Or teach, or speak, or laugh
Their words ignored,
Despairing, unlucky
Haven't someone to help
Or introductions from another
This is the kind of sadness.
Of the people in Site Two

Sovanny – a Site Two resident

After the collapse of the Khmer Rouge regime in 1979, which resulted in the Vietnamese occupation of Cambodia, thousands of starving, emaciated Cambodians flocked across the border into Thailand, seeking assistance. ICRC and UNHCR co-ordinated an emergency relief programme to meet with their urgent needs. Camps to house these people were set up along the border, and as refugees arrived, they were directed to the nearest site. What the people did not know then was that these makeshift camps would prove to be relatively permanent, as it would be thirteen years before the last ones were emptied.

A ruling was made that Cambodians fleeing to Thailand would be classed as 'displaced persons'. This dubious title meant they were denied the status of 'refugee', which would have automatically given them the right to safe haven, protection and acceptance by the country in which they took refuge. But no country was willing to take responsibility for them. This distinction was a cruel blow for the Cambodians, many of whom had fled to the border with the hope of gaining resettlement in a country where they had close relatives. Now they were stuck, unrecognized and unwanted in a land not their own, with nowhere to go.

Site 2, set up in 1985, was the largest of the border settlements and was formed to house tens of thousands of people, who fled when their former camp Site 1 had been mercilessly shelled by government troops on Christmas Day, 1984. Set at the foot of the Dong Rek mountain chain, the camp occupied a dry and barren area of former rice fields. Identified in the distance by a pall of smoke and red dust haze, it posed a dreary sight to arrivals entering from the Thai side. Behind the barbed wire, dirt roads set out in a grid pattern, intersected the confines of the encampment, while bamboo huts lined these roads.

Thai military, TF80 (Task Force 80) and UNBRO, which held joint responsibility, were under the strict control of the Military Supreme Command in Bangkok, which had the ultimate authority over all border camps. Their major issues were national security and the impact of these camps on Thai villagers along the border, while the UN was responsible for the welfare of camp inmates.

TF80 rangers, who guarded Site 2 and the border, wore black uniforms with chequered scarves reminiscent of the Khmer Rouge, thus striking fear into the hearts of the camp people. Rumours flew around that TF80 members were young men, who had broken the law and were given the choice of prison or the dangerous task of working on the border. These stories were never verified, but believed by most with whom they came in contact, as camp people were victims of many crimes perpetrated against them by these rangers. The camp law enforcement system, in the early years was unable to protect the population from the violent abuses of these security forces, bandits and Khmer soldiers, sneaking over the border at night. Despite a curfew, many people were assaulted, robbed and raped after dark and people lived in fear when aid workers left the camp at the end of the day. One of my friends once told me that if a robber entered the house, family members turned their heads to the wall, fearing reprisals should they identify the intruder. After years of complaints regarding the behaviour of TF80 troops, they were finally replaced in August 1988 by a new unit, DPPU (Displaced Persons Protection Unit).

In 1985, Site 2 housed approximately 40,000 Cambodian displaced persons, growing to more than 200,000 people by the early nineties. During this time Site 2 expanded geographically to accommodate these dramatically increasing numbers, causing the boundaries to expand from one and a half by three kilometres to more than six square kilometres. Inside this enclosure were four separate camps, Ampil, Dong Rek, San Ro, Nong Chan, with a small section set aside for Vietnamese. Later, they would be joined by another three groups - Rithysen, Obok, and Nam Yun. Each camp was completely autonomous, run by its own administration, with leaders appointed by the people. They were divided into sections, which contained between one and three thousand individuals, with a leader appointed by administration, to attend to the needs of the people in his section. This leader was responsible for keeping records of all residents under his care, ensuring that they were allocated their correct water and firewood rations, settling squabbles and disputes, following the format adopted by villages in Cambodia.

Life in a displaced persons camp was very difficult. Residents very livelihood, balancing on rations of food, water, firewood trucked in by UN; shelling, landmines, violence, banditry becoming part of their everyday life. Completely cut off from the outside world, their lives were spent in the confines of the barbed wire enclosure, awaiting a political resolution that would enable them to return to their homeland. Once inside, it was almost impossible to leave. Transfers to other camps were difficult to obtain and these limited only to reunification of family members. If fighting was severe, and this happened quite often, the camp would be closed to all traffic, leaving the people without food or water, sometimes for days.

A woman living in Site 2 wrote her version of life inside the encampment:

> *The Khmer people cannot leave Site 2. They are forbidden to go outside the fence. If they try, they may be killed, wounded or raped. Not even only outside the camp, but also inside the camp people are killed, raped and extorted by robbers. What can we do to defend ourselves against these violations of our human rights? We can do nothing, because we have no rights. We are 'displaced persons' - people without a country, without representation, like forgotten prisoners.*

Head Count

Food rationing was very severe in 1985, when I first arrived. The UN, wishing to remain neutral, allocated rations only to women and girls over ten years old or over three foot tall, with girls under this height, eligible for a smaller allowance. Rations were denied to males, as many were KPNLF soldiers and the powers that be decreed that little boys grew up to be men, and men became soldiers. This ridiculous ruling left families with a large number of male members on starvation level. It would be two years before the UN eventually relented and issued family books making all family members eligible for a ration.

Distribution of food, water and firewood was strictly controlled and only released on presentation of the ration card. To gain this treasured document, a headcount was undertaken every three months. I had not been working in the camp long when volunteers were requested to assist with distribution of these cards, so I offered my services, not realizing what I was in for.

On the appointed day, helpers arrived in camp early and were escorted to a compound where thousands of women sat on their haunches in rows of approximately one hundred persons. They had been waiting for two hours when we arrived and already the heat was stifling. About twenty volunteers assembled for a short briefing by a Thai woman worker, before commencement of duties. We were directed to walk down the pathway between the rows of waiting people, looking to each side to establish if any men were in line, dressed as women. If we were suspicious, we were to ask them to stand up, take off their headgear and if still uncertain, ask their name so as to check the voice. I did not see any men in my area and would not have exposed them if I did, as I considered they must be really desperate to take such risks to get a ration.

However, at the finish of this screening, four men had been discovered in the lines and were banished from the compound, enduring the laughter of the crowd, as they sheepishly made their way out.

After this debacle, we were each given a handful of ration cards and allocated a path to take between the rows. We were then directed, on a given signal, to walk down the line handing out cards to right and left, keeping the same pace as other volunteers, lest the women swap lines to obtain an extra card.

At the signal, a loud blast of a whistle, we commenced our duties along the designated paths. I found it to be a distressing experience, as I was beset with pleas for a second card, imploring looks, hands grabbing at me and cries of despair when their pleas went unanswered. Somehow, two of our number had lagged behind and as we reached the end, people surged from the back grabbing cards, nearly knocking us over. It was bedlam, until officials with speakers calmed them down, restored order and the women were guided back to their lines.

By this time, all my cards were gone, snatched from my hand before I had time to respond. I was upset at witnessing and being involved in this degrading scene. Surely, some other way could be devised for distribution. But the humiliation was not over yet.

Next, we were led to an adjoining compound, where rows and rows of small children either sat or crouched on the ground waiting to receive their ration cards. After the whistle signal was given, the children were pushed through quickly, past six scrutineers looking first for boys dressed as girls, then checking heights of any children suspected of not reaching the three-foot standard. Boys had grown their hair long and were decked out in sarongs, with earrings, hair clips and scarves or hats, hoping to pass the identification and be rewarded with a food card. They could be easily picked out; their disguises usually overdone. These interlopers were soon pulled out by Thai staff, who grabbed them down below if they were not sure of their sex. These actions brought forth peals of laughter from the Thais but were looked on with disgust by the foreigners. Some boys were lucky enough to get through despite the surveillance. One little boy received his card before he was challenged. He took off, weaving his way through the crowd, dodging the guards, before he made his escape to the cheers of the people waiting on the other side of the fence.

While this was taking place, children were still being examined, to choose those eligible for the treasured cards. To reach the required height, some little girls wore shoes built up by gluing two or three soles of thongs together. Little ones were standing on tiptoes, others were held up from behind by older sisters, when they were placed under the bamboo measuring stick. At the end of the ordeal, only about three-quarters of the children had passed the test and been rewarded with food cards. After witnessing this debacle, I decided that I would not participate in one of these degrading operations again.

Over the years of my travels around the camp, I witnessed many similar line-ups including one for pregnant women, who were entitled to a special nutritional ration. Nurses were present in a tent, to examine women, to determine if they were more than seven months pregnant, which was the time for eligibility. Many women lined up, some with a pillow stuffed down their sarong hoping to pass the scrutiny and be rewarded with a card. Still another handout was held for babies and children under three years old or under three feet tall. Mothers with these small children would have to wait for hours behind a two-metre high bamboo fence, before commencement of distribution, then, after receiving their card were directed to leave by the gate. However, many attempted to squeeze back in between the bamboo sticks or if this was not possible, to push their screaming toddlers through to mothers already waiting. If found, the women were chased and dragged out by guards, who patrolled the fenceline with sticks. It was unbelievable, the ends to which people would go for an extra ration card.

The population of Site 2 was totally dependent on the UN for their daily subsidies. In 1985, when I first arrived, the ration was very frugal, consisting mainly of rice and canned or dried fish and many cases of severe malnutrition were evident, especially in babies and young children. Over the years, I saw the incidence of malnutrition greatly reduced, when nutritional standards were improved.

By the beginning of 1991, the basic ration given to every family member, consisted of the following:

	Items	Amount	Frequency of Distribution
1.	Milled rice	3.4kg	Every 7 days
2.	Fresh eggs (chicken)	2 pcs	Every 7 days
3.	Canned fish or dried salted fish	210gm	Every 7 days
4.	Mung beans or soya beans	0.5kg	Every 28 days
5.	Vegetable oil	700gm	Every 28 days
6.	Fresh vegetables	500gm	Every 7 days
7.	Salt	280gm	Every 28 days
8.	Wheat flour	700gm	Every 28 days
9.	Fuel (wood or charcoal)	1,725kg	Every 7 days
10.	Soap	120gm	Every 28 days
11.	Water	17 litres	Daily

Although this diet was scarcely above survival level, it was nutritionally sound. It was also deemed to be above the standard in many Third World countries. Camp people, who rarely complained about anything, told me they were happy, as it was much better than the meagre rations to which the people had been subjected during and immediately after the Pol Pot reign.

Trading in Site 2 was illegal in the early days, but this didn't deter the Thai traders, who sneaked into the camp at night, bringing with them cherished items such as brightly coloured sarongs, combs, mirrors, cheap jewellery, tobacco and sugar, to barter these items for UN rations. It was not long before bags of rice, canned fish and vegetable oil, all marked 'not for sale', appeared in the markets in Tapraya and Aranyaprathet, at very low prices.

Food cards and later family books, became a form of currency for the poor, who sometimes sold them to pay debts, leaving family members in dire straits. One ration book would sell for 300 baht (AUD$15), a small fortune for a poor family. Gambling was a huge problem in the camp, where often, these books exchanged hands in card games, resulting in sobbing women seeking help from family service centres because there was no food for their children.

As most displaced person camps were situated close to the Cambodian border, security became a major issue for the Thai military. Access to these camps was strictly controlled, with no one admitted without a pass. Every three months, aid organizations were compelled to submit a list of workers' names to the Military HQ in the nearest town (Aranyaprathet for Site 2) before new passes could be issued for the next quarter.

Over the years, workers became adept at swapping passes or changing dates on expired passes for visitors. Later, Thai authorities became aware of this subterfuge and changed the format to include a passport photograph of the bearer, to be displayed on each pass. Thai soldiers, who inspected the passes, thought all foreigners looked alike, so visitors were still able to gain access many times with a bogus ID. One time, I misplaced my pass so borrowed one from a co-worker, Bob, emblazoned with his photograph, complete with beard. I held my breath when soldiers took the pass and examined it, before handing it back and waving me on. Visitor-entry passes were given sparingly and only after Thai authorities had received notification well in advance.

Aid workers were referred to as 'volags', derived from the general term given to aid organizations 'voluntary agencies'. Security for volags was placed in the hands of UNBRO, whose job it was to alert all camp workers in case of shelling, violence erupting inside the camp, fire, rioting and many other potential dangers. Workers were made aware of strict rules to which they must adhere. All agencies had radios at their camp headquarters, each agency appointed a security officer from their staff, to be held responsible for contacting other staff members should there be a security problem. Many workers carried two-way radios for notification of possible danger, but for those without there was always the 'bush radio' that was fast and efficient. Camp people always knew when there was a radio call for agency staff members, they would alert us, often before we could be located by our own security.

UNBRO sent out the following message to all agencies:

Neither UNBRO nor voluntary agencies appointed by UNBRO as encampment security co-ordinators can be held in any way responsible for possible consequences resulting from a deterioration in the security situation, nor responsible for consequences of any advice or instruction given on security, nor guarantee the safety of personnel or assume any liability in the event of any death or injury of personnel.

Site 2 Security Protocol

UNBRO and volag staff are not permitted to work in dangerous conditions. Relief staff are encouraged not to enter the border camps if they consider the situation to be unsafe.

UNBRO reserves the right to make changes in the exit routes and meeting places according to the specific situation.
Following are the security situation calls to which volags must adhere:

Situation O: *Normal activity, no apparent danger.*

Situation 1: *A warning of possible danger in the camp and/or the immediate area.*

Action:
(a) Stay near your radio for any change in the situation level.
(b) Notify anyone who does not have a radio.

Situation 2: *Will not be used.*
(This situation was scrapped)

Situation 3: *A dangerous situation in and/or around the camp.*

Action:
(a) Relief staff to proceed immediately to their office or the nearest access road for evacuation from the camp. Notify your office as to whereabouts.
(b) Radio use should be reduced to only essential calls.

Situation 4:
(a) Staff are instructed to seek shelter on the ground, in a ditch or bunker.
(b) Stay where you are until Situation 3 call is given
(c) Leave the camp immediately

Staff had to stay within range of radios until the all clear was given.

In the event of evacuations, a meeting place was set up a number of kilometres from the camp. All personnel were required to make their way to this site, where names were checked from the sign-in board by UNBRO security staff, to establish that all workers were accounted for. UN policy of practice evacuations was dropped after reported panic by the camp people, contributing to a number of suicides.

Situation 1 was called if there was an explosion of any description, the cause of which must be identified by UN security before the all clear could be given. This situation occurred so frequently that it became a part of everyday life and volags usually ignored the call. Many times these outbursts were due to truck tyres blowing out, sometimes a landmine triggered outside the camp. Eruptions of violence inside could also result in an emergency being called over the radios. Sadly, violence was an accepted part of camp life.

CHAPTER 2

I wandered around the camp for the next few days, familiarizing myself with the surroundings, meeting the people, observing programmes run by COERR and other agencies, always on the lookout to see where I could best be used.

Camp workers were strictly forbidden to bring anything into the camp, other than their own food and work materials, not more than fifty baht ($2.50) cash was permitted, no extra food, clothes, mail and most of all, cameras, were prohibited. Periodically, soldiers at the entry checkpoint would hold searches of vehicles and workers' bags. The penalty for breaking these rules was confiscation of goods and possible banishment from the camp or in severe cases, from the country. I decided to take the chance to bring in my camera, as I really wanted some photos of the beautiful children. My camera was a small automatic, which I disguised by wrapping it in a scarf, then burying it in the bottom of my bag, hoping it would withstand the searches if I was accosted.

Each day I visited the hospital and made my way around talking to the patients. This was a sad place. In addition to everyday illnesses, people were constantly rushed in, suffering terrible injuries from incidents such as landmine or hand grenade explosions, accidents or domestic violence. Many times, neighbourhood squabbles or family arguments turned to violent clashes with hand grenades, axes or lumps of bamboo used as weapons. Domestic violence was one of the biggest problems in Site 2. Women were often brought in by neighbours after being beaten by their husbands, where they would be stitched up before heading home, frequently to receive the same treatment again. There was nowhere else to go. Families living in such close proximity, and having nothing to do all day, exacerbated these problems. Men, who were used to working long hours out in the fields, were now confined to a few square metres and small disputes often turned into major altercations, resulting in ensuing violence.

I had taken a photograph of the mother and sick baby in the hospital. A few days later, I brought the photo to show her, but was saddened to learn that the baby had died the night before. The little girl appeared to have been making some improvement over the last few days, raising the mother's hopes for her survival, but it was not to be. I was directed to her house by one of the other patients. As I approached, I could hear loud wailing and through the doorway could see the mother, family and neighbours all gathered around a small wooden coffin. When she saw me, one of the women came hurrying over, taking me by the arm and guiding me to where the dead baby lay. She looked so tiny and frail, lying there dressed in a little sarong, the best clothing that could be found. I put my arm around the mother and she clung to me as we shed a few tears together. When she settled down, I handed her the photograph of her baby. She was delighted with it, holding it up for all to see this, the only memento she had of her lost child. All the women gathered around to inspect and exclaim over the photo the mother so proudly held. I was so happy to be able to leave this small reminder with her.

COERR had the largest number of programmes in the camp at this time. Two hospitals, handicapped workshop and agriculture project were staffed and financed by this organization, with funding also directed to the KWA (Khmer Women's Association). Other agencies working there were CONCERN, an Irish organization, which was in charge of sanitation, YWAM (Youth With A Mission), who worked together with JVC (Japan Volunteer Centre) for mother/child health care. Some of these current services were later allocated to other organizations and many new programmes introduced, but now the camp was in its early days and only a few essential services existed.

Nong Chan camp had only been set up a few days before I arrived, so at this time, many people were still living under makeshift shelters of plastic sheeting supplied by UN. Others were busy building bamboo and thatch huts for their families. Enough material to construct a building 4 x 6 metres in size was supplied by UNBRO, for a family of six; smaller families had to share with others. When it rained, houses were flooded unless deep drains were dug around each dwelling. All over this new settlement, men and women could be seen battling the hard earth with hoes, to create ditches around their huts before the wet season got under way in a few weeks.

The KWA was a huge project run by a committee of Cambodian women, helped with financial assistance from UNBRO and COERR. Each camp had its own KWA, run in a businesslike manner by women, who exercised considerable power in the community. Craft and adult literacy classes for underprivileged women were held at these centres, as well as supplementary feeding programmes, social counselling, nutritional education, support for the aged and dying, and assistance for new arrivals and families in need. A child-minding service was incorporated in the compound so mothers could attend classes, giving many women their only chance of escaping from the confines of their hut. KWA centres kept supplies of rice, mats, blankets, mosquito nets and kitchen utensils, for distribution to poor families or for emergencies.

On my forays around the camp, I would often stop to watch the women at work in the KWA craft room, weaving mats, baskets and cloth, dressmaking on treadle machines, handsewing and embroidering shirts. Silkworm cultivation and production of silk was later introduced successfully to the craft programme. The silk woven from this thread was highly prized by Japan and a market set up with buyers anxious to purchase this first-rate merchandise. Mulberry trees were grown in and around the compound to feed the silkworms. All was going well until workers from one of the agencies sprayed these trees without the knowledge of the KWA staff. The silkworms all died after eating the leaves, putting a premature end to this particular silkweaving project.

My First Job

I had only been in the camp for ten days, when Annie approached me with a request to teach health education to a group of Cambodian social workers attached to the KWA. It sounded good, so I agreed to give it a try. I was ready to start work, and pleased that I would now have a definite role to fill. She took me over to meet Mrs Long Lean, who was in charge of that section.

Mrs Long Lean was a small woman in her late forties, very confident, fluent in English, looking more Chinese than Cambodian. She told me that in addition to training social workers for the KWA, she was in charge of the orphanage in Ampil camp. She lived at this centre, where she, together with four staff members, cared for eighty orphans. Before coming to the border, she had been a schoolteacher in Cambodia, but left not long after the Vietnamese took control. The Vietnamese intruders wanted to change Cambodian school curriculums to include their language, which she refused to do. This forced her to make a quick departure to Thailand with her six children, as she feared for her life.

When I arrived at the orphanage it was lunchtime and the children were lined up with their plates for their midday meal of rice, cabbage and fish soup. I was welcomed with smiles and the traditional greeting, with eighty pairs of hands to foreheads. Only two girls could be seen in the lineup. When I asked why there was such a discrepancy in the sexes, I was told that girls were usually snapped up by relatives or other families, to help in the home. However, more importantly, girls were entitled to the prized food ration card.

Cambodian children had distinct roles to fill. Girls were taught to cook, sew, wash clothes and look after babies at an early age, in addition, they were expected to carry water, wood and food rations, whilst the boy's responsibilities were to tend the animals and assist in the rice fields. However, because they were in the camp, boys had no chores, spending their time playing games, swimming and generally enjoying themselves while the girls were kept forever busy.

Now, I was here with Annie and Long Lean, to discuss the classes I would be taking. It would be a good idea for a foreigner to take these classes for a few weeks, they told me, as it would give the students a whole new perspective on health matters. It was decided that it would be best to meet the ladies before planning subjects to be taught. Long Lean, who was familiar with this group, agreed to be my translator. This would help me considerably, as I knew she understood the health situation in the camp much better than I did. We would start the following day.

I was a bit nervous as I accompanied Long Lean to the classroom the next morning, but pleased to have her along to help me through. We headed for the KWA compound where the classes were to be held in one of the bamboo and thatch huts. On entering, we were confronted by a roomful of smiling women, squatting on their haunches on the dirt floor. They all rose to their feet to welcome us with traditional greetings. The room was bare of furniture, except for one bamboo chair, to which I was directed; a large blackboard took up the space along one wall. Long Lean introduced me to the group, explaining that I would be their new teacher for health education. There was much giggling, whispering and excitement when they learnt this. It would be a real novelty for them, as they had had no contact with a foreigner before.

With Long Lean as translator, I told them a little about myself and what plans I had for teaching. I asked if there were any questions and they all started talking at once. Questions were: How old are you? Do you have children? Why did you come here? What is your country like? My answer to the first two questions drew many 'oohs' and 'aahs', and my other answers, plenty of interest. By the time I had given them a rundown on my life, my country and reasons for being there, time was almost up. I agreed to come again next day to give the first lesson, on hygiene. Before I left, they all gathered around to get a closer look, touch my arms and pinch my flesh, all laughing and enjoying this close encounter with their new teacher. I had the feeling it would be good fun working with them.

I soon realized that when teaching health education I would have to go right back to basics, as they knew nothing about everyday hygiene that we take for granted. First lessons reverted to fundamentals - using toilets provided, washing hands after, boiling water, covering food. This initial lesson was followed by instruction on the importance of breast feeding, immunization, malnourished children, sanitation, balanced diet (a difficult one here in this camp) and other health matters. It was all fun to the women, who, during the lesson, could always find something amusing, bringing forth peals of laughter from the class. It was a pleasure to be involved with them and I just hoped that something from the classroom would be remembered and passed on to the community.

Our lesson was interrupted one day by shouts and screams outside, which cleared the room in one minute flat. Everyone was running out of the childminding centre next door, where most of my pupils had left their small children. We soon discovered the reason for this swift exodus. A snake had slithered through the doorway and across the room while the children were singing, causing a huge panic. Nearby workmen appeared and were given the task of finding and killing the intruder. The finder would be really rewarded with this trophy to take home for his family's dinner. Any sort of meat was regarded as a rare delicacy in this camp, where the taste of meat was only a memory.

As well as attending the class, these social workers were busy preparing a puppet show, highlighting the health issues we had discussed. They planned to take this presentation to all parts of the camp over the next few weeks. Each day after class, they were kept busy making puppets, curtains and rehearsing the dialogue. They formulated their own scenario, interspersing the serious parts with some Khmer humour. Annie was busy organizing a generator, sound system and microphones, for the performance. Messages had already been sent to all section leaders, to notify people when the puppet show would arrive in their area.

I accompanied the group on the day of their first performance, held at the rice distribution centre in Ampil camp. By the time we arrived, hundreds of people were waiting expectantly for this big event. Women holding small babies, children running around, a few men, all squatting on the ground, many holding umbrellas to protect themselves from the scorching sun. Barriers were quickly erected to keep the crowd back from the puppet stand, but these proved to be no deterrent. In no time, dozens of small children had slipped under, to put themselves as close as possible to the action. No sooner had the show got under way than the wriggling bodies had dislodged the legs of the stage, bringing the whole construction down on top of them. Everything had to stop while the stand was put together and the show could continue. Adults and children were mesmerized with the presentation, alternating between seriousness and shouts of laughter. The show was a resounding success and continued to be, as it was shown all over the camp. The women were congratulated on their excellent work, receiving a new sarong each for their efforts.

I came to know these women in my class really well. We would often sit after lessons and talk and they would tell me something about their lives before they came to Site 2. All had a sad story to relate. One older woman, Naree, who always brought her six-year-old daughter along, told me that she had lost her husband and five of her six children during the Khmer Rouge years. This little one, the only survivor, was never let out of her sight. Boon Savee, sitting in the back of the room, was very quiet. I asked her to tell me a little about her life. She had tears in her eyes as she held up her youngest, a little boy with clubfeet and deformed fingers. He was one of four children, who had survived from a family of ten. His future was of great concern to her because of his deformities. I asked if she had taken him to the hospital for treatment. She had not. I promised to take them the following day, so the child could be examined.

As luck would have it, an orthopaedic surgeon was on a rare visit to the camp when we took the little boy next morning. He examined him and arranged for x-rays to be taken at KID hospital the following week. He would be performing surgery there in a few weeks and promised to include Savee's son, if the x-ray results showed that an operation could rectify the problem. Sadly, when the results came back, we found that this little boy's condition was inoperable. All he could do was instruct Savee to strengthen the child's good foot with daily physiotherapy.

I had only been in the camp a short time, when I was stopped in my tracks by a loud explosion. I nearly jumped out of my skin, looking around quickly to see what was happening. People in the vicinity were carrying on with their chores, appearing completely unconcerned. I asked some people walking by, what caused the loud bang. Back came the casual answer, 'Only a landmine, nothing to worry about'.

Eventually, I too, became accustomed to these periodic explosions and the background sounds of shelling, which happened sometimes in the day and almost every night in the dry season. It was not long before I learned to differentiate between incoming and outgoing shells, a landmine or hand grenade explosion. Sometimes, shells from Cambodia would land in the border villages inside Thailand, causing the Thai military to angrily retaliate. When the fighting became this close, the whole house would shake and windows rattle. This was a far cry from the life back home, but surprisingly, I soon became accustomed to living with the sounds of war.

TB Screening

Health education classes were only occupying a few hours a week, so I was pleased when I was asked by one of our doctors, Robert Brands, if I would assist him in identifying early cases of TB (tuberculosis). He was very concerned about the spread of this disease in the camp, especially in the families of the TB patients. The programme he suggested that I set up, would assist in identification of family members in the early stages. Any suspects would be referred to the hospital for tests, allowing positive cases to get prompt treatment, thus giving them a much better chance of recovery.

There were approximately one hundred TB patients attending the clinic in Ampil camp. Before commencing the treatment, patients were required to sign a contract agreeing to attend each day to receive medication and continue treatment until completion of the course. This could take anything from six to twelve months. They must take their medication daily in the presence of the medics, to ensure they didn't stockpile and sell it. At the end of each week, patients received a bonus rice ration if they had attended regularly. This procedure was to ensure that patients did not leave before treatment was completed, thus giving that particular strain of TB a chance to become more virulent or immune to the drugs. Dr Rob wanted me to start immediately, as he was worried about the high incidence of this disease in the camp. An interpreter, Sovanna, was assigned to assist me, and together with Dr. Rob, we sat down to devise a plan for the project.

The first step was to obtain a list of patient names and addresses from the clinic. From this list we would choose three patients, who lived in the same area. We would return with them to their homes when they had taken their daily medication, and while there, we would screen other family members for symptoms of TB.

As I waited each day in the clinic for the patients to receive their medication, I would watch the medics at work. TB sufferers arrived and stood in line for their turn while the medics prepared their medication. Eight different capsules and tablets to be dispensed to each patient would be laid out on plastic bags. As the patients stepped forward, they were given their daily dose, which they washed down with water from a communal water barrel, all using the same cup. For babies, pills were crushed and mixed with red syrup in a bottle top, then drawn into a syringe that was placed in the baby's mouth and medicine squirted in. The same syringe was used for the next child waiting in line, with no washing or sterilizing of the instrument.

The first patient we were to accompany home was a thin, sick-looking young woman, who had just started her course of treatment. We asked where she lived and she indicated that it was just a short walk. I was soon to find out that what Cambodians call a short way, can mean anything up to five kilometres. By the time we reached the house more than a kilometre away, we were hot and tired and the poor TB patient was nearly out on her feet. She barely had the strength to usher us into her house and clear a place for me on the big bamboo bed just inside the door. She told us that she shared this hut with seventeen other family members. This was not unusual for Cambodians, where the family unit is very significant. The 'unit' or 'group', whether it be community unit, kinship unit, or family unit, play an important role in Cambodian traditional society. In these extended families, everyone, young or old, share chores around the home according to their role, duty and obligation. The grandparents share the responsibility of rearing children, their wisdom and views being much respected by younger family members. So, this was a fairly typical extended Cambodian family, which we were visiting.

We hardly had time to settle and bring out the papers before every possible space was filled with chattering neighbours, all wanting to get a look at the visitors and see what was going on. All family members came forward to be introduced. The family consisted of the patient, her husband and four children, mother and father, brother, his wife and six children and the husband's two brothers.

Sovanna produced the prepared questionnaire and I proceeded to ask the required questions of the head of the family, the TB patient's father. First, names and ages of all family members were recorded, then questions asked: Did they have a cough? Did they have blood in sputum? Were they losing weight or tired? with the questioning following that line. These forms would be brought back to the hospital, checked out by the doctor, who would then refer any suspects for tests.

In the early stages of this programme, after interviewing the family, it seemed that everyone was a prospective TB patient. I eventually learned that they were enjoying the attention and wanted to make an impression by saying 'yes' to all questions. As I became more experienced, it became obvious, which people were really suffering symptoms of TB and needed referral. It would usually take about two hours at each house, recording all family names, health history and asking questions relating to TB symptoms. Everywhere we went, people were so hospitable, welcoming us into their homes, offering cups of water and generally making us feel at home. Most of these people were very poor, the only furniture in their huts being one or two large bamboo beds on which all family members slept and ate. Bathing was done outside, the women wearing a sarong, the men with a krama around their waist, using water drawn from a large cement barrel given by the UN. Cooking for the family was done on a small claypot stove, under which, a small fire was lit, with wood also supplied by the UN. In the early evening, Site 2 camp could be picked out from kilometres away. This was from the pall of smoke hanging overhead from thousands of these stove fires.

Cambodian women kept their family name after marriage, with the children taking the father's family name. Whilst recording family particulars, I came across many babies named 'Site One' or 'Site Two', depending in which camp they were born. I thought how difficult it would be for these children to live with these names and try to explain them in later years when these border camps were just a bad memory.

During the home visits, people would fire questions at me about their future. They seemed to think that the foreigners were well informed on the political situation, which was not the case. Common questions asked were: When will we be able to return to our country? Is there another offensive coming? Will we be forced back? I could only tell them that the UN was doing their best to protect them, adding reassurance that they would not be forced back against their will. As to the attacks, no one could predict just when the next one would be, though there were always rumours flying around, especially near historic dates.

People, when faced with hardship, become very resourceful. On my travels around the camp I saw many instances of this. One enterprising family with makeshift materials and a lot of imagination had set up a business selling lamp oil they produced themselves. Discarded plastic bags and pieces of plastic sheeting were gathered from around the camp, washed, then placed in a tin on top of a fire, over which a cement hood had been built. The heat generated, extracted the oil from the plastic. The oil then dripped from a pipe protruding from the front of the fireplace into containers set beneath. These bottles of oil, which sold for the equivalent of ten cents each, or a bag of rice, were well sought after in this camp where there was no electricity.

Many families made noodles to sell or for their own use. Rice was cooked, then placed in a homemade stone grinder, which was turned by hand until a paste was formed. This paste would be tied into a krama and squeezed to extract all the moisture before being placed in a tin with holes pierced in the bottom. The dough was then forced through the holes, forming the noodles, which would drop into a pot of boiling water beneath. These noodles were much in demand as a welcome respite from the endless meals of rice.

One of the houses we came upon, had two large marijuana plants growing next to it. Sovanna told me that it was quite common for villagers to grow these plants, using the leaves in their soup. They would invite family and neighbours in to share with them in what they called 'happy' soup. I also found people making their own rice wine, which was very potent.

Gambling in Site 2 was strictly prohibited by the Thai military; even being caught with a pack of cards could land the owner in prison. Some of the more daring men had spirited fighting birds into the camp, and kept them hidden in their homes. On Sundays, crowds of men would gather at these highly illegal contests to watch the cockfights and bet on their favourite. I came on one of these fights as I was walking through the camp one day. There was a real panic when they heard me approaching, but I assured them that I would not inform on them. The poor birds were a sorry sight, very scrawny, almost bereft of feathers, with fighting scars all over their heads. It was hard to see how they could survive another contest.

On the way around the camp, we came across many interesting characters. On one home visit we met a real old mountain man, grey hair down to his waist, playing a homemade violin-like instrument. He played a tune for us and I was amazed to hear such melody coming from so primitive an instrument. This man was very thin; so I asked him did he have a bad cough. He said, "Yes." Did he cough up sputum? He said, "Yes, look," and aimed a big ball of phlegm at my feet. I was nearly sick!

One man, who was questioned, had all the symptoms of the early stages of tuberculosis, but would not visit the hospital for tests. No amount of talking would convince him that he needed to be checked for the disease. I finally extracted from him the reason why. He was a KPNLF soldier and it was illegal for Cambodian soldiers to be in the camp. Officially, the camp was classed as neutral, though it was under KPNLF leaders. Periodically, Thai soldiers came through seeking out these soldiers, who, when caught, would be arrested and put in the cells. Today, they were searching the camp for this reason, forcing all the Khmer soldiers into hiding. These raids were never highly successful for the Thai military, as the word soon spread when they entered the camp.

Cambodian soldiers always kept one step ahead, moving from house to house, where people were only too willing to protect them.

I began to feel like the village nurse making her rounds, as I was approached many times by families bringing sick, blind, crippled or mentally ill members for me to see, asking for my advice or assistance. I always directed them to Sovanna, who was a trained medic and much more qualified than I to give medical help. All I could do was advise them on basic treatment or to attend the outpatients clinic or the hospital, if the illness or injury was severe. We saw many sad cases of children crippled by polio, lepers with missing fingers and toes, war injuries, high fevers due to malaria, sore eyes and children covered in weeping sores, caused by the unhealthy conditions in which they lived.

Over the years I was to work there, I saw how disease took its toll among those living in such overcrowded conditions. Malaria, typhoid, TB, skin infections and abscesses were rampant, deaths from snakebites were also quite frequent in the early days. Many times at night, I would lie in bed and think about these poor people trapped behind the barbed wire, their sad lives, their helplessness, and rue my inability to do more for them.

If the family home of the TB patient was a long distance away, I would requisition a car to take us, as the patients were usually very weak from the disease. For many of these people, it was their first ride in a motor vehicle. It was great to watch the look of wonder on the faces of the children when the car took off on their first ride. However, there were times when children were terrified, screaming in fear and clinging to their mother, until we reached our destination. One day, we left the car but the woman patient remained sitting inside, not following when we walked off and entered the house. I waited for awhile, then returned to the car to see where she was. She was still sitting there, quite distressed by this time, as she could not find how to get out.

This job also gave me plenty of freedom to roam the camp and meet the people. Wherever we went groups of children followed. Bringing in bags of sweets for them had proved to be a disaster, for it had almost caused a stampede of both children and adults. I soon discovered that the children did not expect anything but were just happy to follow me about, keeping a few metres behind, giggling and hiding if I spoke to them.

During my time working on this TB detection programme, more than forty cases of tuberculosis in patients' family members were discovered in the early stages of the disease. Dr Rob was very pleased with the results, because it enabled these TB sufferers to receive early treatment, therefore halting further spread of the disease. Unfortunately, this programme was discontinued when I left camp, as there was no one to take over from me.

Amongst all the sadness and deprivations in the camp there were some shining lights. One of them was the traditional dancing that continued on, despite the hardships, most certainly lifting the spirits of the population. I loved to watch the children's dancing classes conducted each day in an open-sided building. At every opportunity I would stop by, joining hundreds of spectators, to watch the dancers practicing. Khmer dancing, with its intricate hand and graceful body movements, was beautiful to watch. Little girls from six years old, practiced both classical and folk dance here under the watchful eye of their teacher, Voan Savay.

This teacher, who had formerly danced with the Royal Ballet in Phnom Penh, demanded absolute obedience, as well as top-class performance from her little pupils. An incorrect movement could result in a hard whack with a bamboo stick, hair pulled or a twisted ear. While this punishment was being administered, children continued dancing, sometimes with tears running down their cheeks. It always amazed me how they accepted this harsh treatment, fronting up next day full of smiles for their next lesson.

The Orphanage

The orphanage was another place I enjoyed visiting. It was always good to talk to Long Lean, an interesting and intelligent woman. She had adopted twelve of the boys, who lived with her. Her own six children were now in another camp in the south of Thailand. She told me how this came about. The previous year, when Ampil camp inside Cambodia was first shelled, she had to protect eighty-six children in her care. She asked Fr Pierre, "How can I look after the safety of all these orphans and my own children as well?" Fr Pierre promised to find a solution. He spoke to Fr Bunlert in Bangkok, who in turn, used his influence to secure places for her six children in an orphanage in the south of Thailand, where it was much safer. At first, Long Lean was very grateful, but later regretted this decision, as she really missed her children. It would be another four years before she would see them again.

The twelve boys she had taken into her care were aged from fourteen to seventeen. On my stopover at the orphanage, I would often sit in on their daily English classes conducted by Annie. She would write sentences on the blackboard and the boys would repeat them after her, copying her Dutch accent. After instruction was over, I would stay and talk to the boys, who were always keen to practice their English. I became very close to one of them, Phoeuy, who would often accompany me around the camp. He thought he was about seventeen years old. Cambodians from the villages are never really sure about their age, their parents usually remembering the year of their birth by the harvest, good crop, drought, floods or other phenomena. He told me about his life before the Khmer Rouge days, of how he missed his family and normal life. Often, we called into one of the coffee shops in the camp to sit and talk. On one of these occasions, Phoeuy told me that his mother had died and he felt terrible guilt, as he was responsible for her death. I asked him why this was so and he told me the following story.

During the Khmer Rouge years, he had been taken away from his family and put to work with other boys his age, tending the buffalo. These little boys of ten, eleven and twelve had to work twelve hours a day with little food, attend indoctrination lectures every night, sleep outside and were never allowed contact with family members. Though Phoeuy told me he did sneak out at night sometimes. Once, because he missed her very much, he walked miles to the village where his mother had been sent, to make contact with her. Then he had to complete this dangerous mission by making his way back before dawn.

When the Khmer Rouge were ousted, Phoeuy desperately tried to find his way back to his home village. After struggling along bush tracks he finally arrived there, dirty, hungry and exhausted. He was elated to find his mother, father and little sister still alive, but at the time, no news of his two older sisters and two brothers. No rice had been planted, so food was short and the family very hungry. He heard that WFP (World Food Programme) was trucking rice to the border just inside Thailand, so Phoeuy walked the ten kilometres to bring rice back for his family. His mother, who was about seven months pregnant, accompanied him on one of these trips. When they neared the border and were within sight of the trucks, Vietnamese troops opened fire on the people coming to collect their rice. Phoeuy grabbed his mother's hand and they ran, he dragging her along, while the bullets whizzed around them. They kept running, his mother falling many times, and Phoeuy pulling her to her feet until she could run no further. As Phoeuy recounted this story, tears came to his eyes and he became very agitated. He went on to tell me that when they finally reached their home his mother collapsed from exhaustion and her baby was born prematurely that night. She did not recover, never leaving her bed again and a few months later she died. Phoeuy was devastated, blaming himself for her death. Late that night, Phoeuy left home without telling his family. He walked to the border where he joined up with a resistance group - he was twelve years old.

For the next three years, he fought alongside the men, living out in the forest, sleeping under the trees, eating only when kindly villagers gave them food. It was a tough life for a young boy, under constant threat of gunfire, hand grenades and landmines, never knowing when they may come face to face with the enemy. Some people he met in the forest, who were heading for the border, told him about Site 2; where people received food every day, a house to live in and free education. He decided to desert the army and try his luck there. To attend school and receive an education, had been nothing but a dream before.

Now, here he was, four years later, tears streaming down his cheeks as he related this story to me. I tried to reassure him, telling him it was not his fault his mother had died, and that he had to stop blaming himself. A few days later he came to thank me for listening, telling me he had never told anyone the story before and now he felt better about it.

It was very difficult for young camp people, as there was no entertainment for them nor any real jobs to which they could aspire. On Sundays, they would congregate at a large reservoir at the back of the camp, the only place to get away from the dust, dirt, poverty and endless rows of bamboo huts. Here they would sit and talk around the water's edge, sometimes posing for photographs with the water as a backdrop. Some of them would venture in for a swim, others just playing around in the muddy water. This was the only activity open to the youth of the camp, the barbed wire fence the edge of their world.

One day, while sitting talking to Phoeuy he asked me about the young people back in Australia; how did they spend their Sundays? I told him a little about the parks, beaches, sporting events and facilities available to young people there. He sat and thought for awhile, then turned to me and said: "They say the teenage years are the best years of your life, but look at ours. We don't even know what is happening outside this fence. We are like frogs in a well." How true that was.

Primary schools were operating in each camp, at this time out in the open air. Children sat on the ground, usually in the hot sun, holding their slates and chalk whilst the teacher wrote on the portable blackboard at the front. There seemed to be no age limit, with toddlers to teenagers participating in these classes. Pupils displayed a keen thirst for knowledge, listening intently to the teacher, seemingly undisturbed by all the noise and distractions around them.

As well as their lessons, these students were expected to assist with other school associated activities. I would often encounter groups of schoolchildren at work digging dams or clearing land for school use. One day I came upon a group of about two hundred children engaged in a huge excavation. All had their own jobs: loosening the ground with hoes; digging; carting dirt away in baskets; raking. They were completely covered in mud, as it had been raining heavily. This did not appear to dampen their spirits, though, as they went about their work laughing and obviously enjoying themselves. I asked their teacher what was happening and was told that the children were digging a fishpond for the school. Fish would be bred in here to be given out to poor families and when this particular project was finished, the children would start on their next one, a vegetable garden. They attended classes from 7am to 9am, then worked on their project from 9am to 11am. The afternoon group of students also had their two hours tuition and two hours community work.

Qualified teachers were almost nonexistent here; most being killed during the Khmer Rouge years. During that time all books were burned and the entire education system destroyed, Khmer Rouge leaders deeming anything to do with education to be 'Western contamination'. Not only teachers, but anyone wearing glasses, was killed on the suspicion they knew how to read and write. This meant that many of the teachers in Site 2, had only primary school education themselves, thus contributing to a fairly basic standard of education. That was until a year or two later, when the UN took charge of education, building schools, supplying furniture, books and education materials. At the same time COERR opened a teacher training college for existing teachers and trainee teachers. They were trained at both primary and secondary level and it was not long before the first high school in the camp was opened. This was later joined by another two. From this time on, the standard of education improved dramatically.

My work in the camp often took me to the back road, which was at the foot of the mountain. There was a coffee shop on this street where Sovanna and I would sometimes stop for a rest and a cup of coffee. While sitting there one day going over our papers, an older man came over to talk to us. He told me that he was surprised that, at my age, I could still read without glasses, going on to say that he was fifty-three years old but could not read because of bad eyesight. By now, other men at a nearby table had joined in the conversation, telling me that they also had poor vision and asking if it was possible to get them reading glasses.

I promised to look into the matter, assuring them that I would come back in a week's time with the results.

I made enquiries and discovered that I could buy reading glasses in a shop in Aranyaprathet. Further enquiry revealed that the glasses came in five different strengths, ranging from weak to very strong, so I purchased a number of pairs of each strength for the men to try out. When I arrived at the coffee shop the following week, the men were all waiting expectantly, only, by now, there were twice as many. They jumped up from their seats excitedly when I came in carrying the box of glasses, gathering around to get a closer look. There was much ado when I brought out the samples, everyone pushing their way in to be the first to try them on. Cries of joy were followed by looks of delight on the faces of these middle-aged men when they found the right pair and discovered they could read again. One man told me that he was a schoolteacher, saying that it must be his lucky day, as he just happened to walk into the coffee shop at the right time. His eyes must have been very bad as he took the strongest. I watched him as he walked up the street clutching his precious glasses, stopping and showing them to everyone he passed on the way, beaming with delight.

Word soon spread that I was the 'reading glass supplier' and requests came in daily. Because I could not keep up with the demand, I approached COERR office in Bangkok regarding supplies of this commodity. They replied a few weeks later by sending thirty boxes of glasses in a variety of strengths. However, the demand was always greater than the supply. Then I had the idea to write home to friends for supplies of outdated reading glasses. Some church groups in Australia heard about this, put calls out to their members and over one of the radio 'help' shows and soon I was receiving welcome supplies of discarded reading glasses. The people loved the glasses that came in stylish, stronger frames, rather than the cheap black plastic of the local ones. This service, that was to continue over the years, with glasses donated from all over Australia, was very much appreciated by the recipients.

The Mountain Challenge

Whilst sitting in this coffee shop or walking along the road, we would often see men coming down from the mountain. Sovanna told me that there was a KPNLF guerilla camp at the top and these were soldiers returning to visit their families. Because it was illegal for them to be in the camp, they would usually try to return under cover of darkness at or siesta time when the Thai soldiers were taking a nap after lunch. They were difficult to distinguish from the civilians; never wearing full uniforms. Sometimes they arrived in camouflage pants with T-shirt or soldier's shirt with tracksuit pants, either barefooted or with rubber thongs on their feet but always empty-handed, as weapons were prohibited in the camp.

One lunchtime, we met a group of soldiers emerging from the mountain track as we went past. I stopped to talk to them, asking if it was a hard climb up there and if there were any Thai soldiers in the area. They said 'No' to both questions. On the spur of the moment I said to Sovanna that I would like to go up the mountain and have a look, he answered with a big grin, saying that he would like to come, too. So without further ado, we climbed through the barbed wire fence and set out across the two hundred metres of flat scrubland before taking the rising mountain track.

At the start of the trek, the slope was gradual and I thought this would be an easy climb, but I was soon to change my mind, when about a quarter of the way up, the sandtrack turned into a slippery bed of rocks and pebbles and became much steeper. I had to stop a few times to get my breath back, but not so Sovanna, who forged ahead without puffing, only stopping now and then to wait for me. All around us was low scrub with no shelter, all trees having been chopped down long ago by camp people, for firewood. As we climbed higher and the way became still steeper, almost vertical in some places, the undergrowth became thick and tangled, making it more difficult to push our way through. We met a group of soldiers coming down, so stopped for a chat - a welcome respite. They told us that they had just returned from fighting inside Cambodia and had reported back to their mountain base before coming down to visit their families. They couldn't believe that we were making this climb just for the heck of it. After a few minutes rest, we continued on our way. As I looked back, I could make out the pattern of the camp, intersecting roads and rows of huts getting smaller and smaller as we made our way up. How come the mountain never looked so high from down on the ground!

After an hour's climbing, when I was almost ready to give up, we rounded a huge boulder and there we were, smack in the middle of the resistance fighters' camp. We were greeted with looks of amazement from the ten or so soldiers present, astounded to see a foreign woman up there on the mountain. After they recovered from their shock, they greeted me like a long-lost friend, motioning me to sit on a tree stump chair and offering a welcome cup of cold tea. I looked around at this primitive military camp. There were a few small trees up here on the top of the mountain, suspended from these were dark green military hammocks, in which the soldiers slept. The only shelter I could see was a small lean-to made of branches, under which was a cooking fire and a long bench, which was used for a table. Old and rusty guns, which looked completely ineffective, were propped up against the trees, belts of ammunition hung from the branches. Their commander, a man of about forty years of age, told us of the hardships faced by soldiers with the ever-present threat of landmines, malaria and the enemy. He said that this camp was set on the mountain to protect Site 2 from invaders and as a base for returning guerilla fighters. It was a difficult life, but these men were determined to fight on until they had expelled the hated Vietnamese from their country.

After we had finished our tea, one of the soldiers took us on a tour of inspection. First, to a clearing where we had a good view of the camp, which looked like a toy town from where we were, then he escorted us to their lookout, a lean-to covered in branches, from which we could see right over and into Cambodia. A look of longing came into his eyes, as he talked about his country and how much he would love to return to a peaceful Cambodia. He finished by asking the usual question, "You think Cambodia ever have peace?" I tried to reassure him by saying that I was sure that a peaceful settlement would eventually be reached.

Time had come for us to make our descent to the camp. The commander decided to come down with us, as he felt it would be safer for him, with a foreigner present, if we encountered Thai military on the return journey. The soldiers gathered around to say their farewells, waving us off as we left, inviting us to come again for another visit. I could see that it had been quite an occasion for them to have a foreign visitor to their camp.

The journey down was much easier and achieved in half the time. We met more soldiers, two of them women, coming up, stopping to talk to them before continuing on. By the time we arrived at the base of the mountain, it was late afternoon and I was hot, tired, dirty but happy to have made the climb and to have seen another aspect of Cambodian life.

A young medic at the hospital, Yan, would always be waiting when Sovanna and I returned from our rounds. He was anxious to improve his English and invariably had a list of questions to ask, words to be analyzed, pronounced or grammar to be corrected. Other medics, who had finished their work, were always ready to join in and have an impromptu English lesson. These were happy times and we had lots of laughs, as I tried to teach them to say 'sh' or 'v' - always coming out as 's' and 'w', no matter how hard they tried. These sounds were completely alien to the Khmer language. They also enjoyed teaching me a little of their language, laughing uproariously when I mispronounced words or placed them in the wrong context. I came to look forward to and enjoy these sessions with this group of young men, who, although their lives were so harsh, could always find something to laugh about.

Yan lived in the compound behind the hospital with his uncle, aunt, cousins and fifteen other people. I had not been in the camp long when I was invited to lunch at his house. I was introduced to his uncle, Nosai, who lived here with his wife and five daughters. Nosai told me that he had been a high school principal in Phnom Penh, before coming to the border, surviving during the Pol Pot regime by pretending to be a factory worker. He was now head of education in this camp and had just returned from a three-day Education Seminar in Singapore.

While I was talking to him, the women were busy in the kitchen preparing the meal. Every now and then one of them would peep around the corner at me, dissolving into laughter when I looked up. The meal was brought out and consisted of strips of beef which had been dried on trays in the sun, fish in sauce with rice, followed by sweets made of jackfruit, sugar and coconut - a delicious meal, certainly not the usual fare of the camp people.

We were joined by another member of the household, a middle-aged man by the name of Seng Plong. He told me that he was a doctor and had formerly been head of public health in Phnom Penh. The food was laid out before us and I sat there waiting for the women to sit down before we commenced eating. However, I was motioned to begin. I asked if the ladies were going to join us, but was told that they had already eaten. I was to discover that this was the Cambodian custom. The women worked in the kitchen, serving the men and guests but never joining in. At first, I felt very uncomfortable about this, sometimes requesting the women to join us, but after a time I learned to accept this tradition, finding that the women felt too uneasy sitting at the table with guests.

During our English sessions, Yan and I would often sit and chat. One day, he told me a little about his life during the Khmer Rouge time. In the early days of the takeover, his family was moved to another village where they had to work in the rice fields from 6am to 10pm every day, with only two short breaks for meals. These meals consisted of only a small serve of rice. They had not been there long when the Khmer Rouge soldiers came and took his father, who had been a teacher, two brothers and two sisters, who had all been students, and shot them. This left thirteen-year-old Yan, his mother and three younger brothers. A short time later, Yan was taken from his remaining family and sent to another province together with other teenagers. Here, the girls were put to work growing rice, while the boys drove the bullock carts, small children were employed to keep birds and vermin away from the crops and to make scarecrows. When the Vietnamese invaded Cambodia and drove the Khmer Rouge out, all the young men were forced to serve in their army. Not wanting this, Yan, now seventeen, left, walking two hundred kilometres to Thailand with a group of other young men, also desperate to get away. He completely lost touch with his family, now having no idea if any of them were still alive.

About this time, there had been a lot of shelling in the vicinity of the camp and rumours were rife that a big offensive was threatening. Whether true or not, these stories were circulating and the people were very frightened. Everyone in camp had a bag of essentials packed ready to grab if they had to run. The problem was that they were strictly forbidden to step outside the barbed wire enclosure, and there was nowhere for them to run to.

One day around this time, there was a loud, close explosion, resulting in a Situation 3 call over the radios. As we volags piled into the cars ready to evacuate, I looked back. It was terrible to see the look of fear on the faces of Sovanna, Yan and other friends, all watching silently, as we left for safer ground. I felt like we were deserting them when they needed us most. This was a continuing dilemma for foreign aid workers, but we were bound by UN laws to leave the camp when told. The only people, to whom this ruling did not apply, were Catholic priests, and some members of UN staff, who must oversee the withdrawal of workers. Many times, as streams of cars left the camp en route to the meeting point, we would pass Fr Pierre or Fr John racing into the camp to comfort the people. We envied them this dispensation from the rules. I once said to one of my Cambodian friends, how we hated to leave them when there was a dangerous situation, his reply was: "You not worry, you go, this is not your war."

The wet season was under way, bringing more misery for the camp population. Heavy rains every day reduced the areas around the huts to quagmires, making it difficult to stay on your feet in the muddy conditions. On top of this, many of the thatch roofs leaked and rain came through between the bamboo sticks. Firewood supplied by the UN for cooking purposes was never enough, driving many people to risk leaving the camp to search for firewood in the forest. These people took the chance of being caught by the Thai rangers, with the threat of imprisonment or death, also the ever-present menace of landmines, many placed close to the camp. Yet, people still took these daily risks. There was no record kept of where landmines were placed as the responsibility could be with Thai military, Khmer Rouge, KPNLF or Cambodian Government troops. Many times, civilians would be rushed into the camp hospitals before being transferred to KID hospital, with terrible injuries caused by landmines. Nobody knew how many others perished out there after stepping on mines.

My six months was coming to a close and as I looked around, I wondered how I would cope with life back home, and harder still how would I leave all my friends here. My vow to keep the people at arms-length never materialized and here I was with many close friends, whom I knew I would miss terribly. My mind was full of ideas of how I could help them from back in Australia. I had kept up a constant flow of letters to friends and family outlining the problems, harsh conditions and hopelessness the camp people faced. By the letters I received back, all seemed very interested and appalled at the situation. I was convinced that everyone, who heard about the plight of these people, would be anxious to help. How wrong I was!

The last few days I spent in the camp were happy, yet sad. Mrs Long Lean invited myself and Annie to lunch with all the children. I smuggled fruit and sweets into the camp for the orphans. These were real treats for them, many of whom had never seen or tasted sweets before. They would hold the sweet, lick it, then savour the taste with a look of delight on their faces before repeating the procedure, thus making it last for hours. They were all so excited at this rare opportunity of a party, making it a happy occasion for all present. As I said my goodbyes to the children, they begged me to write to them, tell them about Australia and please would I come back to visit them. I made no promises but made a mental note to seriously consider this idea. I felt very sad about leaving Mrs Long Lean and her twelve adopted boys, of whom I had become very fond. They all lined up to shake my hand and say their farewells.

Phoeuy never left my side, missing all his classes so he could spend the last few days with me. I had finished my work with the TB programme, so tried to spend more time with Sovanna, Phoeuy and my 'English' students. I invited them all to the coffee shop for coffee and rice cakes on my last day. This was a real novelty for them and they thoroughly enjoyed it, downing two or three cups of coffee each and six plates of rice cakes. We all sat and chatted.

They plied me with questions about Australia, my life there and my family, making me promise to keep in touch. When it was finally time for me to leave camp, all my friends congregated at the hospital to say their farewells. As the van left and I looked back to see them all waving I wondered if I would ever see them again. It was hard to keep back the tears. I felt so sad to be leaving them, not knowing what the future held.

Sitting in the plane going home, my thoughts were full of the camp. I was not sure if I really wanted to go home. However, all doubts were dispelled when the plane landed and I was greeted by a big group of family and friends. They were all pleased to see me back in one piece and I was happy to catch up on what had been happening in my absence. It felt like I had been away for years not just for six months.

However, it proved to be much more difficult to settle back into life in Australia, than I had imagined. I soon found that life goes on in the rest of the world, nothing changes, even though you know that yours has been changed forever. All my plans to interest people in the terrible plight of the people in the camp fell on deaf ears. I could understand to a certain extent, for I, also, had been oblivious to world problems, but it was their indifference that was hard to accept. At first, I wanted to talk about my experiences, but soon found that no one really wanted to listen. It was not until a few years later when I spoke to other aid workers, I found that all of them had experienced the same attitude from people back home. We realized that what we had encountered could not be compared to anything in their lives, thereby making it difficult for them to comprehend. I soon learned to keep my experiences to myself.

I was involved in the school swimming classes again, a few weeks later. As I saw all these healthy, well-fed children lining up for their swimming lessons, my mind kept harking back to the poor children in the border camps. Although most of the children seemed happy, here and there could be seen a child looking miserable at the prospect of his or her first swimming lesson. It was difficult not to compare these privileged lives with those of the camp children and remember the ever-smiling faces of the Cambodian children, always appearing happy although their lives were so difficult and the future appeared so bleak.

Swimming classes, Christmas, and family kept me busy but Site 2 was never far from my mind. When I went to the beach and saw the white sand, clean water and all that space, I would think of the camp people and how much they would enjoy the freedom here. By the time March came, and classes were soon to end, I had made up my mind I would return for another six months, as I knew my work was not yet finished.

CHAPTER 3

Back for Another Spell

After I had made my decision to return, I contacted Fr Pierre regarding the possibility of work in the camp. He was pleased to hear of my plan to return, telling me to just turn up, as there was plenty of work to be done. That was enough for me and I booked my ticket to Bangkok.

From past experience, I realized it better not to contact COERR head office of my intended arrival. This proved to be the right decision, and I was greeted with cries of surprise and pleasure when I arrived unannounced at the Bangkok office. I was told that, because I knew my way around, there would be no problem about a job, and with Fr Pierre's help, I could decide where I would be most needed.

There would be the usual wait for my camp pass to be processed, so I decided to head for Aranyaprathet and settle in. Being familiar with the whole scene would make it a lot easier this time. I had also learnt my lesson regarding luggage and only brought one small bag, which was simple to manage.

I caught the bus to Aranyaprathet and on arrival, made my way to the COERR office. I was greeted by the new director, Mr Nath, who took me around and introduced me to the office staff. In my absence, many changes had taken place, including an expansion of office space and a growing number of staff. The former bedrooms upstairs had now been turned into offices, so I would have to look for alternate accommodation.

Camp workers had not yet returned, so I sat back to await their arrival. At 6pm the first cars arrived. It was great to catch up with Fr Pierre, Fr John Bingham, Dr Rob Brands, Annie van Zoggel and many Thai co-workers. They told me that other foreigners with whom I had worked, had now moved on and many new staff had been recruited. I was introduced to them as they returned from the camp. The social service team had grown to ten members and there was now a small education team. I met Marie-Claude Cettier, who taught French, Spanish Jesuit brother, Kike, who was in charge of the handicapped centre and Jup, his Thai assistant. During the year, more English and French teachers would arrive to expand the team. The medical team had also grown considerably, with more foreign doctors and nurses and a new group of Thai staff.

When the word spread that I had nowhere to stay that night, a Thai worker, Rucha, invited me to stay in her house, which she shared with a nurse, Yu. I was grateful and relieved that this problem had been solved for the time being. She took me to her house, which was one and a half kilometres out of town, situated right next to a huge pagoda. My room was very small, the single bed taking up all the space, but it would suffice until I had time to look around for something else. I soon realized it was not good living in such close proximity to a pagoda. At 4am I was awakened by the loud ringing of the temple bells, followed by the incessant chanting of the monks. This would be a daily occurrence and impossible to sleep through, but it certainly gave me, a known late riser, an early start to the day.

On my first morning, I rose when the chanting started, gathered my things together and made my way across a small bridge over the river, past the markets, which were buzzing by this time, and on into town. It was still too early for the office to open, so I found a small restaurant where I stopped for a cup of coffee. Already, this place was crowded with local people, who had arrived for their daily breakfast of noodle soup or rice porridge.

After finishing my coffee, I made my way to the office, hoping that somehow I may gain access to the camp, though I had no pass, as yet. I was lucky; Annie had stopped by the office on her way to Bangkok and offered to lend me her pass. This was great, as now I would not be wasting time sitting around in Aranyaprathet.

I was quite excited as I boarded a car bound for Site 2. It would be good to see old friends and check out the changes that had taken place during my six-month absence. We passed KID camp first. Now there was a big empty space where Site 7 camp had previously adjoined. Marie-Claude told me that the people from here were now housed in Site 2 camp. I could see the difference in size as we approached Site 2, for a huge new settlement, built to accommodate the former Site 7 occupants, now named 'Rithysen', had sprung up to the south of the main settlement. We drove along a road dissecting the two encampments, now identified as Site 2 North and Site 2 South. Each had their own separate entrance, with TF80 soldiers in their sentry boxes at both access points, waiting to check passes. I held my breath, while entering through the north access point, hoping my impersonation would not be discovered. The soldiers came out, took our passes and after a quick look placed them in the slots, to be returned to us on departure.

That was a relief - I was in.

The camp population had now grown considerably. Crowds filled the roads, walkways and every conceivable space in between, the noise even louder than before. As I looked around, I felt a wave of happiness come over me to be back again amongst this tough and resilient people. Hopefully, I would find a way through my work, in which to ease some of their hardships. Bunkers had sprung up all over the camp, many families digging their own shelters next to their houses for protection from the constant shelling. It was a grim life for the camp people, used as human buffers on the border, with the ever-present fear of a shelling attack. On one side, Thai military, the other, Vietnamese or Cambodian troops all intent on their own war and with little regard for the safety of the hapless thousands in between. More than anything, these people would love to return to their country, to their villages and their rice fields, but the war made this impossible.

COERR had now built an office in the camp and this was where we headed first. Staff members were dropped off here and headed for their work places. I planned to spend the day renewing acquaintances and finding my way around the now much bigger camp, but first, I would head for the hospital where Yan and Sovanna were still working. A larger hospital had been built by COERR in another area of the camp, complete with consulting room and pharmacy. This hospital would serve patients from the Nong Chan, Ampil and San Ro camps. Another, much bigger hospital, run by ARC (American Refugee Committee) had been set up in Rithysen to cope with the large population here.

By the time I found my way to the COERR hospital, word had already spread that I was back in the camp. Yan and Sovanna, who had heard the news, came running out, faces beaming as they greeted me, saying how happy they were to see me back. It was great to meet with them, and we spent some time chatting and catching up on news before they had to return to the wards. Sovanna had married since I had left and was eager for me to meet his wife, Gnen, so I promised to visit his new family.

Next, I headed for the orphanage to catch up with Mrs Long Lean, Phoeuy and the other boys. I received a tumultuous welcome from all the children when I entered the compound. Long Lean came running out to see what was happening and happily joined in the reunion. The older boys were attending class, so I waited until they had their break before greeting them. It was great to meet up with Phoeuy, Phon, Sok, Rith, Chea and others again. They were full of questions about what I had been doing; what it was like in Australia and anxious to tell me all the camp news. Long Lean invited me to stay for lunch, so that we could all catch up. It was a happy meal with everyone chattering, little ones coming over to pull at my clothes to attract attention and the boys full of stories to tell me. Their English had improved considerably since I had last seen them, making it so much easier to communicate. I passed a happy hour with them before they went back to their lessons and I headed off to look around the camp.

The rest of the day was spent meeting old friends and looking at new projects, which had been set up since I left. I called in to meet Sovanna's wife, who was very shy, giggling and retiring to the back of the house after she had been introduced. Sovanna was living with his wife's family for the first year of his marriage, following the Cambodian custom. His father-in-law spoke a little English, so I sat with them, enjoying a refreshing cup of Chinese tea, while they told me about the wedding and camp happenings since I left. Soon it was time to leave and make my way back to the office for my departure from the camp.

That night after dinner, I made my way to Fr Pierre's house to discuss my work prospects for the next six months. Fr Pierre lived in a large, rambling wooden house on stilts on the outskirts of the town. Stored beneath the house, were boxes of old clothes, bags of donated rice, old bicycles, cartons of shoes and books, most of which were gifts from the people of France. The table, beds, and chairs inside were covered in papers, letters, files, books and clothes. How he ever found his way through all this mess was hard to say, but amazingly, he managed to put his finger on what he wanted immediately.

Fr Pierre was seventy-three years old and had served in India for forty-two years before coming to work on the border. A caring and compassionate man, he was admired and loved by camp residents. His clothing consisted of a couple of old baggy shirts, still baggier pants and shoes, with the backs worn down, his heels always over the top. He drove an old battered utility to and from the camp. When he arrived in Site 2, crowds of people followed him in, running alongside to keep up. He always had time to listen to a sad story and a seemingly endless supply of money to give for a needy cause. Other foreigners sometimes told him that he was a 'soft touch' and shouldn't give money to everyone coming with a sad story that could often be concocted. His reply was, "I would rather give. After all, it may be true and they may really need it."

He would tell visitors or journalists, who flocked to him for his views on camp life, "Site 2 is vast, overwhelming; it is at once filled with beauty and suffering, danger and violence." After telling them of his love for the Cambodian people, he would implore interviewers to respect the people, saying, "If you wish to speak to the people, emphasize their greatness and their dignity, not their suffering. If you wish to help them, do so with respect, otherwise you would do better to stay away."

Every Saturday, he held mass in a Catholic church built in the Vietnamese camp and later in a small church in another section of Site 2. His mass in the Vietnamese camp attracted hundreds of camp people, along with many foreign workers, who came to participate in the service and also to listen to the beautiful singing of the choir. Fr Pierre did not speak Vietnamese, so he required a translator for his mass.

As well as many stories about Fr Pierre's kindness, we relished the humorous side of many of his deeds. He would often become very emotional while giving mass and talking about the sad plight of the camp people. During one such session, he was impressing on his congregation that as Christians, they must show compassion; practice compassion in their daily lives; in their work; with their family and friends; they must spread the word about compassion. He wondered why everyone in the assembly was looking at him in stunned amazement, while he continued to talk about compassion with tears coursing down his cheeks.

After the session, Fr Pierre noticed that people were walking out of the church shaking their heads. He questioned one of his English-speaking Vietnamese friends about the sermon and received the answer, "Father, I cannot believe what you said. Do you really feel that way?"

Fr Pierre assured him that he did. The man was obviously shocked and Fr Pierre could not understand why. It wasn't until later that he discovered that his translator had mistakenly used the word 'corruption' for 'compassion'. He found that he had been telling his followers to practice 'corruption' wherever they went; not only that, but to spread the word around as well! This was a laughing point amongst the foreigners for years. It was a long time before Fr Pierre was able to live that gaffe down.

Another 'Fr Pierre story' that we all remembered, happened at Christmas when the camp was only two years old. Cambodia is a Buddhist country, so they do not celebrate Christmas. Some of the foreigners working in Site 2 came up with the idea to present a Christmas pageant on the outdoor stage to show the people a Christian story, so they could understand why we celebrated this event. The plan was for the foreigners to perform the nativity play, followed by an address by Fr Pierre. The group, with the help of Fr Pierre, practiced for weeks for the big occasion. There had been quite a lot of publicity about this event, so when Christmas Day arrived, thousands of Cambodians had taken their place outside the stage, awaiting the big presentation. Out came the foreigners dressed as Mary, Joseph, shepherds, wise men, angels, and the story got under way. A translator was standing by giving a rendition in Cambodian language of the Christian story. Shreds of tissue paper had been scattered around the stage to depict a snow scene, as the story was unveiled.

No sooner had the performance commenced than the rain came down, soaking the actors to the skin, making the tissue paper stick all over them - nobody had heard of snow anyway - people forgot their lines, the crèche holding the baby Jesus fell over and through it all there was not a sound from the audience! Nobody laughed, cried, clapped! It was a disaster! The organizers were aghast; what must the Cambodians think of these foolish foreigners? Oh well, they had saved the best till last, the audience would understand this part.

Fr Pierre came on the stage surrounded by the cast and the applause was thunderous. They all loved Fr Pierre and waited anxiously for his words of wisdom. He proceeded to make one of his impassioned speeches about peace for Cambodia; what wonderful people they were and how much they deserved peace so they could return to their homeland and now he would pray for peace to come to their troubled country. He said a short prayer, before being handed two white doves. He held one bird in each hand, as he called out in Cambodian language, "Peace for Cambodia!" then swept the birds towards the sky. They took a few feeble flutters before both crashed to the ground. Fr Pierre picked them up and repeated the performance, calling out, "Peace. Peace." Again they fluttered and fell at his feet. By this time, he realized that their wings had been clipped and they would not be flying for peace or anything else. The foreigners were now trying to suppress their laughter, but soon everyone, audience included, saw the humour of it and dissolved into laughter too.

Another peace effort had failed!

Now I was here to talk about work with Fr Pierre, who cleared a place amongst the clutter for me to sit, before we got down to business. We discussed many work possibilities, finally coming up with the decision for me to centre my work in the San Ro section of the camp. We chose San Ro, for it was the home of the poorest people, mainly families of soldiers. What my work would be, we had yet to decide, but next day I would go to San Ro and meet with the administrator, Mr Lay Khek, to discuss with him my future role there.

The following day, I fronted up at the office of Mr Khek. I was greeted by a slightly overweight Cambodian man in his forties, who spoke English quite well. I introduced myself and went on to explain why I was there. His face lit up. He told me there were many problems in his camp; the people being so poor they welcomed any help that was available. It was obvious that he really cared about the welfare of his people and was genuinely pleased to hear that I had come to work in his camp. His suggestion was that I make a house-to-house survey, finding needs, recording them and we would work from there. My hours would be from Monday to Saturday, with Wednesdays off. Wednesday was rice distribution day in San Ro camp.

Rice distribution was an important day in the lives of the people, each camp being allocated a different day to receive their ration. A large field was set aside in each camp as a distribution centre, where family members assembled with their ration card, to receive their weekly allowance. On each section's appointed ration day, schools would close and work would stop for the all-important task of collecting the weekly supply. People would queue for hours in the hot sun, waiting for their rice and tinned fish handout, which was carried home, balanced precariously on the heads of the women, with the children following, carrying vegetables and whatever other rations were due at that time.

I relished the idea of a free day in the middle of the week, giving me a chance to check out other programmes and meet with friends in other parts of the camp. Mr Khek promised to appoint a permanent translator, who would accompany me on my daily rounds. This would be tiring, hot work but I felt happy that I would be working with the San Ro people, assessing their needs and hopefully, able to ease some of their problems.

A few days later, I was prepared, having set myself up with books, paper, files, pens, bag, hat and walking shoes, for the long job ahead. When I arrived, Mr Khek introduced me to Sarath, who would be my translator. Sarath, a young man in his mid-twenties, was tall for a Cambodian, with very dark skin and a nice, pleasant face. Little did I know then that I would have a long association with this young man, he becoming almost a member of my family. But now I could see that he was very ill at ease in the presence of a foreigner, so I tried to alleviate his discomfort by asking him a little about himself. I found his English quite good when he proceeded to tell me about his family. I learnt that he was married with a five-month-old son, and that his parents and sisters also lived in San Ro camp. We talked about the job ahead, what it entailed and how we would go about it. We decided that first we would make up a questionnaire and print separate copies for each household we visited. Sarath was well aware of the many problems that existed in this camp, so was able to help a lot with the type of questions to be put forward.

The office supplied me with a map of San Ro, containing eight sections set out in rows, with a population of around 6000 people. When I looked at the map, I realized that we had a huge task ahead if we were to cover this whole area in the six months I was to be here, so we would need to get on with the job as soon as possible.

The San Ro KWA had their centre close to the administration block and I was offered a room in their building. The room was very small, containing only a bamboo table and chair, but it would be good to have a base, somewhere to come back to for lunch and at the end of the day. This KWA centre catered for the poorest women of San Ro, teaching them sewing, weaving, knitting, crocheting and other crafts. Their classes were from 8am to 11am and 2pm to 5pm, under the supervision of Rucha and her Khmer teachers.

By the time I arrived in the morning, the place was buzzing with activity and the noise of twenty treadle sewing machines going flat out amid the constant chatter of the women. They all stood up to greet and welcome me to their centre when I made my first appearance. I was escorted around the room by the president of the association, where she showed me, with much pride, the work being done by the ladies.

Before long, all was prepared and Sarath and I set off for the first interviews. We had decided to start at section eight, the most distant, and gradually work our way back to the office. This meant that we would have to walk about a kilometre along the road before we reached the section, then in about another three hundred metres. I would be on my feet out in the hot sun most of the day, so the work would certainly keep me fit.

It had been raining heavily the night before, which did not affect the surface of the gravel road, but we soon found this was not so when we turned into the track between the houses. The ground surface here was clay, and held pools of water, turning it into deep mud in parts. It was really difficult to hold your footing and I found myself slipping and sliding, making progress very slow. We finally reached our goal, the house in the far corner of San Ro camp, and Sarath explained to the occupants, our reason for being there. There was a flurry of excitement when the people realized they would be entertaining a foreigner in their home and they busied themselves making a place for me to sit. Within a few minutes, the usual crowd had formed outside all openings, anxious to listen in and discover the purpose of our visit. We would record names and ages of all family members, find out how many food rations they were receiving, if the children were attending school and what their most urgent needs were.

We only managed to visit three families the first morning. Lunchbreak for the Cambodians was from 11am to 2pm, during which time they ate their meal, had a shower and a sleep. This meant that we would have to be on our way back to our office by ten-thirty each day, so that Sarath would be back in time for lunch with his family. I realized that we would just have to get going earlier in the morning and work a bit faster or we would never get the job done in the time. However, that was easier said than done. After the first day, word spread about our mission and families would be waiting expectantly for us to arrive. They enjoyed these sessions so much that they did not want us to leave and would engage in long conversations, telling us all about their lives, families and needs. I enjoyed these discussions but it did slow us down.

By the end of the first week, I realized that these people had many serious problems. Because of the UN policy at that time of only allocating rations to women and girls, families with a large number of males were in dire straits. One lady, who had a husband and five sons, therefore receiving only one ration, told me that her children woke up every night crying with hunger. Neighbours helped out a little, but their rations were only sufficient to support their own families. As well as this problem, there was a shortage of clothes, mosquito nets, cooking pots and other household items. When families first arrived in the camp the KWA was meant to supply them each with a coir sleeping mat, mosquito net, blanket and one cooking pot. Many people arrived illegally at night and were afraid to front up to authorities, so were bereft of these essential items. I also found that a vast number of children in San Ro camp were not attending school. The reasons given for this were many and varied, but I could see that a large number of them, especially girls, were being kept home to carry water, look after younger siblings or help with household chores. But I soon realized that the most acute problem was the shortage of food, which would need to be tackled immediately.

I went to see Fr Pierre about this dilemma and other problems that faced these poor people. When I told him about the hungry children, he immediately handed over 1,000 baht (approx. AUD$50), which he surmised would be enough to buy rice for sixty needy families immediately. He agreed to donate more money, as required, for these impoverished households. I would arrange for Mr Khek to buy some supplies in the camp, then I would send selected families to the distribution centre nominated by him. When I told Fr Pierre that many families lacked clothing, he told me to go ahead and help myself to the boxes of clothes downstairs. Cooking pots, etc. I would organize with the KWA president.

I made my way down to the undercroft to start this task. I was shocked, when I opened the boxes, to find that rats, mice, spiders and cockroaches had already made their homes there, destroying many of the garments. Others had been ruined with damp and many pieces were unsuitable for Cambodian people, but I realized that I should be able to salvage quite a few usable items. I planned to spend the day sorting and washing the clothes. I would have to apply for a pass to bring them in, which would take a week or more to be processed. In the meantime, I realized I would have to find a suitable place to store the clothes in the camp. I made my way to the handicapped centre, which now had a furniture workshop, and told Kike of my needs. He promised to have a bamboo cupboard with shelves made and ready within a week. My next purchase was a padlock to go on the outside, knowing that the clothes would not last long unless locked away when I left the camp.

Now that we had supplies, Sarath and I decided it would be best to distribute items to needy families as soon as their needs were recognized, which would mean setting aside some time each day for allocation. I would do this in the lunchbreak, for I certainly did not need three hours off then. I could do this alone, leaving Sarath time to spend with his family and have a sleep.

By the time the boxes arrived in the camp, I had found many families desperately in need of clothes. At the UN clothing handouts, each person received an item of clothing, regardless if it was for man, woman or child, leaving it up to them to swap with others for something suitable. I decided not to do the allocation this way, but there certainly would not be the time for people to pick and choose. I had sorted the clothes into men's, women's, large, small, girl's, boy's and baby's. I distributed them this way and was pleased to note that recipients seemed happy with what they received. However, the needs were so great in this camp that after two weeks, I was dismayed to find that my supplies had almost run out.

I was relating the story of these needy families to an American couple, Cynny and Bob Robinson, who had just finished their work in the camp and were leaving to go home. When they heard of the dire needs of the San Ro people, they immediately gave a donation of US$50 for the purchase of more clothes. A Vietnamese lady visitor also heard about the problem and donated US$30 for the same cause. I decided it would be best to spend this money at the market in Bangkok, where the clothes were much cheaper, and I desperately needed to restock.

I made my way to Bobe market in Bangkok the following weekend. Here everything was sold in bundles of twelve. With the donated money and some of my own, I was able to purchase supplies of men's shirts, tracksuit pants, women's blouses, sarongs, and children's and baby clothes. I hired a tuktuk to take me to the bus station and loaded my purchases aboard. The people who received these articles of clothing were overjoyed. For most of them, it was the first time they had ever had brand-new clothes.

Soon Bangkok office heard about my work with these disadvantaged people and sent down boxes of donated secondhand clothes and shoes for distribution. This enabled supplies to always be on hand when required.

Getting children to attend school was not always easy. As most of the parents in this camp had never attended school themselves, they could see no reason why their children should; also, they always gave the excuse that the children had no suitable clothes to wear to school. Sarath and I set up a system to encourage school attendance. When the parents agreed to their child's participation, we would go with them to visit the principal of the school to request admission. When this was granted, on the afternoon before the child's first school day, they would receive a new set of clothes. This system worked in most cases, though sometimes we found that the children would only attend for a week, then their clothes would be sold. However, we were too busy to do a follow-up and trusted that at least some of them would benefit.

On my return to the office one day in May, I was saddened to hear that Site 8, the camp south of Aranyaprathet and housing Khmer Rouge families, had been shelled the night before, with eleven people killed and many wounded. This put fear into the Site 2 people, who had also heard shelling during the evening and expected that their camp may be the next hit. For the next few nights, many families slept out, crammed into their bunkers, where they felt safer below ground level. However, heavy rain one evening filled the bunkers with water, forcing the families back into their huts. They would repeat this move many times when shelling was close.

Sarath was waiting in the office when I arrived for work, telling me that a shell had landed next to a neighbour's house the night before but had not exploded. He took me over to see it. Right next to the building was an angled hole in the ground, with a cordoned off area around. On looking into the hole I could see the tail fins of an unexploded rocket buried about half a metre down. The family living here had no idea about their lucky escape, until they went out in the morning and found the shell buried. Had it exploded, the family and many of those around would have been wiped out. Thai military had been notified, and they sent bomb experts to defuse and remove the missile later that day.

Three friends from Australia, Ros, Betty and Winsome, who were to holiday in Thailand, requested a visit to the camp. I made the application to our head office a few weeks before their arrival and was pleased when approval was granted for a one-day pass. I had recently moved into a house closer to town, which I shared with Marie-Claude, who was now on vacation in France, so there was plenty of room to accommodate my guests.

The day of their arrival, I caught the bus to Bangkok. It was great to meet up with old friends, hear the latest news from home, receive mail and a box of new Australian T-shirts for camp children. These had been donated by my sister, Jeanette's friend, Peg Eaton, whose family ran a small factory in Perth. Over the years, many more T-shirts were kindly donated by this family and well received by grateful Cambodians.

I spent the next two days with my friends, doing the rounds of Bangkok, before we headed back to Aranyaprathet by bus. COERR had given me the loan of a car for the day that my friends would be in the camp. This would make it much easier because I had planned to take them to as many places as possible in the short time we had. Earlier, Ros had written to ask if there was anything she could bring from home for the camp people. I suggested that she bring some cosmetics, as I knew the girls in the sewing room would love them. Our first stop in the camp was to this centre, where I took the visitors to meet the students. The girls all gathered around in excitement when Ros opened her bag and they saw the lipstick, eyeshadow, powder and rouge. One of the girls offered to be a model while Ros demonstrated the art of applying makeup. It was an interesting and exciting session for the young women, who never had the chance to own or apply cosmetics before. It was still more thrilling when Ros presented each girl with an item from the supply for them to keep. After their impromptu lesson, the students proudly escorted the visitors around their workshop to show their handicrafts, presenting each of them with a small gift of their work, as a memento.

Next, I took my guests on a tour of the camp. They were treated to a performance of both classical and folk dance presented by children, accompanied by musicians using traditional instruments, and supported by a group of singers. They performed the classical blessing dance, which was always presented first on the programme for the purpose of welcoming guests, finishing with the dancers throwing flower petals at the feet of the audience. This was followed by the popular coconut-shell dance, which was performed at all kinds of ceremonies but most often during weddings in Cambodia. The dance was presented by a team of boys and girls in bright green and gold costumes, each holding empty halves of coconut shell that were clapped together in time with the music. The small performers put on a faultless demonstration, pleasing and amazing the company with its professionalism, all lining up at the end of the performance to take their bows and meet the guests. We rewarded them with a supply of soft drink and biscuits, a rare treat for the children.

Sarath had invited us all to his home for lunch. It was a big occasion for Cambodian families to have foreign guests and the ladies had been cooking all morning. Sarath and his father joined us for a delicious lunch, after which, Ros, who loves to sing, told the family that it was an old Australian tradition that guests always sang a song to thank the hosts. She lined us all up and we sang 'Waltzing Matilda', while the family stood open-mouthed watching this 'strange' tradition. I am sure they didn't know whether to laugh or cry. The atmosphere was cleared by Ros, who soon had everyone laughing with her jokes and antics.

We spent the rest of the day visiting homes of many people I knew, including one family of fifteen children. The mother, a large happy woman, was delighted to entertain the foreigners in her home, telling us the story of her life and introducing the children one by one to the guests. We visited the orphanage, handicapped centre, hospitals, TB clinic and coffee shop, all unique in their own way. My friends found it all rather mind-boggling, but an interesting and inspiring day. By the time we had made the long journey back to Aranyaprathet, everyone was exhausted. To perk them up after an hour's rest, I took them to one of the many beauty parlours in town, where they had their hair shampooed - a most refreshing experience. This shampoo includes a massage of the head, shoulders, arms and back, taking almost an hour and costing the equivalent of sixty cents Australian.

My friends and I spent the next few days relaxing at the beach. It was great to breathe in the fresh, salty air and swim in the clean ocean again after the dust, dirt and squalor of the camp. All too soon the holiday was over and they were ready to return home. On departure Ros, Betty and Winsome, all assured me that they had found their Site 2 visit to be the highlight of their holiday, describing it as an incredible and unique experience they would never forget.

When I returned to the camp, Sarath, who was waiting at the office, greeted me with enthusiasm, telling me how pleased he was that I had come back. I found over the years of working here that when you left the camp for any length of time, the people never really believed you would return. Sadly, they had been let down so many times in their lives they never really trusted anyone.

While at the beach, I had gathered a bag of shells to take back for the camp children. I soon found that they were a hit with children and adults alike, most of whom had never seen the ocean, let alone the shells from it. Wherever I took them, I was mobbed with people wanting to get a closer look, feel and examine them and hear the story of the beach from where they came. It made me realize that things we took for granted had never been experienced by these people with their lives so cloistered, both here and back in their own country.

On arrival at my office, one of our Cambodian sewing teachers brought a pretty little two-year-old girl to meet me, explaining that she was her new daughter. I knew that she and her soldier husband had no children of their own, so asked how this had come about. She told me that this child was not wanted by her parents, who already had five others, so she had bought her for 300 baht (about AUD$16). I was to find that this was not an uncommon practice in this camp, where life was very tough for big families. Sometimes, on my travels around, when I would speak to or admire a small child, the mother would offer them as a gift, begging me to take the child home to Australia, saying, "I want you to be the little one's mother." It was hard to make them understand that it was impossible to do this, sometimes incurring the displeasure of the mother when the offer was declined.

During my rounds, I was confronted by the smell of meat cooking at the house I was visiting. This was so unusual that I went out the back to see what it was. I came across a group of people sitting around a claypot fire, over which was suspended a wire frame holding long, thin pieces of meat. I was horrified to discover they were skinned rats that had been caught in the camp and claimed by those present to be a rare delicacy. There was a look of delight on the faces of the group as they waited, mouths watering, for the feast to follow. They could not understand my look of revulsion and cry of horror when I learnt what they were!

Vietnamese Refugees

On Wednesdays I would often call to see Phoeuy and we would visit the Vietnamese compound. Here there was always plenty of activity, for they are very energetic and hard working. As we made our way between the homes, people were always busy, whether working on their huts, digging, chopping wood or playing games. Markets, stalls, barbershops, restaurants, were set up in every possible space and a general air of liveliness prevailed. In contrast, their Cambodian neighbours would more likely be found reclining in hammocks or relaxing at home.

Buildings in the Vietnamese camp were quite different, consisting mainly of large, long huts made to hold fifty people. Inside, along each wall, a bamboo bed stretched the length of the building to accommodate its fifty occupants, each person's belongings piled at the top of their allotted space. Here and there curtains were hung to give some privacy. Sometimes, a shelf was built above the bed to hold possessions or even to sleep on, but overall, this was crowded, uncomfortable communal living. Later, when the Vietnamese camp was moved to Site 2 South, these large buildings were replaced by small huts each holding four to six people, allowing for more comfort and privacy.

This camp, unlike its Cambodian counterpart, housed many more single people, mostly young men. Families in Vietnam would pool their resources to send a family member to the border of Thailand and Cambodia with the hope of gaining resettlement, establishing themselves in the new country, then sending for family members to join them. It was an arduous and dangerous journey to undertake; some never making it, others robbed of all possessions. Many women were abducted and raped by Cambodian or Thai soldiers, but still they came by the thousands, always hoping for that chance of acceptance into a third country.

I was approached by a young Chinese/Vietnamese man when walking through this camp one day. He was very friendly, just wanting to talk to me and practice his English. He told me his name was Ronald (this name adopted since he arrived), that he was twenty-four years old, and had come to the camp from Saigon one month before, with his two sisters, because he said, "Living conditions under communism are unbearable." It had taken them two weeks to find their way from Vietnam, across Cambodia to Site 2. During this time they had walked for many kilometres, rowed across rivers, finally paying a Cambodian guide to get them across the border into Thailand and so into the camp.

I would often meet up with Ronald when I visited here, usually making our way to the coffee shop, where he would talk for hours about his life and family back in Vietnam. On one such visit, he told me that he had written some letters in the hope of gaining entry to a safe country, asking me if I would post them for him. I agreed and he handed them over, telling me they were very important and not to lose them. I hid them in a book in my bag, as we were not allowed to handle mail at all, so I didn't get a good look at them until I took them out in Aranyaprathet to post. When I did, I was amazed to see the addressees - CIA, FBI and Ronald Reagan (then US President). He certainly believed in going right to the top! Maybe this new approach worked, for about a year after this, he told me that he and his sisters had received approval and were off to settle in the USA!

Being classified as political refugees, people from Vietnam had much more chance of resettlement than Cambodians. This ruling enticed many Cambodians to register as Vietnamese, with the hope of getting through the tough interrogation process. They would change their names, fabricate a life story, attend Vietnamese language classes, all with the hope of bluffing their way through the interviews, which, surprisingly, many of them did, until more stringent screening methods were later adopted.

Interviews to gauge eligibility were held about every two months at a centre not far from KID camp, to where those selected for questioning would be transported by bus. Before being classed as suitable for resettlement, these people would have to survive at least three interviews, mainly to determine if they were political refugees, therefore, making it too dangerous for them to return to their country. After completing this process, many people failed the test and were then rejected which sent them deeply into depression, and there were many suicides in the camp. Those rejected, felt they had failed their families back home, and the disgrace was too much for them to bear.

For the successful ones, it was very exciting. When the time came to leave, they turned up in their best clothes, clutching their meagre possessions, to board the buses transporting them to Phanat Nikhom camp, about four hours away. Crowds of well wishers gathered early in the morning to farewell family members, friends and neighbours. As the buses pulled away, as well as the farewells and cheers, there would be tears and sobbing from people waving goodbye to their loved ones, with the realization that they may never see them again.

A young Vietnamese man, Thach Sen, with whom I had become very friendly, had come to the border two years before, leaving his wife and three children behind. He was desperately wanting to gain entry into another country, settle in, then send for his family to join him. However, after three interviews, with rejections each time, his chances seemed slim. He was feeling quite dejected, when the opportunity came for him to help ICRC at the interview centre to weed out the impostors, with the promise of resettlement in Denmark for his assistance.

He accepted the offer, though fully aware that he could be putting his life at risk. The requirements were for him to be present at interviews, conducted by English speakers with a Vietnamese interpreter. He was to listen in, to determine which accents of those being questioned were Vietnamese or which ones had a Cambodian inflection. The Cambodian impostors would then be renounced and sent back to their camp. Rejection was so distressing to many of these people that they became quite violent, causing Thach Sen to be moved to KID camp for his safety. He thought this a high enough price to pay for his promised resettlement.

After a month of his attending the interview centre, I called to visit him at his new address in KID, only to find him in deep depression. He had just received word that his application to resettle in Denmark had been rejected. Now he was still under threat, his chance of resettlement gone, away from all his friends and living in a camp completely occupied by Cambodians, who deeply resented Vietnamese people. He was devastated.

I promised I would look into the matter for him. I contacted ICRC representatives, urging them to honour their promise to this man, but they denied offering him resettlement, saying it was up to the country involved, not them. I reluctantly returned to tell Sen that though I had done my best, my pleas had fallen on deaf ears. I visited him many times after that in KID camp, trying to lift his spirits by bringing gifts and letters from friends in Site 2. However, these efforts only brought a momentary relief from his despair. Many of his countrymen in the camps were in similar situations, but they at least had the support of friends around them.

COERR workers had just arrived in camp one day when there was a loud explosion. Situation 3 was called on the radios, which meant we had to leave the camp immediately. No one was sure what it was all about until we had reached the meeting point, about ten kilometres along the road to Tapraya. A message over the radio informed us that a young woman had stepped on a landmine while walking across the rice distribution centre next to the Ampil hospital. At that time, no details of her condition were available.

This incident caused the camp to be closed to aid workers until the whole area was searched and the all clear given. During incidents such as this, 'limited medical access' only was allowed; meaning that only a restricted number of medical staff were permitted to enter the camp to attend to urgent cases. We were to learn later that the woman landmine victim, who was seven months pregnant, survived the blast but lost her foot, resulting in the eventual amputation of her leg. Amazingly, her baby survived. It transpired that the mine had been laid by a soldier after a dispute with the police about use of the field for volleyball games. This type of incident was all too prevalent here, where landmines or grenades could be bought very cheaply at the market.

While still unable to enter Site 2, I paid a visit to the hospital in KID to see how the woman was faring. She was in a ward with dozens of other landmine victims, both male and female. They were lying on hard wooden beds, some with bloody stumps where their legs had been, others with no arms, all with multiple lacerations from the mine blast they had experienced. A depressing sight, but made lighter by the looks of delight on the faces of the patients when I made my way between the beds. I found this a most humbling experience; here was I, able-bodied and fit, visiting all these severely injured people and they greeted me, smiling with pleasure that I had stopped to talk.

I went first to the bedside of the injured woman, who was sitting up and appeared to be quite happy and content, though she must still have been in a lot of pain. She showed no malice towards the minelayer, telling me that she was just unlucky to be there at the wrong time. After spending some time with her, I went to talk to the two men in the beds near her, who had each lost a leg. They told me that they were soldiers in the same regiment, who had been on patrol inside Cambodia three days before. One man said that he had stepped on a landmine when he went to a creek to have a drink, his friend in the next bed, had rushed to help. This man stepped on another mine when he reached for a tree branch to make a stretcher to carry his friend. So the sad stories continued, as I made my way around the ward talking to other victims. The surprising thing was that none of the injured seemed depressed or angry, but accepted this as their fate, or as Cambodians call it, their 'karma'.

Mine victims would stay in this ward for about ten days before being transferred to another centre in the compound, where they would assist in the production of their own prosthesis, or wheelchairs, if they were double amputees. The prosthesis for a single amputee was made with a wooden frame filled with plaster for weight, then covered with leather, finished with a layer of rubber under the wooden 'foot'; altogether very basic but functional. At one end of the building was a pathway between two handrails, where the amputees practiced walking with their new 'legs'. They appeared to adapt to these artificial limbs quite speedily and in no time were happily playing volleyball, bounding about on their new prostheses. The chairs for double amputees consisted of a wooden frame with bamboo slats for seat and back and bicycle wheels each side. The users became very adept at zooming around the gravel roads in their heavy chairs. They had many problems during the wet season, though, when the muddy ground made it hard for them to propel their chairs through the sludge.

Joined by my Son

Four days after the explosion the all clear was given, for workers to return to the camp. I was busy trying to complete the home visits, wanting everyone to have the same opportunities before I left. However, I soon realized that I had no chance of finishing the rounds of San Ro camp before my contract terminated in four weeks.

About this time, I received a letter from my son, Tim, who told me he had decided to come for a month's visit. I was thrilled at the prospect of having one of my family with me, for I missed them a lot. It would also help them to understand what kept me working here. Through COERR, I was able to secure a camp pass for him, then waited anxiously for his arrival. I had told friends of my son's visit, and they were looking forward to meeting one of my family.

On Tim's first day in camp I took him on a tour of inspection, accompanied by Sarath as our guide. Our first call was to the orphanage where we were soon surrounded by the residents, who had been waiting anxiously to meet my son. After their initial shyness, the English speakers were soon talking flat out, telling him about the camp, their jobs, study, etc. and asking many questions about his life. After spending some time there, we continued on to the hospital to meet Yan and Sovanna. They took us around the wards, introducing us to staff and patients and giving us a rundown on hospital procedures, before going on to meet Sarath's family. The rest of the afternoon was spent at the KWA centre and in my office, where Tim met staff and workers. At the end of a busy day, we headed back home in the medical van, Tim saying that he had found it very interesting but confusing, and difficult to absorb everything in so short a time.

He accompanied me on the daily rounds of San Ro camp. On one of these days, Sarath greeted us with the news that forty-one men had found their way into the camp the night before, arriving about midnight. They had left their families, making a quick exit when they heard that government troops were heading for their village, forcing all men deemed eligible, into the army. We went over to the hut where they were staying, to see if they needed help. Here we were confronted by a sorry sight. The thoroughly exhausted men were lying on the dirt floor, all attempting to rise when we entered. They looked tired and sick, so I motioned them to stay where they were. Their spokesman told us that they had walked for ten days to reach the camp, the last four without food. They finally reached the outskirts of Site 2 only to be robbed of all their possessions, even their shoes, by TF80 soldiers. Sarath told me that camp administration knew of their arrival and they were now waiting for a meal of rice, which was being cooked by the KWA ladies.

I shall never forget the day I presented each these men with a pair of thongs; a most touching experience. Their leader arranged for them to stand in a line while I handed each a new pair of cheap rubber thongs. I was rewarded with a huge smile, some of the men close to tears as they gave their thanks. For some, it was their first ever footwear, still others their first ever new ones. They tried them on, wiped them clean, sat down and turned them over in their hands, examining them all from front to back, top to bottom, before putting them on their feet to be examined again and tried out with a few steps, before wiping them clean and placing them back in their individual plastic bags. It was unbelievable and very moving to see the pleasure these grown men were getting from the gift of a pair of simple thongs.

While visiting the homes, we heard many stories of crimes, humiliations and financial gains executed by the TF80 soldiers against the camp people. They told us that a Cambodian man had been shot and killed by Thai soldiers, while collecting wood outside the confines of the camp. No enquiry would be held, the soldiers maintaining that they did their duty, when he was breaking camp rules. Some of the orphanage boys told us that TF80 soldiers had found an older man and woman outside the fence and forced them, at gunpoint, to lie down in the mud and 'swim' while they all stood and laughed at the couple's distress. Observers, fearing retribution, would not intervene or report the offences.

Site 2, North and South, was controlled by internal checkpoints that camp people were not permitted to travel between on weekdays, unless they had a work pass issued by TF80. The only time for free travel between north and south was eight hours on Sundays, but even then, rangers could make it very difficult for people to pass freely. Many people had family and friends in the other camp, so it was not long before they found a way to overcome this problem. A hole was cut in the barbed wire fence about two hundred metres from the military station through which people would climb, then hurry across the road when soldiers were occupied. However, the soldiers soon found out about this subterfuge and set up their own illegal checkpoint at the roadside, charging people one or two baht (5 or 10 cents) to go through. If Sarath and I were heading to Site 2 South, we would go through this way, taking a group of waiting people with us, much to the delight of the people and anger of the soldiers, who could not charge while a foreigner was present.

There was not much for women to do during the day hours so they would gather together outside their huts to socialize. I would come across groups of young women, babies in their arms, some hanging off the breast, where they seemed to be constantly feeding, all laughing and talking. Groups of older women met daily to chew betel nut and gossip, not missing anything that was happening in the vicinity. The pastime of chewing betel nut appeared to only be undertaken by the elderly women, easily identified by their red-stained and blackened teeth. Maybe this was the reason the young women avoided it! It was interesting to watch the ritual of preparing the betel nut, which was first ground into a thick paste, then spread carefully over leaves brought down from the mountain behind the camp. These leaves were then meticulously rolled and folded before the product was ready for use. One of the women asked me if we chewed betel nut in Australia, urging me to try it when I told her that we didn't. I put a little on my tongue but could not stand the bitter taste and the coating of betel nut in the mouth, which stayed with me all day.

We had just finished visiting the homes one day and were passing the outpatient clinic when we were stopped by a woman's screams. Outside the building, on a bench, lay a little boy about three years old, his mother next to him holding his hand and crying out. The child was blue in the face, obviously not breathing, while a medic was applying heart massage. I realized he needed mouth-to-mouth resuscitation as well, but not really confident, I held back. That was until Tim urged me on, saying, "Go on, you can do it, that is what you have been teaching for years." I had to lean over a bamboo barricade to apply expired air resuscitation, which I did, working together with the medic. We worked on the child for two or three minutes before realizing our efforts had been successful, when the child vomited into my mouth! This did not concern me at the time, as I was elated to see the colour come back into his face and know he was breathing again. However, I did spend the rest of the day repeatedly rinsing my mouth! The mother was relieved and overjoyed, picking up the crying child and hurrying off, not realizing how close to death her son had been.

A Wedding Celebration

I had received an invitation to attend Yan's wedding, to be held a couple of weeks before I was due to leave. I was looking forward to this occasion, for it would be my first time as a guest at a camp wedding. The Buddhist marriage service was a long affair, usually starting early the day before and finishing mid-afternoon, after which, the wedding guests were invited for the feast. Yan was attired in a black suit, white shirt and tie. His bride, Sophie looked beautiful in a gold brocade dress, gold bracelets, necklaces, rings and an elaborate hairdo, with the similarly attired groomsmen and bridesmaids. All were standing outside the wedding venue to welcome the sixty invited guests, when I arrived. The bride would change into many different outfits during the day; the number of these she wore, depicting the affluence of her family and their standing in the community. Because of this, many families would put themselves into deep debt, borrowing from moneylenders, who charged huge interest rates. Some even sold the family ration book to pay for a lavish wedding.

Sheets of bright blue plastic had been hung from the roof of Yan's uncle's house across to neighbour's roofs, while beneath this canopy were set tables and chairs for the guests. Decorations comprising branches of leaves, balloons and paper streamers cut from exercise book pages, were strung over the tables to give a festive atmosphere. Tables were covered with doilies, also cut from books, paper plates, plastic forks and spoons, bottles of soft drink and Mekhong whiskey and handwritten menus in Khmer and copybook English. The menu read as follows:

MENU

Dry Peanut	Desserts
Roast Chicken	Fresh Fruit -
Chicken Mix	Orange
Fry Chicken	Hairy Berry
Chicken Soup	(rambutan - a prickly red fruit)

When all the guests were present and had been seated, the celebration began. Dishes of food were brought out and guests were soon enjoying this feast, a far cry from the rice and tinned fish of their daily diet. It was not long before Western music, bellowing from speakers, in turn with a live band with traditional instruments and a lady singer were competing with guests' voices becoming louder as Mekhong whisky found its way down throats unaccustomed to alcohol. Halfway through the meal, the bridesmaids mingled with the company, handing out envelopes for guests to enclose their wedding gift, which was always money. The fun was starting now, as groomsmen tucked these gifts high up into the canopy overhead. Now it was up to the married couple to reach them. There were shouts of laughter as Yan lifted his wife, who retrieved the envelopes in her mouth. Cigarettes placed in the mouths of each guest by the bridegroom were then lit by the bride; even non-smokers having to take a puff to wish the bride and groom a long and happy marriage.

By now everyone was really enjoying themselves, teasing the couple and trying to get them closer together. Yan and Sophie were given a banana, and took an end each in their mouth. They were urged on by the laughing guests, to eat until their lips were touching, but the game ended before this happened, despite the encouraging cries of the crowd. All too soon, I realized that time had run out for me and I would have to leave, for it was approaching camp closing time. I said my farewells, thanking the bride, groom and parents for a great day and wishing the newlyweds every happiness for the future. I left to the sounds of laughter and hilarity, great to hear in this often sad and gloomy border camp.

Tim had been enjoying his days in the camp, with he and Sarath becoming firm friends. As we were making the rounds, he confided in me that he would love to stay on and continue the work in this camp. I suggested he consult with Mr Prapon, who was now director of programmes in Aranyaprathet, also speaking with Fr Pierre if COERR approval was given. I really hoped that, because he was now familiar with the work, he would be accepted, as he understood the problems, was compassionate and I knew he would do a good job. I would be able to leave, knowing my work would carry on and the whole camp could be covered, something that was not possible in the time left to me.

There were only two weeks now before I was due to leave so I had my fingers crossed for him. Tim had gone to Bangkok to meet with Fr Bunlert, who would make the final decision. A few days later, an elated Tim returned to tell me he had been appointed to the position for the next six months. I was so pleased, as now I knew I could leave, secure in the knowledge that my work would carry on.

I was kept busy saying my goodbyes, sad to be leaving my many friends. On my last day in camp, I was overwhelmed by the kindness of my camp friends. They came to see me off, bearing gifts, many of which they had made themselves - carved apsara dancers, a beautiful painting of the camp, kramas and woven baskets, gifts I would treasure as a reminder of my Cambodian friends and Site 2 camp.

I spent one day in Bangkok before boarding the plane for home, feeling sad to leave, but looking forward to seeing my family, eating Western food, enjoying hot showers and most of all sitting on a toilet again!

CHAPTER 4

Soon after returning to Australia, I was teaching swimming again. As I took my classes through their paces, my mind would drift back to the impromptu swimming lessons I had given in the camp. After a particularly heavy downpour, deep muddy pools appeared in the drains around the camp roads, and soon filled with the naked bodies of small boys frolicking in the water. Many times, I would stop, roll up my pants and wade in, placing the children in a line before giving a quick swim lesson. This delighted the children, who would follow my instructions, laughing as they lapped up the attention. I could not help but compare the two situations. In Australia, in clean, unclouded pool water, children lined up in an array of expensive bathing costumes for their weekly lesson, but in the camp, in muddy drains, naked brown bodies splashed and enjoyed themselves though swimming in a virtual cesspool.

Try as I might, I found it increasingly difficult to dissociate myself from the past and my time spent on the border. Frequent letters from Tim kept me up to date with details of the situation and work developments, making me even more 'homesick' for the camp. Maybe, if I returned, I would get it out of my system for good; or that was what I thought when I made the decision to give it one more try when my swimming classes were finished. After my resolution was made, I felt happier and relaxed, and set about making preparations to leave.

By the time I arrived in Thailand, Tim had completed his contract and was preparing to leave for home. I was able to spend a few days with him in Bangkok, catching up on the latest camp news, before he flew out.

I received another welcome reception from the COERR staff in Bangkok, who sent me on my way with the usual instructions to go into the camp, determine where the most need lay and go from there.

I had been invited to share a house closer to the camp, in the village of Tapraya; fellow residents being two Australian nuns, Srs Bernie and Fay, Fr Vincent from Belgium and an American teacher, Mary Sutphin. On arrival, Sr Bernie, who had just returned from the camp, showed me to my quarters in a big wooden house. I had been allocated a large upstairs front room, containing the usual hard base bed, one wooden cupboard with two shelves, a desk and chair. Quite spacious compared to previous lodgings.

The education van full of COERR teachers had returned by the time I had unpacked, so I made my way downstairs to meet them. I had heard that many new education programmes had been introduced since I left, including numerous English and some French language classes. I met English teachers, John, Mark, Bob, Jake, Josie and Sharon from USA; Australian Brian; Ashley from Ireland; and French teachers, Beatrice and Veronique. The van driven by Ashley, stopped off at this house each morning en route to the camp to pick up Tapraya residents, returning them in the afternoon before continuing on to Aranyaprathet. By now, most of the COERR overseas staff lived in Tapraya village, preferring the much shorter, twenty-five-kilometre daily drive to their workplace.

Tim had already informed Sarath that I would be returning. He was waiting at the office in the camp when I eventually received my entry documents, and told me that he had been there every day for the last week, hoping I would be in one of the cars. He asked if he could work as my translator again. I explained to him that I had no definite job as yet, but he assured me he would be willing to wait, because he really wanted to work with me. That would suit me, for he was a good translator, as well as being very honest and reliable.

Since I had left, camp population had grown, more bunkers were in evidence due to recent shelling attacks, agencies had set up numerous new programmes and many more foreign workers were visible. As I wandered around the camp for the first few days checking out all the changes, I felt like I was home again.

I found that Mrs Long Lean had been granted resettlement in USA and was now living there. Her six children were still in one of the border camps, though she was trying desperately for approval for them to join her. Phoeuy and the other boys, who had been adopted by Long Lean were now living in quarters behind the COERR office under the care of Mr Viseth, the new office manager. It was great to catch up with them again and hear all their news. They told me that high school education had now been introduced, so they had taken advantage of this opportunity and were all studying hard.

A new co-ordinator, Fr Alfonso, had been appointed to lead the Education and Social Service team. Fr Alfonso, a Spanish Jesuit priest, who had lived in Thailand for the last twenty years, regarded himself as more Thai than Spanish. He was a tough man with whom to work, having lived so long in Thailand he was accustomed to the servility of Thais towards their superiors, which he did not receive from the foreign workers. This caused many clashes over the years. There was a lot of friction among staff, caused by Fr Alfonso's attitude towards foreign workers and his harassment of certain staff members, culminating in a meeting being called by a number of disgruntled workers to see what could be done. A vote of no confidence in Fr Alfonso's leadership was cast and presented to head office, requesting that staff responsibilities be taken from him. It took some time, but he was eventually relieved of his duties on the border and summoned by his superiors, to work in Bangkok, much to the relief of most foreign staff.

Camp people were now finding many different ways to make money. Two coffee and noodle shops had opened, small stalls had been set up along the road, where vendors sold rice cakes, noodles and small items such as combs, toothbrushes, shampoo, small mirrors and sarongs. Bicycle taxis had appeared on the roads. For the sum of two baht and perched on the metal carrier behind the rider, you could be taken anywhere in Site 2. One enterprising man had set up a homemade chocolate wheel, charging one baht a spin, the winner taking a handful of sticky toffee, which was pulled out at arm's length until it broke off. I always stopped and had a spin of the wheel, invariably winning a prize, which I gave to the children who quickly gathered. I'm not sure if I was always eligible for this reward, or if it was given because I was a foreigner but it did not matter, as the children were always delighted with this sticky offering. One blind ex-soldier had acquired a hand-held speaker. He walked around the camp, led by his little son, stopping here and there to tell Cambodian folk stories, sometimes accompanying the stories with a tune on an old Cambodian-style guitar. In no time, a crowd formed, listening intently to the tales. At the end, his son would hold out his father's hat for donations. I loved to stop and listen to him, always receiving his thanks and 'God bless you' when I gave my contribution.

A Camp Survey

Not long after I returned, I was approached by Prapon (COERR's Aranyaprathet director) to conduct a survey of camp people over fifty-five years old. An English organization, HelpAge, was interested in funding a programme for the elderly in Site 2, if it was deemed necessary. I was to choose a broad section of the camp in which to hold this study. Its purpose was to establish the percentage of elderly, age brackets, state of health, support systems and activities. The job would have to be done in haste, with only two months to complete the survey and submit a written report with recommendations.

All too often, these rush jobs were made here, resulting in insufficient details being collected, but I accepted anyway, happy to have a definite role to fill. Sarath was also pleased that he could work with me again. Questionnaires were quickly prepared, so we could start as soon as possible on the door-to-door survey. COERR had now invested in bicycles for staff members, so this would make it quicker to get the job done and certainly easier on the legs.

Not long after foreign workers had left the camp a short time later, we were shocked to learn that Site 2 had just been shelled. Details were sketchy, giving no indication of casualties, leaving us all terribly concerned for our Cambodian friends, staff members and camp people. UNBRO announced that there would be 'limited medical access only', to the camp until further notice.

We all stayed close to the radio in Tapraya that evening and the following morning, hoping to elicit more information about the attack. We had to wait until medical staff returned in the afternoon before we discovered the extent of the shelling. One shell had landed in Site 2 South and four in the north, killing five people and injuring twenty others, many seriously. San Ro camp had taken the brunt of the attack with three shells exploding between the houses in a heavily populated area, leaving me very concerned for the safety of Sarath and his family.

It was another two days before the all clear was given and we were allowed entry into the camp. After checking that Phoeuy and the boys were all right, I made my way to Sarath's house. I was relieved to find that his immediate family were unhurt, but sad to hear that two of his relatives had been killed and another two wounded. He took me to where three shells had landed, all in the same vicinity. One of the shells had exploded on the pathway between the huts, leaving a small hole, considering the terrible damage it caused. Two huts nearby were completely demolished, and others within a radius of ten metres were pockmarked with shrapnel.

Sarath's uncle, who had lost his son and daughter in the attack, was holding a service for the deceased. Candles and incense were burning over photos of the dead siblings, below which family and neighbours were kneeling in prayer. A funeral service had already been held at the pagoda and the bodies cremated. I was approached by the mother of one of the wounded, who begged me to visit her twenty-year-old daughter who had been taken to KID hospital with severe facial and leg injuries. I promised her and other families that I would visit their loved ones and report back on their condition.

Mr Khek showed me photos taken at the camp hospital on the night of the shelling. Dead and badly injured people, including three children, were pictured lying on bamboo beds while medics attended to them by torch and candlelight. They were given emergency treatment before they were lifted onto truck trays to be transported to KID hospital. One of the medics shown, was attending to his seriously injured sister, who later died in hospital. The pictures were very graphic and brought to mind just how isolated, alone and unprotected the camp people were when we left at night.

I visited the wounded in KID hospital a few days later. I found that one person had died, a young man with chest, leg and abdominal wounds was still unconscious, with little hope of recovery, but all others were doing reasonably well, considering the extent of their injuries. One man, whose wife had been killed in the shelling, was attending to his own two badly injured children, plus another child, who had been hurt and sent alone. I had brought my camera and received permission to take photos of the injured to show to their families. These photographs would reassure them that their loved ones were still alive. Sometimes it would be days before relatives were notified of a death in KID.

When I took the photographs back, the families were relieved to see them and discover that their loved ones were improving. The mother of the young woman with severe facial injuries was especially pleased to see the photo of her daughter and find that doctors had done such a good job repairing the damage, which would result in only minimal scarring.

While in KID, I called to see my Vietnamese friend, Thach Sen, who was still languishing there a year later. He didn't know I had returned, and his face lit up when I came to his door. I took him to lunch in the camp restaurant, where we sat down and had a long chat. He told me that he had been quite miserable with nothing to do all day, but was cheered recently by the news that he had been selected for the next round of interviews. It was the old story, with people's emotions always on a roller coaster ride; up and down, up and down. I just hoped for his sake that this time he would be successful and receive the longed for wish of resettlement.

The survey kept me busy going from house to house daily, interviewing the older people and checking out their circumstances. It soon became evident that many of the elderly had a good family support system, although they confided in me that they missed the comradeship of village life and despaired of ever seeing their homeland again. For the few elderly people I found who were living alone, life was very tough. Some told me they had lost all their children during the Pol Pot years, now having no family structure to which they could cling, feeling they had nothing to live for, their lives filled with grief. Traditionally, in Cambodia, the elderly are respected for their wisdom, revered as family heads and their advice sought, but here families had been split and old customs were dying.

Life was not so difficult for the older women living in a family situation, where they were kept busy looking after grandchildren and assisting with household chores. However, time fell heavily on the hands of older men who were accustomed to spending the daylight hours out in the fields. They sat around idle and depressed, smoking innumerable cigarettes, dreaming of the day when they could return to their villages and their rice fields. The greatest fear expressed by all the elderly being that they would die in a foreign land.

Sometimes, all the misery around would get too much, for listening to the sad stories, made me realize there was not a single family left untouched by the genocide of the Khmer Rouge. Families had been torn apart, people uprooted from their homes, rejected as refugees; now living within the confines of a dusty, squalid camp. I could not help but admire the courage of these people and wonder how I would have coped had I been in the same position.

People, when they spoke of the past, always referred to it as 'before, during or after Pol Pot'; the terrible years forever imprinted in their memory. They did not talk of them often but when they did, a look of incredible sadness would come into their faces.

When I first arrived and saw all the problems surrounding the camp population, I wanted to solve the lot, but as time progressed, I realized that you cannot move mountains but must be patient, working on them bit by bit. It took some time for me to come to this realization and gain patience, but it was considerably easier when I had been through this slowing down process.

The Boarders

I was receiving regular mail from Tim, who was having great trouble settling back in Australia. He had managed to find some interested people, who donated money and books for the 'boarding school'. He wrote, sending the money and informing me that a shipment of books was on the way.

The boarding school was a centre set up for boys and young men, who were alone in the camp and were keen to study. The ages of these young people ranged from sixteen years to early twenties and they all had a common interest; a burning desire to learn. For most of them, this was their first opportunity to attend school after growing up during the Khmer Rouge occupation, when education was banned.

More than fifty of these young men lived in a large hut under the guidance of their Cambodian teacher and mentor, Keo Song. They attended classes each day at the school set up in the compound. Fr Vincent, who also taught at the school, took a great interest in the welfare of these young people. He was concerned that the food they were receiving from the UN was not enough for growing boys, arranging with COERR nutrition centre to supplement their diet with extra vegetables and some meat brought in each week. One of the boys once said of Fr Vincent, "He is a very strong influence in our lives, gives us food, teaches, helps and cares for us like a real father."

When I told the students about the gift of books from Tim and friends, I was met with cries of delight. Books were highly prized in the camp; the only ones available were textbooks, also in short supply. The boys were very excited that the books were written in English, enabling them to improve their language skills. They gathered around, firing questions at me about Tim: What is he doing now? Where did he get the books? When will he come back?

I enjoyed visiting the boarders and sitting in on their English class run by an affable young American, John Henderson, who had a great knack for teaching. His students always achieved top marks, while enjoying the classes and his humour. John's classroom could always be identified by the laughter issuing forth. John and I would often have lunch with the boys, bringing along extras such as fresh fruit, cakes or biscuits; a real treat for them. We introduced them to the game of charades that brought forth much hilarity, as they had never experienced word games before. It was always a pleasure to be involved with these intelligent and interesting young men.

I became very close to one young man, Saren, at this school, adopting him as one of my Cambodian 'sons'. Saren, a good-looking young man with a charming manner, was in his early twenties and came from a middle-class Cambodian family, all of whom had died or been killed during the Khmer Rouge takeover. He was fifteen years old after the Khmer Rouge fled, with nowhere to go, he wandered the countryside alone, eventually finding his way back to the street in Phnom Penh, where he had lived with his family, only to find the house was gone. He headed for the Thai border where he joined up with a team of smugglers, supporting himself by shuttling goods across the border. After narrowly escaping with his life when caught in a gunfight between rival groups, he decided the life was too risky, so he followed a group of refugees into one of the border camps, finishing up at this school. He was so happy to have this opportunity of an education, staying up till all hours of the night studying by candlelight on his bed under a mosquito net. I spent many happy hours with Saren and the other young men - Boney, Sararith, Savan, Sombath, Ratanak, Veasna and Vily - who were always bright and cheerful and loved to have company.

I had given Tim's money to Keo Song, and by the time the shipment of books arrived, a new building had been constructed, with a sign over the door naming it: 'TIM'S LIBRARY'. The boys had built shelves from bamboo and soon the books were all in place and documented, with a lending system set up, which would give access to the books for all students at the school. Tim collected many books over the next two years, which were added to the library, resulting in a quite large book centre that was enjoyed and appreciated by the students.

An incident, which happened while I was still working on the survey, brought home to me the vulnerability of the camp people. Sarath failed to come back to the office after lunch one day. He was usually very reliable, which made me concerned at his non-arrival. However, I soon dismissed my fears, thinking that something at home must have held him up. It was not until the following day that I discovered the reason for his absence. He told me that he was sleeping in his hammock outside his hut, when a drunken TF80 soldier came up and spoke to him. He did not wake, which made the soldier angry. His shouting finally roused Sarath, who woke to see a gun pointed at his head. The soldier berated him for not answering, made Sarath get down on his knees in the mud while he held the gun to his head, threatening to shoot. Sarath's wife, who witnessed this from inside, ran to the administration office to alert his father and Mr Lay Khek. They came hurrying back to find Sarath still being held at gunpoint. After remonstrating with the soldier, Mr Khek managed to calm him down before sending him on his way, leaving a very shaken Sarath and family.

When I heard the story next day, I was horrified to learn that incidents like this happened frequently but were never reported. I asked Sarath if he wished to report the matter to the ICRC, whose mandate it was to protect the people. If so, I would make the necessary arrangements. He agreed, so I contacted the head of the ICRC and arranged a meeting for him with Sarath.

After listening to Sarath's account of the incident, the head of this organization turned to Sarath and said, "The best thing is to forget that this happened, otherwise the soldier could come back and wreak his vengeance on the whole family." I was stunned. No wonder these poor people felt that nobody cared about them and they had nowhere to turn.

Work with Leprosy Patients

In the meantime, Josie, an English teacher, approached me with a request to take over her classes for leprosy patients as she was due to leave. I would enjoy the challenge of teaching English and the involvement with this group, who were shunned by their countrymen because of their disease. I invited Sarath to assist me, but he declined, for, like all Cambodians, he was fearful of contracting leprosy.

Working with these unfortunate people proved to be an interesting and rewarding experience that I will always remember. The classes were held in one corner of the ward for leprosy patients, and away from the main hospital. The building was the usual bamboo and thatch construction, containing about thirty beds for patients undergoing treatment for unhealed wounds and minor infections. More serious cases were sent to the special leprosy ward in KID. An outpatient clinic was attached to this building, where patients came to receive their daily medication or for dressing of wounds. There seemed to be a constant stream of leprosy patients with cuts and abrasions waiting here each day. I asked one of the nurses the reason for this and was told that the disease deadened the feeling in the affected parts, usually toes and fingers first, then feet, hands and so on as the disease advanced, unless treatment was sought. Because there was no feeling, cuts, burns, blisters and abrasions were not felt or attended to until infection had set in, which did not take long in these unhealthy surroundings.

I arrived at the classroom on Josie's last day, to be greeted by about twenty students of all ages. They stood up with a look of anticipation on their faces when I entered. Josie introduced me and I looked around at my students. Their ages ranged from teenagers to elderly, most of them with glaring evidence of leprosy. Many had no fingers or toes, badly deformed hands, feet and faces, no eyebrows and brown patches on their skin, obviously they had been suffering from the disease for a long time. In Cambodia, there had been no treatment for leprosy, so those afflicted just had to suffer, gradually becoming worse. Many leprosy sufferers were now coming over the border when they heard that they could receive treatment for their malady in Site 2 camp.

After introductions, the class got under way. It was soon evident that there was quite a mixture of levels, a few speaking good English, others not understanding a word but enjoying the involvement. Josie had managed to procure some basic language books which she used together with the blackboard. I had never taught English before, so was interested in getting a few ideas. I soon realized that I had a challenge ahead of me, considering the difference in levels of comprehension.

I turned up ready for my first class the following day. One of the students, Jin Jolin, who spoke good English, offered to translate for me. I soon found that the people in the class were more interested in listening to me speak, checking out my history, family details, etc. than learning English and were thoroughly enjoying the attention they were receiving. They asked me to draw a map of Australia on the board, show them where I lived, where Cambodia was situated, continuing on to population figures, industries, leisure, etc. They seemed interested in everything, as it was all new to them. I was not a very good teacher and many of them never advanced beyond the basics but they all seemed to enjoy the classes, turning up every day. I did manage to teach them the days of the week, having a good laugh when they repeated them after me, adopting my Australian accent.

After a few weeks of English classes, I decided it would be good to have a change from the daily lesson, electing to hold a music day. When I suggested this and enquired about instruments, some of my students offered to borrow them from friends. We planned the event for the following week when they could round up the instruments. I invited John Henderson along to play a tune on his mouth organ. John always carried his harmonica in his pocket, often stopping to give an spontaneous performance on the side of the road, where a crowd would soon gather to enjoy the music.

The music day arrived and my students filed in, all empty-handed. I asked where the instruments were that they had promised to bring, and was met with a number of excuses but no musical implements. What could we do? I couldn't let them down, because all the class, as well as bed patients, were looking forward to this musical interlude. We would just have to improvise. We gathered a few empty fish cans, which we filled with stones. Someone produced a large tin, tying a blanket over the end to serve as a drum, with a piece of bamboo for the drumstick. Bedends would double for a xylophone; strands of wire pulled firmly over a wooden frame would represent the traditional khim, and our band was ready.

John started the session off with a couple of tunes on his harmonica, which they all enjoyed, responding with loud applause. This was followed by the band playing traditional music on their makeshift instruments, producing quite a remarkable sound, not unlike the traditional ones. They soon got into the swing of things and thoroughly enjoyed themselves, playing one tune after another, much to the delight of the patients. It was gratifying to see all these people having such a good time, for there was not much pleasure in their lives.

Seeing the happy faces and joyous response of these leprosy patients to the impromptu concert inspired me to request some musical instruments from the handicapped workshop. Kike kindly agreed to have them made and donated for this good cause. It was not long before the leprosy ward had its own set of traditional musical instruments and some of the keener ones had learnt to play, entertaining the patients in the ward each afternoon, after language class.

My brother, Bruce, had planned a visit to Thailand, so I applied for a camp pass for him. It was good to have time away from the camp, to make the trip to Bangkok and spend a few days there before heading back to the border.

On his first day in camp, he was invited to join other guests at a camp wedding, a great opportunity to see this traditional ceremony. Weddings were always fun; a time for camp people to forget their problems and enjoy themselves, usually resulting in some having to be carried off after imbibing in alcoholic drink, to which they were unaccustomed. The celebration was well underway with guests relishing the festive atmosphere, when we heard a loud explosion. This was followed by a call over the radio, informing us that the situation was 'Number 3', meaning we must leave the camp immediately. On the street, people were running for home, some already in their bunkers, wedding guests quickly dispersed and we foreigners headed for the nearest vehicle to take us out. A sad finish for the bride and groom on this special occasion, and a dramatic introduction to Site 2 for Bruce!

We were not allowed back until two days later. It was then that Bruce met many of my friends, was taken on a tour of the camp, watched traditional dancing and sat in on my English class. He enjoyed talking to the people, displaying patience when people approached him to practice their English. He spent three days before heading back to Bangkok, then home. This was to be the first of many trips that Bruce made to the border camp over the years.

The border situation was very tense at this time, with constant shelling, almost daily Situation 1 calls and a number of camp evacuations for volags, when shelling became close. Site 8 camp was shelled again, putting more fear into the hearts of the Site 2 people, who were afraid that their camp would be the next target. The camp was in its third year and the strain of confinement was starting to show. A feeling of fear and desperation lay heavily in the air. The camp was dark from 6pm to 6am and if there was a storm during the night, a mine or hand grenade explosion, panic spread quickly. One of my workers once told me, "People in Site 2 live in constant fear. We are afraid of bandits, shelling, TF80 rangers, Cambodian soldiers, even our own leaders."

KID camp was situated quite a distance from the border and never under threat of shelling, so when the camp was closed I would make the trip there, to visit the hospital patients, the handicapped centre and my friend, Thach Sen. On one such visit, I was greeted by an elated Sen, happy to tell me that his interview had been successful and he had been accepted by Australia, to be located in the state of South Australia. I was very happy for him, knowing how hard it had been for him alone in this camp for the past eighteen months. He would leave KID the following week for Phanat Nikhom, where he would undergo language and orientation courses before his departure. He was very excited and looking forward to my coming back so he could visit me at home, being quite disappointed when I explained to him that I lived in Western Australia, which was thousands of kilometres away, making daily or weekly visits impossible.

It was August and should have been well into the rainy season, but this year had been very dry, resulting in an acute water shortage in camp, and problems for the farmers around Tapraya. The rice had already been planted and would be under threat if the rains did not come soon.

An American friend, Therese, who had previously worked in Site 2 and now lived in Bangkok, had come back for a visit to Tapraya. It was Saturday night, with nothing much to do in this small village, so together with Bob Maat (a US Jesuit brother), Antonio (a visiting Spanish brother), Kike and Jup, we organized our own amusement. Jup brought out his guitar, playing some popular Western songs, while everyone joined in the singalong. It was good to relax with fellow workers after the daily stress we each experienced. Suddenly there was a roar, causing us to rush to the door, just in time to see the rain begin to fall in torrents. People were running out in the streets shouting gleefully at the sight, dancing in the rain, secure in the knowledge that their crops had been saved. We joined in too, immediately drenched to the skin, but unconcerned, as we participated in this joyful occasion with the locals.

I was enjoying my classes in the leprosy ward. My students, Jin Jolin, Som Pak, and Kong Ros all spoke good English, so I would give them an extra lesson apart from the others, though they always joined the basic class as well. Each of these three men suffered advanced cases of leprosy, with hands and feet badly affected. The medication they were now taking, halted the spread of the disease, but could not repair the damage already done. They were very self-conscious about the appearance of their hands, with only stumps for fingers, always hiding them in their pockets away from hostile eyes.

Cambodians were terrified of catching leprosy and no amount of talking could convince them that the disease was not highly contagious, nor could they be infected if they touched an afflicted person. Those with leprosy were treated with disdain and avoided at all costs by camp people, even their huts being built in a compound away from the rest of the population. Life was very tough for them. I always made a point of shaking hands with the patients or touching them to show that I was not afraid of contamination. They appreciated this small gesture.

A new English teacher, Liz Bernstein, had arrived in Site 2 and was setting up classes. As I knew I would be leaving soon, I approached Liz to ask if she would take over my lessons when I left. She agreed to my request. This was great, because I wanted the classes to continue after my departure and I knew all other teachers were busy. Now I could leave, knowing my students were in good hands.

I decided I would like to do something special for my class before I departed. To leave the confines of the camp, even if for a short time, was the desire of most of the camp residents, so I thought along these lines. I finally came up with the idea of a picnic in the forest outside the camp, if it could be arranged, but first I would have to get permission from the Thai military.

I made an appointment to meet with the commander of TF80, Colonel Boo. I told him about the classes I was taking with the leprosy patients and of my desire to take them out of the camp for a picnic on my last day. He had never had a similar request and had to think for a few minutes before saying, "I give my approval, but only if I can come, too!" What a surprise! I agreed with alacrity; this would certainly be something different, only hoping that his presence would not frighten my students. I did not tell the class about the plan, just to be ready on the day and we would have a celebration for my departure. Not sure how many would turn up, I bought a plentiful supply of soft drinks, ice, fried rice, fruit and biscuits in the morning and arranged for the use of two vehicles, Mark promising to drive the other.

When we arrived at the leprosy ward next day, we were greeted, not only by my twenty students, but forty-three excited people, who had been waiting hours for our arrival. We managed to squeeze them all into the van and the back of a utility and set off for TF80 headquarters where I had arranged to meet the commander. He was waiting in his car with a number of soldiers, informing me that he was bringing them to reconnoitre the area as a safety measure. By now, my charges were looking a bit dubious when they realized the soldiers were coming with us, but soon settled down when we took off. As we drove out the back of the camp, I could hear the excited voices trying to guess where we were headed. We drove along a track on the top of the reservoir till we could go no further, waiting here while the commander sent his soldiers off to check around the area for landmines or bandits. After twenty minutes, the all clear was given, so we gathered up our supplies, including musical instruments and set off on foot. By this time, hundreds of mystified people lined the fence, peering through the barbed wire strands, trying to work out what was going on.

It took us about half an hour to reach our destination, a shady spot up high on a small hill where we had a good view of the camp, the mountain behind and the bush around us. In no time, the musicians had unpacked their instruments and the music started, everyone joining in singing their traditional songs with gusto. It was a great atmosphere, all enjoying this little bit of 'freedom'; the happy faces telling the story. The arrival of John, who immediately produced his harmonica and joined the band, then Aiden and Kike added to the party mood.

Kike told us later that one of the men said to him, "I am so happy, I feel like a bird, I feel free." The commander joined in too, talking to the people and enjoying the music. Before saying his farewells he thanked me for allowing him to join, saying, "It was a pleasure to be involved with these people. I have never been close to a leper before and I was not even frightened!"

It was well in to the afternoon before we packed up to start the walk back to the cars. Progress going down, being much slower, as many of the patients took this opportunity to gather roots and plants that would be used for traditional medicine. It was a happy but tired group, who were finally dropped off at their centre, one man saying, "This was the happiest day of my life, and one that I will always remember."

I had said my goodbyes to my friends during the week. Now, as I drove out of camp for the last time, I looked back wondering if I would ever see these people again. I had decided to stay home this time, emergency work in the camp was finished now and it would be more difficult for me to find employment. Maybe I would return for a visit one day. With these thoughts, I said my farewell to Site 2.

CHAPTER 5

Back in Australia, I settled back into life, spending many hours on the beach before it was time to teach school swimming classes. I was determined to stick by my resolution to adjust to life here and forget about working in the camp. That was until a few months later when I received a letter from Paulette, who was in charge of the fine arts (traditional dance, drama and music programme) in Site 2. In her letter, she told me that she was soon to leave Thailand with her husband, Alex, who had been offered a job in Holland. She was concerned about the continuation of the programme she had developed, asking if I would come back to fill her role as co-ordinator of the fine arts programme.

By the time this letter reached me, swimming classes were almost over so I reasoned there was nothing to keep me here and the lure of camp work was too strong. I jumped at the opportunity. So much for my resolution!

This time it took longer to organize things at home. I realized that I would have to make a longer commitment now that I would be in charge of a permanent programme. A few weeks after swimming classes finished, I was on my way to Thailand again.

My first concern on arrival was to catch up with old friends, making my way to the quarters behind the COERR office to see Phoeuy and other boys to hand over letters and gifts sent by Tim. The boys gathered around to greet me, all present but Phoeuy. I asked where he was and was dismayed to learn he had disappeared from the camp four months before, nothing had been heard from him since and nobody knew where he had gone. They were mystified, saying maybe he had gone back to Cambodia or illegally into Thailand, but he had given no indication to his friends that he was leaving and I could only hope that he was safe. Unexplained disappearances were always a worry in this environment.

Next, I made my way to the boarding school to visit my friends, and distribute books and letters from Tim. The boys gathered around, all talking at once, bringing me up to date on camp happenings since I was last here. I finally tore myself away to continue the many visits I still had to make, promising to come back over the next few days.

Sarath was working at the ICRC family tracing office, so I headed off hoping to find him there. He had not heard of my return, jumping up and knocking over his chair in surprise when I walked in, before giving me a big hug. It was good to chat with him, hear news of his family, find that he had settled into his new job and was happy with it. It certainly felt good to be back and to meet up with old friends.

Traditional Dance, Drama and Music

Before the fine arts programme had been formed by Paulette, there had been only one Site 2 dance and drama group, which received a small amount of funding from the Jesuit priests, Frs Pierre and John. Paulette was concerned that dance and drama presentations were not being brought to the people, through lack of centres big enough to accommodate large audiences. With this in mind, she approached COERR with a request for them to support a fine arts programme. They agreed to its installation on the condition that a donor could be found to fund the project. It would be a few months before this would happen, Caritas Switzerland eventually agreeing to donate funds for this new project, resulting in the birth of the fine arts programme.

Paulette called together representatives from all six camps and devised a plan to form a full dance and drama programme in each division. Ampil fine arts group, headed by Meas van Ruon and his wife, Voan Savay, already had a small repertoire of traditional dances, which their group practiced, but they lacked costumes, musical instruments and equipment required for a good presentation. They agreed to share their expertise with the new dance groups.

The group of representatives then put their heads together and decided that first, before fine arts centres could be set up, it would be essential to have the correct music for each of the many traditional dances and background music for the drama. As Cambodian music has no notation system of its own, relying only on memory, they would have to locate some of the older people, who could remember the authentic tunes. After much scouting around, six people, who could recall the correct melodies, were found, and brought together with the musicians. From then on it was a long, slow haul, listening to the tunes being hummed, putting the music to them, going over and over until they got it right. Finally, after a lot of patience on all sides, the musicians came up with a repertoire of dance and drama music approved by all. Now it was time to form fine arts groups, recruit teachers, dancers, actors and musicians so that teaching and practice could commence.

By the time I received the call to take over, the programme was well on its way. I was a bit concerned about accepting this position without having any previous experience whatsoever in this field. Paulette assured me that, because I understood the people and the culture already, which was a decided advantage, I would be able to manage. I was keen to give it a go, for it sounded like a real challenge.

I realized that I would have to become orientated quickly, as Paulette was due to leave in another ten days. My duties entailed scheduling monthly meetings, listening to and sorting out problems, organizing performances, purchasing supplies, arranging building construction and generally assisting with the programme.

Leaders of each of the six dance and six drama groups were called together to be introduced to their new co-ordinator, discuss the month's work and present a list of materials required for the following month. It was a very informal meeting, with each group leader presenting his monthly report, followed by discussions on construction of new buildings, food rations for workers, materials and equipment essential to the programme.

Some of the groups had new training buildings by the time I came on the scene, others still practiced in makeshift shelters. Rithysen already had an outdoor stage, which drew thousands of spectators each week to watch the cultural performances.

Paulette left at the appointed time, and I was kept busy riding my bicycle around the camp seeing to the construction of buildings, purchasing materials and visiting all the centres. Only four of the programme leaders spoke English, so I soon realized that I would need an interpreter. One of the group leaders, Pen Chenda, stood out from the others with his good command of English and unselfish attitude, so I asked him if he would assist me with translation, when required. He readily agreed. In time, I was to become very close to Chenda, spending many happy hours with his family.

The conditions under which the dancers now trained were much improved from when I first arrived and watched them practicing outside. New dance teachers were enhancing their skills under the watchful eye of Voan Savay and passing these skills on to their students. As I visited the centres over the weeks, I detected the gradual improvement in the preparation of the new dancers, though, I could see that it would be quite some time before they would be challenging the Ampil dancers in artistry and skill. There was such a lot to learn.

Classical dance or ballet was only performed by selected pupils. These dances required many more skills, poise, balance and dedication to learn the numerous intricate and graceful hand, body and foot movements. Classical dance dates back a thousand years to India and Java, combining Hindu myths and Buddhist tales and was routinely

Making the most of a rain shower in Site 2. Photo: Tim Grant

Photo: Margot Grant

People were living under plastic sheets in the first days of the camp.

Giving a swimming class in a camp drain Photo: Tim Grant

School lessons were held outside in the camp's early days.

Photo: Margot Grant

Photo: Tim

Site 2 artist, Dao Lary, with painting, on canvas I smuggled in.

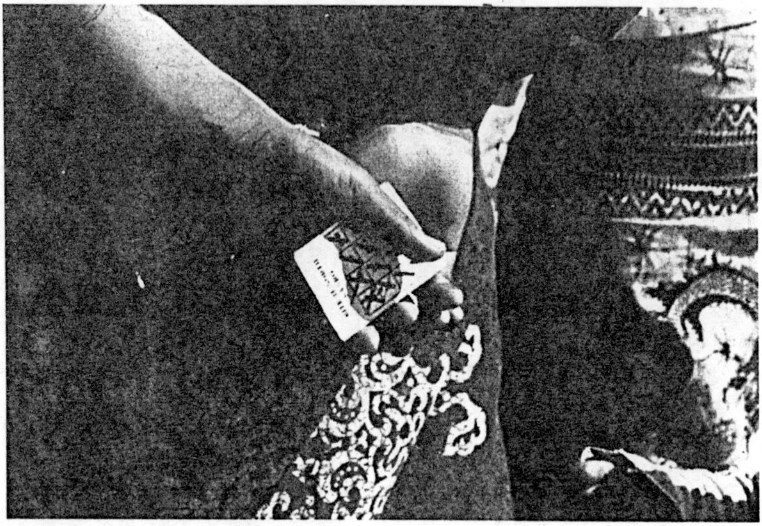

Holding on to the treasured rice card. Photo: Tim Grant

Rice Distribution Day. Photo: Margot Grant

Traditional Cambodian greeting.

Photo: Tim Grant

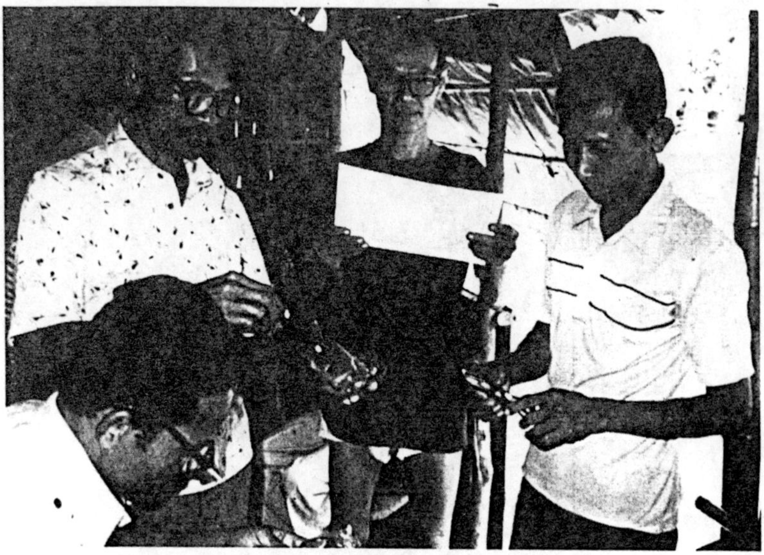

Seeing – at last! The welcome gift of reading glasses. Photo: Margot Grant

Refugees making their way into Site 2. Photo: Margot Grant

A patient being brought to the hospital. Photo: Margot Grant

Hospital ward shared by patients and chickens. Photo: Margot Grant

Father Pierre with some of his little charges. Photo: Tim Grant

Waiting in line for the daily water ration. Photo: Margot Grant

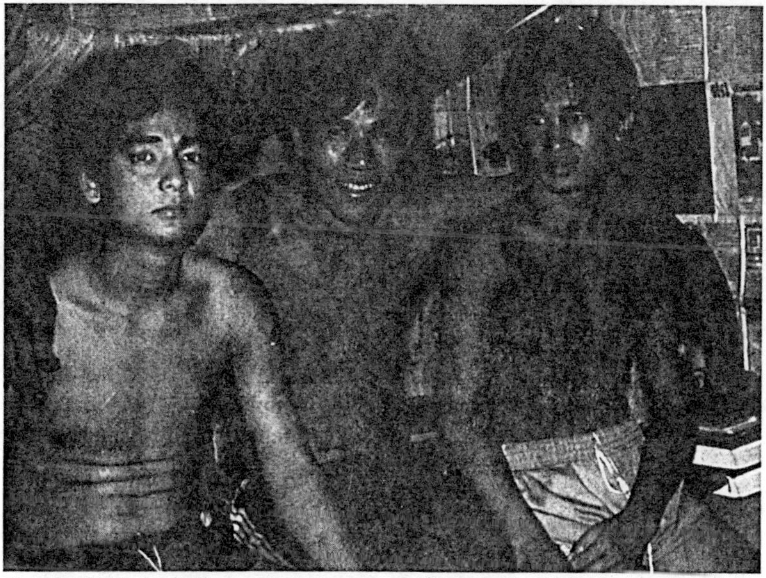

Sombath, Saren & Sovann – young men from the boarding school.

Boarders outside Tim's Library. Photos: Margot Grant

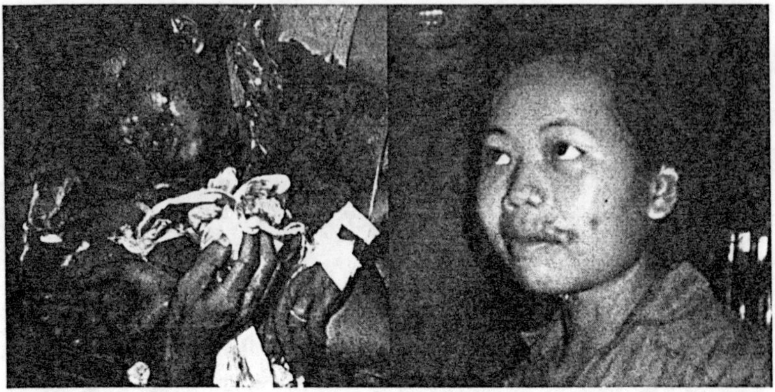

A young woman injured by shelling in the camp …
… and a few weeks later after treatment at Khao-i-dang hospital.

Photos: Margot Grant

Photo: Tim Grant

11-year-old Ly, injured by a rocket. With his mother in KID hospital.

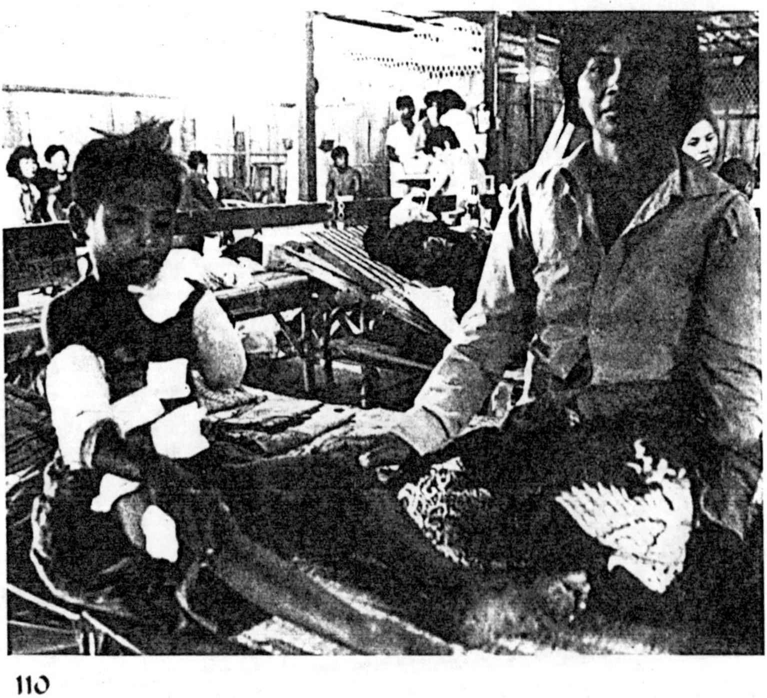

Tim at Sarawath's wedding. Photo: Margot Grant

John Henderson playing his mouthorgan for the crowd. Photo: Tim Grant

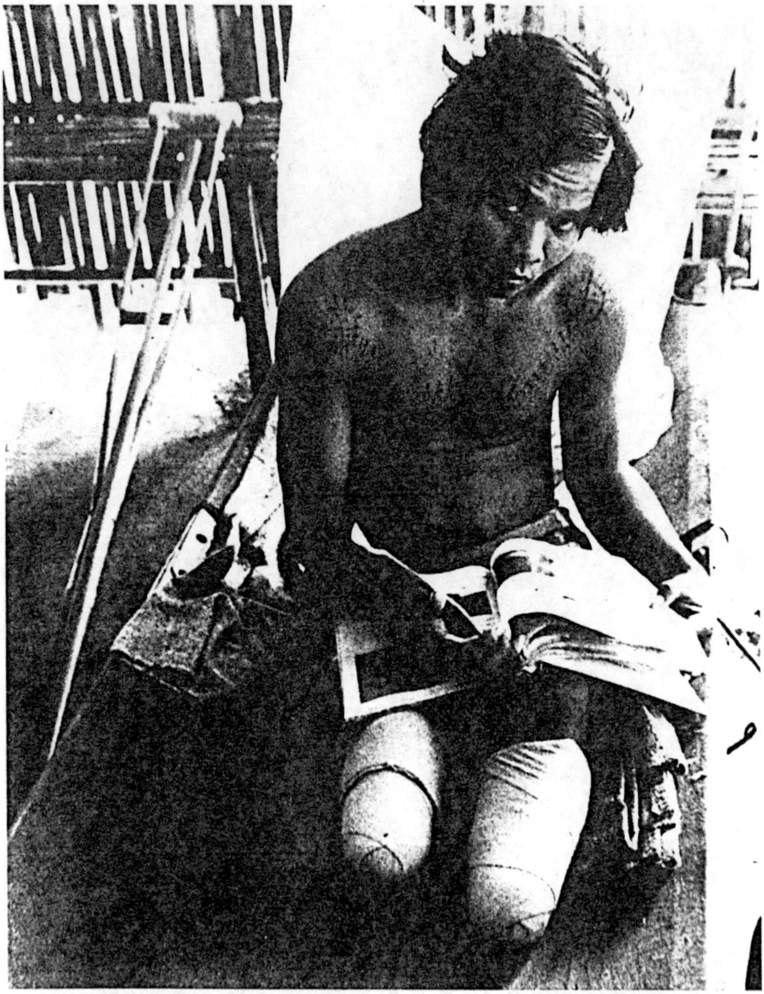

Amputee with tattoos. Photo: Tim Grant

performed before royal courts in Cambodia. Classical dancers must start their preparation at an early age, with the dancer required to bend the hand back until the fingers almost touch the arm, taking a large amount of practice and quite some pain during training. As well as this, the fingers must turn up from the top joint to complete the artistic hand movements. It is not unusual to see little girls pressing their hands and fingers back as far as they could, longing to achieve the correct hand positions in the hope that one day they may be chosen to perform these intricate movements.

In contrast, folk dance is bright, lively, colourful and full of fun. Originating in the villages, folk dance is solely of peasant origin and considered to be an integral part of village life. It is a realistic art, with special dances for different occasions, be it a wedding, funeral, during planting and harvesting, hunting, fishing, rice husking; each one depicting an important aspect of village life. Each of these dances is devoted to a particular province; dance motifs based on local legend and the activities in that region. Folk dances are designed to invite humour and laughter; villagers believing that they bring good luck and prevent disaster. When the rice harvest was completed in Cambodia, villagers celebrated with dance, song and music.

Camp people, who were mostly from Cambodian rural areas, thoroughly enjoyed watching the groups practicing their dance routines and would line up at the bamboo walls, craning their necks to catch a glimpse of the dancers through the gaps. They particularly loved watching the folk dance, which brought back memories of village life, never failing to gasp, chuckle or burst into laughter at the same parts of the performance, even though they had seen these dances many times.

While the dance teachers were preparing their groups, drama teams were also working hard to learn their roles in the 'basak' - Cambodian folk stories. These traditional stories, passed down from generation to generation, can be very violent, portraying battles, stories of love, jealousy and bravery. The crowds enjoyed watching these powerful dramas, performed by different groups each week, on the outdoor stage in Rithysen camp. They would come in their thousands, not concerned that they must stand in the hot sun or sometimes in the rain, to watch these folk stories being enacted. It seemed that the more brutal they were, the more the audience responded with claps, cheers, sighs and laughter. You imagine that these people would have experienced enough violence in their lives, but they never seemed to tire of watching and enjoying these powerful and often savage dramas.

Our monthly meeting was always an exciting time for the group leaders, when supplies for the programme were distributed and orders placed for the following month. Each group would present their monthly report outlining their activities and requests. One of the English speakers must have assisted them with their letters. I had to decipher many of the requirements, getting lots of laughs along the way. They asked for 'sand pepper', 'wheels of cotton', 'eyedraw pencil', 'twinned wire', 'flywood' and 'wire fire'; always ending their requests 'with high information', and signing off, 'Yours fatefully'.

Many metres of coloured cloth, sequins, reels of thread and makeup were brought in and dispensed to the different centres. It took me a few months and my budget a few thousand baht before I understood which materials I was purchasing were essential to the programme. This realization came about after a visit to the market where I saw boxes of makeup and metres of the same cloth for sale. I soon realized they were taking advantage because I was new to the job, grossly inflating the amounts in their orders. When confronted with this disclosure they burst out laughing - it was all a game to them, trying to outwit the foreigner! It was difficult to be angry with them but I vowed to be more careful in future, for I had a budget to control.

Each group had a number of seamstresses employed making costumes. Classical dance robes were the most elaborate. Made from velvet, satin or brocade cloth, meticulously sewn with gold thread, covered with handsewn sequins, one costume taking three or four workers up to two months to complete. Folk dance costumes were made of cheaper, colourful material, each dance having its own particular style and colour according to the theme.

A few months after I took over, outdoor stages had been erected and were in operation in all camps, bringing performances to tens of thousands of camp people each week. UNBRO, currently on a big budget, agreed to donate musical instruments, sound and light equipment and generators for use by the groups to upgrade these performances. It was an exciting day when this equipment arrived (156 pieces in all). Included, were sets of musical instruments for all dance and drama groups, mixers, alternators, stage lights and wiring to go with the generators.

There was great elation when the boxes were opened. Chenda turned to me, saying in a quivering voice, "We have never seen all this equipment before; even in Cambodia, musicians never had a full set of instruments like we see here. We are so lucky!"

Not long after I started with the programme, I received a visit from a very agitated dance teacher, Mom, accompanied by her sister, Och, saying that they would like to speak to me in private. After we were seated in one of the outer rooms, Mom produced a letter she had received the previous day. It was written in Khmer and I could not read it, but a tearful Mom told me that the letter contained death threats to them both, stating they would be blown up with a hand grenade. She went on to tell me that the reason for this threat was the new dance centre built in Nong Chan camp, of which she was in charge. The fence erected around the compound was built over a path used by nearby residents to carry water from the tanks alongside the road. Some of the people were unhappy because now they would have to take a much longer route with their heavy burdens, so the threat was made. Mom and Och were very frightened that this threat would be carried out. I told them I would meet with the administrator of their camp to see what could be done about the matter.

After meeting with the camp leader, Chai Kim Hour, next day, a plan was made to move some of the houses to a different area, rewarding them with a cash incentive and new furniture. They refused. I went back to talk to Mom and Och but no amount of reasoning could convince the sisters that the problem could be solved and they refused to return to their house again, preferring to stay with their brother in another part of the camp where they felt safer. The dance building was eventually moved to another section and a new teacher appointed. Mom remained adamant that she would not return.

Now that so many people were taking advantage of the weekly entertainment, it set me thinking how this exposure could be best utilized for the good of the people. Maybe we could use this avenue to impart significant messages regarding camp problems to the population. It would be worth a try!

Notices were sent around to various agencies and a meeting day organized for aid workers to present their ideas. Representatives from a number of organizations attended with many suggestions and ideas for dramas proposed. As a result of this meeting, plans were made to present a drama each week depicting a problem that needed to be addressed within the camp.

The first of these dramas, due to go on stage in two weeks, would be a story about leprosy, the impact on sufferers and its treatment. This theme was prompted by my work with the leprosy patients and an incident that happened while I was engaged in teaching them.

After class one day, I took my friend, Som Pak, to a restaurant for coffee. Before he could hide his hands in his pocket, the waitress came up, took one look at his deformed hands and with a look of disgust on her face, refused to serve him. I asked why and she answered, "Because I can't have him using our cups; the customers may catch his disease."

I could see she didn't believe me when I told her that it couldn't be caught that way. She did eventually relent, reluctantly giving him his coffee but I knew it was only because of my presence. I felt embarrassed and sorry for Pak, who brushed it off with a wry smile, saying, "I'm used to that, it happens all the time."

With this encounter in mind I arranged for the leprosy drama to be performed first, realizing the public desperately needed education regarding this disease.

I presented this idea to the German doctor in charge of the ward, who thought it a great plan, sending me off with a host of literature on the subject in both Khmer and English. Actors were brought over to meet with leprosy patients to plan a story that people could understand and associate with their lives. They came up with a great story of two people living in Site 2, who discovered they had leprosy, one person seeking treatment, the other ignoring it and the following consequences. The story depicted the abuse with which the sufferers were faced and told how it was only possible to be infected after prolonged and close encounters with an afflicted person.

When the story was presented, it met with a good reception from the audience. As usual in Cambodian drama, it was interspersed with humour that had the crowd laughing. It was also apparent that the audience were interested to learn about the treatment, showing that if it was caught in its early stages the progress of the disease would be halted and no disfigurement would result. I could only hope that a lesson would be learnt by this presentation and some good would result.

The leprosy drama was followed up with stories about domestic violence, breast feeding, rabies, cholera, the handicapped, human rights, alcoholism, landmine awareness and many other current social, community and health problems. These weekly presentations proved to be a vital source of information for camp people and were enjoyed by the large crowds attending.

Meanwhile the fine arts teams were showing good progress. All groups now had their practice buildings and held regular performances for school groups, agency staff and visitors, as well as the weekly stage performances. Workshops were being held for hair styling, makeup application for the dance teams, mask making and training for costumers. Preparations before dancers could take to the stage, would take a team of six costumers and makeup experts at least three hours. Dressing for the classical dance took the longest; yards of material had to be carefully pleated before being wound around the body and up between the legs then caught at the waist. Dancers would stand patiently for hours while the costumes were meticulously sewn in place by seamstresses, so they would fit tightly to the body. Because they could not sit once their costumes were in place, makeup would be applied while dancers were still standing. Folk dancers were much easier to dress, their costumes consisting of loose tops, pants or sarongs, heavy makeup also being applied to complete their outfits.

A market had now been approved and opened between Site 2 North and south with access for both. On our travels around the camp, Chenda and I would often call in to this centre that was not unlike the market in Aranyaprathet. A wide range of goods was for sale here, bought from Thai traders, who came in each morning with cartloads of merchandise. This was great for camp people, making it more like village life where people congregated in the morning to shop, drink coffee or stop for a chat. I enjoyed the atmosphere prevailing here, with plenty of hustle, bustle and camaraderie. Life for camp residents was gradually improving.

I missed the company of my friend Phoeuy as I made my way around, often thinking about him and wondering where he was. I thought he might have gone to Bangkok to look for work; a few of the camp people had done this before. In this city there were frequent roundups of illegal immigrants, who, when caught, were thrown into Suan Plu prison.

On my last trip to Bangkok, I had visited this prison, checking to see if Phoeuy was there. I made enquiries at the prison office, looking through the list of inmate's names, but Phoeuy was not on their list. I went in to see the prisoners just in case he was there under another name. It was a terrible sight, with hundreds of prisoners of all nationalities living together in eight large cells, sleeping on the cement floor, only one shower in each cell and one rice meal a day. When I came in, many prisoners rushed to the bars, all demanding my attention and talking in many different languages.

Eventually I located the cell holding Cambodians, 250 altogether, some telling me they had been there for eight months already. I told them for whom I was looking, but they knew nothing of Phoeuy. It seemed that he had just vanished into thin air! When I told the prisoners I was from Site 2, many of them said they had come from there, quickly scribbling notes for me to take back to their relatives. I also visited the women's cell where four Cambodians were incarcerated. They looked so sad. It was hard to communicate with them, but at the mention of Site 2 they all perked up, two of them writing letters for me to take back. I took all the messages back to the camp, finding most of the people. They were so pleased to regain contact with their loved ones, even if it was from the prison. Eventually, Thai authorities would return the Cambodian prisoners to Site 2 camp.

Fr John had brought a video machine into camp and hooked it up to a powerful generator. At present he was using it for his English class, but he had also made it available to other groups. I had brought back some video tapes Tim had chosen, so I booked the video room to play the tapes for the boarding school boys. Because there would be at least seventy of them filling the room, I made a rule that the viewing would be by entry ticket only, otherwise the screening would be invaded by hundreds of outsiders, leaving no room for the invited. Saren and Savan agreed to make these tickets out of cardboard with a COERR stamp to ensure all those eligible gained entry to the show.

On the appointed day, all invited boarders turned up, clutching their entry tickets and full of excitement at the prospect of watching their first video. I started the show with an old Charlie Chaplin movie, causing them to almost fall off their chairs with laughter; they loved it! This was followed by a Tom and Jerry video. Surprisingly, they did not find it funny at all and watched in dead silence. We finished up with 'The Three Stooges' and this really appealed to their sense of humour, laughter echoing forth again and drawing crowds to the outside of the building to see what was going on. At the break between films, we had lucky ticket draws, giving out prizes of calculators, books, pens and pads donated by co-workers. There were cries of delight and disappointment when the lucky numbers were drawn, their first ever raffle. I only wished I could have supplied prizes for all of them.

Saren had been urging me to stay overnight in the camp. Tim had already done this and it had been a real treat for the boys at the boarding school. I agreed, but told him it must be kept secret as it was highly illegal. Saren now had his own house, sharing it with Sombath and Savan, so it was agreed that I would stay there.

When I came into camp on the elected day and the sign-in board was handed over at the gate, I did not put my signature against my name, therefore I would not be required to sign out on departure. I followed this procedure, knowing UNBRO would not close the camp until all workers had been located. Saren came to the office and picked up my overnight bag during the day. Just before closing time, I made my way by bicycle to Saren's house. Sarath had been invited to join us for the evening meal, which the boys had cooked for this special occasion. We were sitting, chatting after dinner and waiting for the sun to go down when shelling started quite close to the camp. I could see the boys nudging each other and looking at me, waiting to see my response or signs of fear.

When I ignored it, Saren turned to me and said, "You hear the shelling?"

I told him that I could.

Sombath asked, "Aren't you afraid?"

I said that I knew they would look after me, so I was not afraid. They thought that was great and all relaxed then. Everyone joined in to play the game of Scrabble, which I had brought in with me, bringing forth much laughter as they thought up the most unbelievable words to use. None of the other boarders knew that I was in the camp, so when it became dark I dressed in a sarong with a krama over my head and made my way over to the boarding school. It was so quiet and dark outside, only the faint glow of candles could be seen burning inside the huts. I looked up, not a cloud in sight, the sky a picture of glittering stars, each one standing out so clearly, I could even pick out the southern cross shining far in the southern sky. It was a beautiful sight with no streetlights to spoil the image.

The boys were all studying on their beds by candlelight when I came through the doorway, asking them in Khmer, "What are you boys doing?" I was greeted by a stunned silence, then cries of delight when they realized who it was, amazed to see me in camp after nightfall. We stayed and chatted for awhile before they went back to their studies and Saren and I went on to visit Keo Song and family.

There was an eight o'clock curfew in the camp. By this time it was really quiet outside, the only sounds to be heard were from battery operated cassette players, occasional baby cries or people talking in low voices. It seemed so different to the noise and flurry of the day.

I took my shower Cambodia style, outside in a sarong, before settling down for the night on a bamboo bed under a mosquito net, by now it was quiet all around. I slept really well. Cambodians are early risers and very noisy people, so I was awakened at four-thirty by sounds of activity: wood chopping, children playing, and the babble of voices as people went about their early morning chores. Saren, Sombath and Savan had already been up studying for an hour. I had to stay inside to avoid being seen by Thai soldiers, so we sat and talked until it was time for the boys to go to their classes at 7am. I waited until eight o'clock, then made my way to the COERR office, arriving there just after other staff members.

No one realized that I had not come in with one of the vehicles. It had been quite an experience to taste life after camp closure.

Mailmen to the Rescue

Restrictions placed on the camp population by Thai authorities were many and varied, being particularly harsh in the early days of the camp. Maybe the worst of these regulations suffered by the people was the complete banning of all mail, both inward and outward, effectively cutting them off from all contact with the outside world. Not to be daunted, the internees soon found a solution, this coming in the guise of our intrepid priests, Fathers Pierre and John. These men set up a mailing system whereby letters could be sent by camp people to overseas family members, giving the return address of the priests' respective post office box numbers in Aranyaprathet. They ran this mail service knowing full well that if caught, they could be banned from the camp or even the country, but took this risk as they deemed it to be an essential service.

Random searches of workers' bags and insides of vehicles were periodically held by soldiers, so the risk of detection was always there. Letters would be furtively collected in the camp by the priests, hidden in books, files or pockets to take out, then stamped and mailed in Aranyaprathet. Ingenious methods were employed to bring overseas mail into the camp when cars were more likely to be searched. Lining inside the vehicle was removed and letters placed inside before the panels were screwed back into place, floor mats sometimes hid postal articles, inside shoes or the waistband of pants were other popular places to secrete mail.

Many camp people had relatives living overseas and letters to these kin were usually sent to request money to boost the living conditions of the family inside Site 2. Whenever letters arrived from overseas, family, friends and neighbours would crowd around to see if there was a cheque enclosed. If so, there were always cries of, "How much did you get?" from the bystanders; if none, they all, including the recipient, lost interest. Sadly, mail could not be sent into Cambodia, as the government there would not allow mail from Thailand, assuming it came from the camps. People who made it into the camps could not notify relatives that they had made it safely. Their only alternative to make contact, being through soldiers going inside to fight, but this was never reliable.

It was not long before some resourceful camp people set up their own illegal 'post offices' inside their huts. Their services included addressing or writing letters in Khmer or English for the non-speakers or illiterate, arranging to have the letters posted (usually with the priests, who would also pay for stamps), charging the sender a fee for the service, plus cost of postage stamps. These shrewd operators were the people who eventually made money, either this way or another, ultimately becoming the 'middle class' of Site 2.

Cheques from overseas for camp people were cashed with a trader in Aranyaprathet, by the priests and other aid workers. This method was preferred by the people, as they knew they would receive all their money, unlike cashing them with Thai traders, who entered the camp illegally, charging a huge interest rate.

Many humorous stories emerged of aid workers bringing in contraband. Fr Pierre had an appointment with the head of the Thai military in Aranyaprathet on his way to the camp one day. In Thailand it is the custom to take off your shoes before entering a room, so Fr Pierre dutifully followed this custom, shedding his shoes at the door. However, he forgot that he had secreted a wad of money inside. There it was exposed for all to see. He looked around to see if he had been caught, but luckily no one was in sight, so he quickly donned his shoes, foregoing the 'no shoes' custom in his haste to avoid detection.

I had purchased twelve pairs of shorts for the boarding school soccer team and was bringing them into camp in the van a few weeks later. We arrived at the entrance to find many vehicles lined up at the gate and rangers carrying out a search of vehicles at the front of the line. When car occupants realized what was happening, there was a rush to hide letters, money and other contraband that many of the workers were carrying. Letters and money were concealed under shirts, and small goods were hidden, but what was I going to do with twelve pairs of shorts? Then I had an idea. I handed them around to other staff members who pulled them on. By the time the van was searched, occupants were sitting demurely attired in a pair of football shorts over their jeans. Obviously, the searchers did not think it unusual or funny that all the people aboard were wearing bright green and white shorts as they waved us on! The boys loved the story when I told them, enjoying hearing how the TF80 had been outwitted again.

Another time, I had been asked by an artist, Lary, who was doing some paintings for me, to bring in three metres of canvas. I realized that the only way I could get past the guards with this bulky package would be to wear it, so I wound this heavy material round and round my body before putting a big shirt over the top. I made it past the guards but lost copious amounts of sweat on the way. I finally delivered the canvas to Lary, rather the worse for wear. Years later when he was settled in USA, he wrote, thanking me for helping him in many ways, and for the risks I took for him, especially noting the time I wore the canvas. It was good to know that these episodes were appreciated and remembered many years later.

Eventually Fr John's luck ran out and he was caught with a huge pile of mail when entering the camp. A meeting with the head of the Thai military ensued where he was brought to task, lectured about the foolhardiness of attempting to cheat the system and warned that if he transgressed again, he would be completely banned from camp. The fear of banning was enough for Fr John and he terminated his postal service.

Later, COERR, with the permission of the Thai military, opened a legal mail and banking service in Site 2, run by a Thai employee. This service was set up in an office, with each section of the camp being allocated different mail days. All mail was opened under the watchful eye of Thai soldiers with details of all cheques recorded. A rule was made that recipients of cheques were not allowed to draw more than US $100 per month. If the cheque was for a larger amount, the difference was kept in a banking account for that person for the following month. It was not long before people lost faith in this system when cheques started to disappear or access to their funds was denied, and people went back to relying on the foreigners.

By early 1988 the first group of students had completed their high school studies and graduated. The only avenues open to them now, were in the field of teaching or nursing. COERR had recently opened a Teacher Training College (TTC) run by an Australian nun, Denise, so Saren, Boney, Vily and others, who had graduated, applied to study here, although confiding in me that teaching was not the career they really wanted to follow.

About this time, Fr John Bingham's nephew, Ken, arrived. A New York lawyer, he had resigned from his job on Wall Street, volunteering to work in the camp after hearing his uncle's stories about the plight of the people and their needs. When he arrived, he had no idea in what capacity his skills could be used, being prepared to work in any field. After meeting up with high school graduates, Ken realized there was a lot of talent going to waste in the camp, so decided to set up a centre where students could learn some aspects of law, administration and management skills which should be useful when they returned to Cambodia. COERR together with KPNLF agreed to fund this project. Classrooms were erected in a compound in the middle of the camp, with teachers from France - Rodolphe, Bryce, Stefan and Agnes recruited to teach together with Ken. The new centre was named the Institute of Public Administration (IPA).

Classes in engineering were also made available to graduates at this time, giving them a greater choice of professional training. These classes were taught by engineering graduates from France: Thomas, Gilles, Jean-Michel, Guillaume, and Alain; each teacher staying for two years before being replaced by another from the same school in Paris. Saren and some of his friends chose to attend the IPA, Boney and Vily preferring to study engineering.

A good thing happened for the people of Site 2 about this time. TF80 rangers were replaced by DPPU. There had been many reports of atrocities committed by TF80 over the years, resulting in the US State Department urging the Thai Military to replace them, promising to pay wages and supply uniforms to outfit a new group if the Thai Military undertook the recruitment. They were only too happy to do this and now was the changeover time. Thai Military held a reception in their quarters in Aranyaprathet and invited interested volags to come along to meet the new replacements. We had been told that the new DPPU staff members, both male and female, were better educated and trained and there should be no further problems.

On the day TF80 rangers left, thousands of people lined the roads as the trucks carrying the rangers drove out. It was eerie, not a sound could be heard. The people just stood and watched, not really believing they were leaving, never to return.

The DPPU did a good job at first, but over the years their effectiveness as protectors slowly deteriorated. However, they were never feared as much as the previous unit members.

All workers were required to drive the cars at some time, so I decided to go about securing a Thai driver's licence. Ken also wanted to get his licence so we planned to go together. It turned out to be quite an ordeal to secure these documents. First, we had to have a letter from our employer, a letter from our landlord to say how much rent we paid, three passport photographs, a copy of our current driver's licence from home, copy of our passport and visa. These papers had to be taken to the district officer in Aranyaprathet, who, on approval, would write a letter. Then we were required to fill out more forms before driving two hundred kilometres to Prachinburi, the capital of our province.

We found our way to the police station where we presented the paper work, filled out more forms, had our fingerprints taken, paid 150 baht, then waited one and a half hours before finally being presented with our

Thai driving licence. After all this paperwork and numerous formalities, no driving test was required. No wonder the Thais were such terrible drivers!

Due to more shelling, the camp was closed, and being at a loose end, I decided to visit KID. I called into the leprosy centre to see Jin Jolin, my ex-student, who was receiving treatment at that time. He told me there was a young man, who had been brought in to the hospital two days before, with horrific injuries from a landmine explosion, and asked if I would visit him as he was very depressed. Jolin took me to the ward where I met 24-year-old Phin Saroeun for the first time. The terrible injuries he suffered, had resulted in the amputation of both legs above the knee and one arm above the elbow, in addition to this, his body was covered in gaping shrapnel wounds. A KPNLF soldier, he had been on patrol, walking through the forest when this accident happened. It was hard to know what to say to cheer someone in this state. I did my best to be positive and cheerful, but all he could say was, "Look at me, I can't walk, I can't work, I just want to die!"

I pointed to Jin Jolin, who had no fingers and could barely walk on badly deformed feet, saying, "Look, Jolin is also handicapped but he is getting on with his life."

Saroeun answered with, "But he can walk and he has two hands!"

He looked so sad lying there covered in bloodsoaked bandages; his face now wet with tears. It was taking all my might to hold the tears back myself, so I quickly made the excuse to get him some things from my car. It would do him no good to see me break down also. While there, I made an effort to compose myself before heading back with some Khmer books and oranges. I promised to come back to visit him in a few days.

That night I went to visit Fr Pierre to tell him about this poor man, asking if he could visit and help in any way. Fr Pierre was to spend many hours with Saroeun, helping him to cope with his handicap and get his life back on track again. This day also started a long friendship for me with this young man, who became another of my 'adopted' sons.

While at the hospital, I visited two of the shelling victims from Site 2. They were still receiving treatment but the young man with serious injuries had since died. I was pleased to see that the woman with leg wounds and a child with stomach injuries, were both well on the way to recovery, thanks to the excellent medical treatment they received in KID. They were due to return to Site 2 in a few days' time.

To Honour the Ancestors

Pchum Ben Anniversary

In the early morning
The cocks crow waking people up
To wrap rice cakes
For the Khmer anniversary holiday.
After cooking delicious foods and desserts
People dress in colorful clothes
And take the food
To the gigantic and noisy pagoda
That they have decorated with flower blossoms.
There is a mixture of colors
Of peoples clothes
And religious flags waving.
Merry birds are flying
In the floating colors,
Absorbing the flowers,
Giving a concert
Among lightfooted students.
The crowd moves back and forth,
Bikes swarm uninterruptedly
On the roads.
People are eating, praying,
Giving merit,
As audiences.

by Sophal (a Site 2 student)

Pchum Ben time was drawing near. This is a moving but happy event for the Cambodian people, held for two weeks from the end of September, for the purpose of honouring their ancestors. For the Pchum Ben celebration, hundreds of people, all dressed in their best clothes, form a procession carrying gifts wrapped in orange cellophane paper to be placed before the monks as offerings for their ancestors. Names of dead family members are called and a prayer chanted by the monks. This ceremony is held to ensure that the dead family members will be at peace and can look forward to a better life when they are reincarnated, according to the Buddhist belief.

Women are kept busy for days before this big event, making 'nom som': rice cakes filled with corn or banana then wrapped in banana leaves, a delicacy made only for special occasions. These, with many other traditional dishes, were prepared for the feast following the Buddhist ceremony, then, there would be time for games and fun. For this celebration, the grounds of the pagodas were filled with stalls with drama and dance performances being presented on stages set up in the enclosure. The camp curfew is lifted at this time and celebrations go on until well after nightfall.

A couple of weeks prior to this celebration, I had written a letter to the commander of the Thai military in Aranyaprathet, requesting permission to stay overnight in the camp for the Pchum Ben ceremony, giving as my reason that I needed to be there to oversee the dance and drama performance. Two days before Pchum Ben, I was surprised and pleased to receive notice that my application had been approved. This was a first time this permission had been given to a foreigner; maybe because no one had ever asked before, but I was elated and thrilled to have the opportunity to join in the celebration with the people. This time I would be able to walk freely in the streets and not have to hide like the time I had stayed before.

The family of So Sayornn, head of the drama programme in Dong Rek camp, whom I often visited, begged me to stay with them for the night. I agreed, looking forward to observing at first-hand, real family life in the camp. Sayornn lived with his mother, sister, wife and three children, next door to his widowed sister and her four children. An uncle, aunt and cousins lived nearby, making up the traditional Cambodian extended family. I was particularly close to Sayornn's mother, who was about my age. I would often sit and talk to her in my halting Khmer or we would attempt to communicate in sign language that would end with us both in fits of laughter while trying to understand each other.

I made my way to Sayornn's house, as I had promised to join in the pagoda ceremony with his family. All family members were dressed in their best when I arrived, with the children full of excitement, busily packing gifts to be offered to the monks. The ladies hovered around, dressing me for the occasion in a fancy white blouse, embroidered sarong, and a white scarf wound around the neck and over the shoulder. When all was ready we joined the procession on the road, laden with offerings, headed for the pagoda; my presence in the cortege attracting a lot of attention along the way.

At the pagoda, the crowd broke up into groups, each branching off to different buildings where the monks held their blessing ceremonies. We headed for the house of the oldest monk, who was well known to the family. Incense sticks were lit by family members and prayers offered for the restless souls of their ancestors, before we sat on the floor to wait our turn for the monk's blessing. Then it was time for Sayornn's family. Gifts of incense, candles, cigarettes, rice cakes, cooked food and money were handed to the monk. Names of dead family members were called and holy water sprinkled, before prayers were chanted by the monk to chase away the spirits. The family left happy with the knowledge that they had paid their respects to their ancestors, enabling them to now have a better life after reincarnation.

We made our way back to the house after the ceremony, where the women busied themselves preparing the food consisting of many different authentic Khmer dishes. specially cooked for this occasion. Sayornn had invited four male relatives and other guests to join us for dinner. A huge feast was set before us. It was amazing, in the camp with so little, how the people could come up with this array of food, but many families somehow managed to find something extra for this special celebration. Sayornn was one of the lucky ones, having a brother resettled in USA, who regularly sent money to aid his family, allowing them to live with a little more dignity.

As the sun was setting, we headed for the pagoda where the fun part was starting. The group consisted of Sayornn and his wife; Pierun, his eight-year-old son, LaTin, and daughters Phaktra, aged four, and baby Lieta; his mother; Near Lon and myself. I imagined that everyone in Nong Chan camp must be there, for the grounds were packed with people when we arrived.

A traditional drama was being presented on the stage, with hundreds of intrigued onlookers hanging on every word and thoroughly enjoying the story. There were food and drink stalls, games being played and trestles set up, holding trays of food and rice for everyone to help themselves. Small children were running around filling plastic bags with food to take home to their families. Sayornn told me that this food was donated by camp people for the poor who couldn't afford to buy extra food for Pchum Ben. It was such a different atmosphere to the day hours when it was all business, with the roads full of agency cars, trucks and water tankers.

We spènt a happy couple of hours here, people stopping to talk, enjoying having a foreigner in their midst for this special event, before leaving to walk back to the house at 8pm. By this time, the children were very tired after a busy and enjoyable day and the excitement of being out after dark.

The family had prepared a place for me to sleep on a bamboo bed that doubled as their table in the day. On top of this was a folded blanket covered by a sheet on which I would sleep; a pillow with frilly cover and a mosquito net draped over the top, completed my boudoir. The family soon settled down and I lay listening to camp noises gradually fading after people returned to their houses. In the distance could be heard the steady boom, boom, of shelling not far over the border; the sound these people went to bed with most nights.

I felt like I had just gone to sleep when I was wakened at 2.30am by Pierun, telling me it was time to get up and head off to the pagoda. By now, all family members were awake. We joined the crowds of people on the road, headed for the temple for the continuation of the Pchum Ben ceremony. The pagoda was a large structure consisting a bamboo frame supporting a thatch roof and open on all sides.

Inside this building, hundreds of people were already sitting on the wooden floor facing three rows of seated monks in their bright saffron robes, shaven heads and bare feet. We found a place to sit and waited for the ceremony to begin.

It was not long before the monks commenced their chanting in a nasal monotone, followed every now and then by responses from the congregation, continuing for an hour. By this time, I was very uncomfortable trying to sit in one position on the hard floor. Every now and then, I would have to change position, much to the amusement of the people around me, for they had no trouble sitting in one place for unlimited periods.

After what seemed an age, the prayer service was over and we lit sticks of incense, then carried them outside. Here we joined the procession to walk around the temple three times, placing food on stands positioned around the pagoda. As each offering was placed, dead family members names were called so that they would know these were for them. If not fed on this day, their spirits must wander for another year. It was an impressive scene in the pre-dawn light, hundreds of people shuffling around singing, calling out names, the air heavy with the scent of incense and a haze of dust thrown up by hundreds of feet. I felt honoured to be invited to join in this moving ceremony. It was 5am before we headed back to the house, the whole camp alive with activity by this time.

Coffee shops are great meeting places for the men. They have breakfast, coffee, smoke endless cigarettes and exchange gossip. Sayornn and I headed for one of these venues to have morning coffee and 'babor', a tasty Cambodian rice porridge. We were constantly being stopped along the way, with greetings from many people, telling me how pleased they were to have me join in their celebrations, causing our progress to be slow.

Shelling continued and seemed to be getting closer. Everywhere I went, people asked if I was afraid, but I assured them that I was not and that I could put up with it if they could. There were loud bangs when two shells landed close to the camp making the ground shake and sending people scuttling for their bunkers. After breakfast, Sayornn and I headed for the office, where I had arranged a nine o'clock meeting with fine arts representatives.

We were greeted there by Viseth with the news that the camp had been closed to all outside workers, due to the threat of an attack. So that left me inside, with all the other foreigners out. There was nothing I could do about it; so I decided I would make the most of it.

All the guys from the fine arts groups arrived for the meeting, and though I had decided to forgo it because of the situation, they assured me they wanted to stay, so we sat and chatted. They told me of their hopes for when they returned to Cambodia and their fears that, maybe, they would not be accepted because they had been in the camp. Some of them wanted to continue with fine arts work, with one man keen to return to rice farming, but worried he may have forgotten how to farm after so many years since he had been in the fields. Others hoped to set up small businesses selling goods in the market; the English speakers keen to work with the foreigners. "Because they pay more money," they laughingly told me.

By eleven o'clock, I realized that no one was coming in to get me, so, together with the fine arts guys, I headed for the restaurant, treating them all to a lunch they thoroughly enjoyed. There was still shelling but not so close now and only intermittent. I realized that I would have to find my own way out if I wanted to get home that night, so I headed for the main gate hoping to secure a lift back.

It was not long before a water tanker appeared so I hitched a ride with the Thai driver to Tapraya. This was not the most comfortable journey, sitting up on a hot iron cover over the motor, but better than walking. Back in the village, everyone was pleased to see me safely back, Fr Alfonso telling me that the UN chief had called him on the radio, knowing I was in camp. They had decided that I knew how to look after myself, and there would be no need to send someone in to get me. The UN guy said, "She is okay. She is a sturdy woman." I was not sure if I should have taken offence at that!

Black Magic

A very distressed Chenda was waiting in the office when I arrived a few days later. He told me that the drummer in his band, Bun Sakorn and his wife had been stabbed to death the night before, the killer had absconded and could not be found. Chenda knew his identity and was afraid he would come back to kill more people, including his family. They felt more frightened because the man responsible, an ex-soldier, was covered in tattoos that they believed would protect him from being killed by bullets, knives or explosives. Soldiers could always be identified by their tattoos, displaying designs of a sun on each shoulder connected by Buddhist symbols across the chest, to protect the body. Tattoos of animals then continue down the legs, to safeguard these limbs, with more symbols covering the arms. Sometimes, I would visit a tattooed landmine victim in hospital, asking about this protection and why it did not work. They would come up with the excuse that 'My karma was not good on that day', or 'I failed to believe strongly enough in its power', but never admitting that this magic had failed.

I asked Chenda the motive for the killing but he was too frightened to talk about it, saying it was all to do with black magic and I would not understand. He and his family had moved out of their house, were living with friends, and feared for their lives.

UNBRO protection officers were investigating the crime, but had no leads on the whereabouts of the killer, finding it difficult to obtain any information, with neighbours too fearful to be involved. This man did not return to the camp, so was never apprehended for the killing.

Black magic and spirits were very real to the Cambodian people; the fear of the supernatural deeply ingrained in their subconscious. When visiting Nong Chan dance group one day, I found all staff members busy building a spirit shrine to hang over their stage. They told me that the spirit of an old dance teacher, who lived before the 13th century, had entered the body of one of their male dancers the day before. He had been writhing and dancing around crazily as the spirit took control of him. I asked if the shrine was to drive the spirit away, but was told, "No, to keep it here so the group will dance better." People were bringing in incense and candles, praying to appease the spirit, whom they feared may be angry with them.

When a family member died, it was important to have the body, or some part of it, so a ceremony could be held, as they say, "If people are not buried, their spirits cannot rest and ghosts can be cruel."

My first full year was coming to a close and I decided that I would go home for a few weeks to spend Christmas with my family. Before I left, I wished to reward the Fine Art leaders with some celebration as they had achieved enough through the year to warrant a memorable celebration.

Unbeknown to them, I had written to the DPPU requesting a pass to take fourteen people to Aranyaprathet for the day, citing as my reason 'to familiarize them with Thai culture!' This day pass was approved and I set about plans for our 'cultural' trip.

None of these leaders had been out on the Thai side of the camp since they had arrived years earlier, so there was much excitement when I told them of the plan. Ken agreed to have the day off and accompany us, volunteering to drive the van.

We arrived in the camp at 8.30am on the appointed day. Fourteen beaming faces confronted us when we pulled up at the office. All of them attired in their best clothes, surrounded by wives and friends waiting to bid them farewell and remind them of shopping they wanted done. Before we left, I handed around car-sick tablets that many of them took straight away. There was a ninety-minute journey ahead and they were unused to car travel. Needless to say, we still had to stop by the roadside going there and back, waiting while some were sick. As we drove through the countryside and farmland, all were glued to the windows pointing to everything in sight, saying they felt like they were back in Cambodia as the surroundings were so similar.

On reaching Aranyaprathet, we took them first to the big pagoda in town. They knelt and prayed before the statue of Buddha, before going on to the very ornate Chinese temple. This was very different, with big statues, colourful paintings, sculptures and ornaments. Next we took them on a tour of the COERR office, where they all got stuck at the photocopying machine, the first one they had ever seen; intrigued by its function. We split the group in two, Ken and I taking seven each. They were not used to traffic, so it took us all our time to marshal them across the roads and guide them through the streets whilst constantly checking for stragglers. It was an age before we made two blocks, after they stopped and looked at everything in the shops, fascinated by the display of goods.

We finally made it to Ploens restaurant where I had made a booking for lunch. I asked if they would like beer to drink but all declined. The waitress came over and I ordered a variety of dishes from the menu, to be placed in the middle. When the food arrived, there were many more dishes, plus bottles of beer, Mekhong whisky and packets of cigarettes. When I showed surprise at these extras, I found that the men had also been ordering, choosing the most expensive food, including lobster! More and more dishes kept coming and they kept eating and eating. I just hoped that I would have enough money to pay the bill!

After lunch, we headed for the big market where they could spend the money they had brought with them. They loved the market and the huge range of goods on display, buying sarongs, thick jackets (don't know where they would wear these!), children's clothes, tricycles, schoolbags and food. By the time we had made our way through, and they had exhausted their money supply, it was getting late so we headed back to the car.

They amazed me on the way back, by consuming a huge tin of biscuits and bottles of soft drinks. It was hard to believe they could fit any more in after the huge meal they had eaten in the restaurant. We had some time left so stopped in Tapraya, where I took them to see my house. They thought it was great, poking their heads in every room, running up and down the stairs and commenting how beautiful it was.

We treated them all to ice-creams before heading back to the camp, just making it by 5pm. As we drove through the Site 2 entrance, Pen Chenda turned to me with a sad look on his face, saying, "You opened the gate for us this morning, but now we're back in prison!"

As I left Site 2 a few days later, on my way home, my thoughts were with the camp people. Here I was, able to come and go at will, but they were stuck within the confines of the barbed wire enclosure. They would have to endure the long, hot days of dull routine, the nights full of fear, and listen to the constant thunder of shelling while all they wanted was just to have the opportunity to return home, as I was doing.

CHAPTER 6

It took me a while to get back in the swing of things, with long lists of goods to be bought and many problems to be sorted out when I returned to the camp. Although I had left instructions for the dance and drama group leaders to carry on with the meetings while I was away they had not done so, with the result that no performances had been held and dance lessons and workshops had stopped operating. It would be a couple of weeks before the programme was on track again and back to normal.

By now, Site 2 had been in existence for five years, and many changes had taken place. Television sets, powered by car batteries or generators, had sprung up all over the camp, their antennas looking so out of place perched atop the bamboo and thatch huts, battery charging services set up by enterprising camp people with battery rentals also available. The only programmes accessible were all in Thai, but that didn't seem to worry the people, who crowded around the television sets intrigued and not the least bit concerned that they could not understand a word. Video halls had been introduced, ticket boxes and drink stalls out the front. While inside, rows of bamboo seats were set up to accommodate the ever-increasing crowds, all willing to pay an entrance fee of ten baht to see a movie shown on a television set perched up front on a bamboo table. After years of being cut off from the outside world, the people just couldn't get enough of these movies, packing out the theatres daily. Bloodthirsty Chinese movies, purchased from Thai traders in the market, were the most popular.

Vietnamese Refusal to Leave

A new compound named 'Ban That' had now been built at the back of Site 2, to house Vietnamese refugees. Ban That was completely separated from the main camp, having its own checkpoint where entry could only be gained with a specially stamped pass. Most of the former Vietnamese residents of Site 2 had now been relocated here, but about 400 people were still in the old camp, refusing to be moved to Ban That, believing it was a 'closed' camp. Fearful that if they agreed to be relocated, there would be no more interviews or chance of resettlement and they would lose their refugee status. This was not so, but no amount of talking by UN officials and Thai military could convince them otherwise. Buildings were being demolished around them and a departure deadline given. At this stage, the gates to Ban That were still open to them.

Concerned for the safety of my friends in this section, I made my way over to the camp to speak to my staff member, Thach Ven, the director of the Vietnamese dance group. I found him cowering in one of the remaining buildings, fearful of the consequences of his stand, but determined to hold fast, saying he would die rather than go to the new camp. He handed over musical instruments and other fine arts equipment, imploring me to keep them safe until these problems could be resolved. I stayed with him for an hour, pleading with him to see reason, but his mind was already made up. He would sit tight.

Knowing the deadline was next day, I called over again to see the remaining people. By now, more buildings had been pulled down by the DPPU, with only a few public buildings, including the pagoda, still standing. This building only being spared because one of the monks had threatened to kill himself if it was destroyed. Fearing he may carry out his threat the soldiers left it alone. Confusion and anger reigned among the remaining people and knowing they would be no match for armed Thai soldiers in the event of a confrontation, I hoped they would keep calm. I had not been there long, when six DPPU guys came along, and spying me, angrily ordered me out, saying that no foreigners were allowed in this compound. I reluctantly said goodbye to my friends.

There were still close to 300 stalwarts standing firm next day, many desperate, some staging hunger strikes, others lying on the road and refusing to move, one man had stabbed himself in protest and the monks were threatening self-immolation. UNBRO cancelled food and water supplies, hoping to force the people to change their minds, but they would not relent. Protest banners adorned remaining buildings and loudspeakers were being used to broadcast their complaints. The situation was becoming very tense.

Remaining buildings were set on fire the following morning, and fanned by strong winds the flames spread quickly, placing the whole camp at risk. UN cars drove through the streets directing through loudspeakers, that volags leave immediately. As we made our way to the waiting vehicles, flames could be seen leaping from burning buildings and a pall of smoke hung over the whole area.

Agency cars formed a convoy heading out, instructing volags to assemble at the Situation 3 meeting point about fifteen kilometres away, where they were to wait until all workers had been accounted for. After a headcount had been made and all workers found to be present, UNBRO officers announced that the Site 2 was closed, giving us no choice but to make our way home.

I left for work next morning, only to get as far as the village of Khok Prek and there be told by an UNBRO staff member that the situation in the camp was very tense, resulting in 'limited medical access only', until further notice.

Word came out over the next few days that the people were still maintaining their stand and talks with the UN and DPPU had failed. It was a worrying time for us, stuck in our village, for we all had friends in this section and were concerned for their safety. It was to be another five days before we gained entry, and still the position remained the same. Now the remaining people were living under strips of canvas and all roads to this section had been sealed off, with armed soldiers on guard.

A very disturbed and frightened Thach Ven came to see me in my office two days later, saying he had escaped from the enclosure at 3am, and had been hiding since. The UN was now sending in rice and water for the people, but DPPU was holding it from them, forcing them to sneak out of the compound at night to buy supplies, as they were very hungry. This was a risky exercise as they could be shot or beaten if found leaving the compound. After supplying him with food and clothes to take back, I hid him in a back room where he would stay out of sight until darkness fell and he could return safely.

Trucks sent in by Thai military entered the section at midnight a week later, waking the remaining people, then forcing them aboard before transporting them to the grounds of the pagoda where they spent the rest of the night. Next morning they were transferred to a compound near the border road. Leaders were called up and given their last chance to make the decision, on behalf of the people, to go to Ban That camp. They flatly refused.

On a visit to the new compound, I found all the people still there but living under mats, plastic, blankets, thatch or any cover they could find. They complained about not receiving enough food and water from the administration, even though regular rations had been approved by UNBRO. In spite of all the existing deprivations, they were still adamant that they would not be coerced into moving to Ban That. It took some time, but eventually supplies of bamboo and thatch were brought in, enabling them to erect more substantial shelters.

Reluctantly they settled into this encampment, ostracized by both the DPPU and Cambodian neighbours, whilst a large number of their counterparts, who had gone to Ban That camp, were approved for resettlement. It took a few months before these people realized the error in their refusal to relocate, but by then it was too late. They were to remain in this compound for another four years before being transferred to Si Khieu, a holding camp located far away on Thai soil. Eventually these people were sent back to Vietnam.

While we were banned from the camp, I took the opportunity to visit KID camp, making my way first to the OHI (Operation Handicap International) workshop to catch up with Saroeun. At the entrance I was greeted by a smiling Saroeun in his wheelchair, his leg stumps had healed and an artificial limb had been fitted to his arm. He seemed to have come to grips with his handicap and appeared to be more content, telling me he was attending English classes and was looking forward to soon talking with me in that language.

Saroeun had a nice open face, winning everyone over with his lovely smile, especially the foreign nurses who all fell for his charm, willing to help him wherever possible. Fr Pierre had visited, giving him a radio that had become his prized possession; he kept it next to him in the chair, even though the batteries were flat. He requested a pair of jeans to cover his scars, and more batteries, which I promised to bring on my next visit.

My medic friend, Yan, his wife and baby daughter were now living illegally in KID so I went next to visit them. Yan told me how they had found their way to this camp.

A Thai guide met them outside the fence of Site 2 at 4.30am, leading them through the rice fields for three hours, before coming to a village where they waited until night came. A car which was to take them the rest of the way failed to turn up, so they walked the remaining forty kilometres in complete darkness.

Yan told me that the huge lights and guard boxes of the KID made them cringe with fear, but luckily they managed to slip through the fence unnoticed. They were fortunate to have made it as there were many others, who paid, then were robbed and left to find their own way; still others, who had been robbed then killed. Although without a job or food rations, Yan still believed it was worth the gamble, as there was always a chance of entry to another country from KID, so he thought! These people never ceased to amaze me with the risks they took, for the outside chance of gaining resettlement. In time Yan secured a job as a medic in the hospital. This entitled him to a worker ration, but he never made it to a third country. He and his family were eventually repatriated to Cambodia with other border people.

Phoeuy Found

Out of the blue one day, an ex-COERR worker, Brian who now lived in Bangkok, came to tell me that he had found Phoeuy. He was walking through Bangkok's Pratunam market when he was nearly swept off his feet by someone cannoning into him, then wrapping arms around him, head buried on his chest. When he finally disentangled himself, he found it was Phoeuy. He kept saying, "Father Brian, Father Brian, I am so pleased to see you."

I was delighted with this news. As I planned to visit Bangkok in two weeks, I asked Brian to arrange a meeting for me. Meantime, I told Viseth and his camp friends that Phoeuy had been found alive and well. There was much jubilation when they heard this news, as by now they had convinced themselves that he was dead. They all wrote letters for me to give him.

A few days later, I was greeted in Bangkok by Brian and an Australian visitor, David Ashwell, with the disturbing news that Phoeuy had gone missing again. He had gone to Surin in the north of Thailand and should have returned a few days before, but there had been no word from him and now they were quite concerned. Another two days of waiting brought no more news. I could delay no longer and was preparing to leave when I received a phonecall from Brian with the news that Phoeuy was back.

Because Phoeuy had no idea I was in Thailand, it was a big surprise for him when I opened the door. After the initial shock, he wrapped his arms around me in a big hug, saying how happy he was to be reunited with his foreign friends from Site 2. He had grown so muscly from his hard work on the building site that I hardly recognized him.

He told us his story. His job had finished in Bangkok, so he joined his friend, Noeurn, to travel to Surin for the funeral service of Noeurn's father-in-law. Many Cambodians were attending, most of them illegal immigrants. When, at a gathering after the funeral, the police burst in with drawn guns, causing the Cambodians to run in all directions. Phoeuy climbed out a window hoping to escape that way, only to jump straight into the arms of the police waiting beneath. They promptly arrested him and threw him into prison, along with many others without Thai ID cards.

After sitting in a cell for two days with little hope of release, he called in one of the guards, showing him the gold chain he had managed to conceal on capture. After some negotiation, the guard agreed to assist his escape, in return for the chain. When all prisoners were asleep that night, the guard opened the door for Phoeuy and he ran for his life. Afraid of recapture, he hid in the rice fields for two days, until hunger and thirst finally drove him out. Desperate, he approached a local farmer, telling him of his plight and the man, poor though he was, gave Phoeuy his train fare to Bangkok. This was when I caught up with him.

I had brought a pair of jeans and a shirt from Aranyaprathet and I gave them, together with letters from his friends and one from Tim. His face lit up when he saw this mail, sitting with the envelopes in his hand, studying the outside for a long time, before opening them to read. This would be the first contact he had had with his friends from the camp for one and a half years. He looked very sad after he had finished reading.

Fr Mark, the Jesuit priest in charge of the Bangkok office, joined us when he heard the story, ready to offer his assistance. He asked Phoeuy what he would like to do. After giving it some thought, Phoeuy said he wished to return to Site 2. Fr Mark promised to contact the ICRC for advice on how to get him back. He did that next day, only to be told to "Bring the person involved to this office and we will hand him over to DPPU officials." I did not agree with this, knowing how cruel these officers could be with Cambodians, especially when they were illegal immigrants, so I thanked Fr Mark for his efforts, telling him that I would solve the problem my way.

That evening, Brian, David and I, took Phoeuy out for dinner and he told us what had happened to him since he left Site 2, nearly two years before. "Noeurn and I didn't tell anyone about our plans to leave as we were afraid we would be stopped. We waited until dark, then crawled through the barbed wire fence and made our way over the mountain behind the camp. It took us six days, walking at night and hiding during the day, before we made it to the town of Buriram. Here, we worked in the fields to earn enough money to support ourselves, then we moved on to Surin. We found jobs and stayed there until we had saved enough for our fares to Bangkok."

What a shock it was for two country boys when they landed in this huge metropolis, never having seen a city before. Phoeuy said, "We couldn't believe our eyes. So many cars, shops, buildings and so many goods for sale! We spent all our time at first, just looking in the shops!"

Both spoke good Thai but still had difficulty finding work without an ID card. Eventually they took jobs that no one else wanted, cleaning street sewers. This work entailed long hours, dirty work and very little pay. They met up with other Cambodians living illegally in the city, so moved in with them, sleeping on the floor, ten people to a room.

Phoeuy went on to tell us: "After a few months we had saved enough money to follow our plan, which was to get to the fishing town of Phuket in the south. While there we planned to work and save our fares to America!"

It was not long before they found jobs on building sites, where they worked very hard for the next six months. They now had enough money, they thought, to follow their plan. They headed for the harbour where they asked the crew of a fishing boat to take them to the USA! They could not understand why the fishermen laughed at them. When this plan failed, they decided to go back to Bangkok.

They met up with other Cambodians in the city, who told them that a demolition team was hiring illegal immigrants, so they fronted and got the jobs. This work was very hard - ten to twelve hours a day, for very little pay. They were living on the site, amidst of the roar of machines working around them twenty-four hours a day. Their foreman, a Chinese/Thai, gave them capsules each day, which Phoeuy said 'stop the pain'. It was not long before they had become dependent on these drugs, leaving wherever they were at night to meet their 'friend' for their next dose. Now they were working long hours, with barely two to three hours sleep each night.

Phoeuy went back with Brian and David to stay at their house that night. I received a phonecall from Phoeuy later that night, to tell me that he was having second thoughts about going back to the camp and asked if I could get him a job in Aranyaprathet or Bangkok. I told him that this would not solve the problem; he would still be an illegal immigrant and would forever be looking over his shoulder. Later I received a call from David, telling me that Phoeuy had gone out to meet the guy who supplied the pep-up pills.

When Phoeuy came to see me the next day, he was still undecided about going back, saying he was having problems sleeping. I explained to him he was being drugged with amphetamines to make him work harder and that this was probably the reason he could not sleep. I told him how wrong it was of his boss to give him these drugs. Phoeuy replied, "But he is my friend. He gives them to me so I can't feel the pain!"

We talked for a long time. I stressed that it was no life for him in Thailand as an illegal on the run all the time, with the likelihood of a prison sentence hanging over his head. I told him Site 2 was a lot safer now, with little shelling - I was soon to eat my words! - that the TF80 had been replaced by a much better group, that he would be among friends and could continue his education. He finally agreed that it would be in his best interests to return, but on the condition that I get him safely back, saying he would come to see me the next day to discuss it further.

Now that the decision was made, I knew it would be better not to let him out of my sight. The guy feeding him the drugs would not want to lose this source of cheap labour and may hold him there, so I made arrangements for him to spend the night at the JRS (Jesuit Refugee Service) house where I was staying.

We made our way to the building site in the middle of the city the following day, to fetch his belongings. Phoeuy told me to wait at the gate, but I said I would come with him, making the excuse that I would like to see where he had been living.

At the building site, huge machines were making a terrible uproar and the ground under us was shaking. We picked our way through the rubble, sending scavenging rats scuttling, as we made our way to the small corrugated iron huts where the labourers lived. I followed Phoeuy into his hut to reach his allocated floor space and retrieve his few pitiful possessions, all the time stepping over people lying on the floor. These tiny huts were unbearably hot inside, bare of furniture, each one housing ten or more workers, mostly illegals. I could not imagine how they could possibly sleep with the constant roar of demolition and construction machines working all around them.

As Phoeuy gathered up his belongings, his foreman came in to see what was happening. I moved forward, saying I was a friend and that he was coming with me. Phoeuy collected his gear, the guy still watching, trying to get Phoeuy alone, which I would not allow. As we left the site and he realized his worker was checking out, he became very angry, calling him back, then shouting abuse at us until we were out of sight.

It was a relief to get away from this hellhole and head back to the quietness of the guest house. Now, my problem was how to get an illegal immigrant back through many towns, villages, army checkpoints and then into Site 2!

An ICRC van travelled to Bangkok every week from Aranyaprathet with medical specimens and mail. Aid workers were permitted to use this facility if seats were available. I had booked my seat to return the following day, so I rang, hoping to secure a seat for Phoeuy. I heaved a sigh of relief when this was successful, believing it would be easier to get through military checkpoints under the mantle of the ICRC, rather than on public transport. I booked him under a Thai name, knowing that the ICRC would not agree to harbour an illegal, just hoping no other camp workers, who may recognize him, would be aboard.

On arrival at the take-off point next morning, I was dismayed to see one of the Thai nurses, who worked for COERR; then she saw me and came over. Spotting Phoeuy with me, she turned to him, asking in Thai where he was from. I held my breath. Luckily, he had the presence of mind to say he was from Tapraya and had been visiting Bangkok. His Thai was very good and she accepted this. The next problem would be at Wattana, about fifty kilometres from Aranyaprathet, where soldiers from a military checkpoint held up vehicles and checked the passes of all aboard.

I was very tense as we approached this guardpost, Phoeuy seeming very relaxed, as he did not know what lay ahead. We reached the checkpoint, stopped, and the driver opened the door for a soldier. By this time, I was in a cold sweat. The soldier put his foot on the bottom step, took a look around at the mostly foreign occupants, stepped down and waved us on. My relief was apparent, causing Phoeuy to say, "Why you so nervous?" I was sure he was not aware of the hurdles still to be crossed, before he was back safely in Site 2. We reached Aranyaprathet without any problems.

I had rung Fr John from Bangkok to ask if he would risk driving us back to Tapraya. Always one for taking chances, Fr John said it would be no problem, and he would be happy to oblige. He met us at the bus on arrival in Aranyaprathet. We waited until it was dark, sat Phoeuy between us in the front of the car and took off.

We would have to pass the first military base not far from Aranyaprathet. At this checkpoint, soldiers always looked at passes and checked the contents of vehicles. When we arrived, we handed over the two passes and waited. The soldiers did not even look inside as they checked the passes then waved us on. We were relieved to drive off.

Marie Claude and I were sharing a house in Tapraya, so I would need her permission to keep Phoeuy in our house until I could get him back into Site 2. When approached, she agreed to allow Phoeuy to stay for as long as it took to smuggle him back to camp.

I left for work next morning, giving Phoeuy strict instructions to stay in the house all day. I didn't want anyone reporting him to the authorities. As I walked out the door he was playing tapes, and enjoying his last bit of freedom before returning to camp life.

After making enquiries, it seemed that it would be more difficult getting someone back in than taking them out! I spoke to Fr Pierre and together we came to the conclusion that it would be best to bring him in openly in the education van with other workers. First, I would need permission from staff members, who would be travelling in the van, for everyone could be in trouble with the Thai military if Phoeuy was caught. They all agreed, even enjoying being part of the conspiracy.

We placed him in the middle of the van with workers all around, so he would be harder to detect. We would have to get through a checkpoint at the village of Khok Prek, another at the gates of Site 2. At the checkpoint, workers gathered around Phoeuy, talking, while the driver spoke to the soldiers. We made it through there. Next was the Site 2 entry, where the van stopped while workers signed in. There was a queue of cars ahead and soldiers were busy, so did not apply the usual headcount, only checking the passes while workers signed in. What a relief, we were in! We congratulated each other. Quite some achievement to smuggle an illegal from Bangkok and back into Site 2, right under the noses of the Thai military!

Viseth and Phoeuy's friends were waiting for him at the office when we arrived. They clustered around, one of the boys saying, "Our family is complete again!" as he gave Phoeuy a big hug to welcome him back. I could see there would be lots of stories to tell, so I went back to work, leaving a happy Phoeuy talking nonstop with his friends.

Champagne, Elephants and a Brothel

So far, this year had been very stressful, with consistent shelling, bandit attacks in the camp, a rise in domestic violence and another year to add to the misery of the people away from their homeland. It was impossible for camp workers not to become involved one way or another in these problems. Periodically, we needed some kind of relaxation to ease the built-up tension so we could cope with these traumatic times. Dorcas was soon to leave after two years working with COERR; a good reason to plan a big party.

Dorcas and I put our heads together to work out what to do for this special occasion. We decided to plan a party that people would enjoy and remember. Guests would be requested to come in formal evening wear giving everyone a chance to dress up, which would make a welcome change from the sloppy gear we wore into camp each day. We agreed to keep the details of the evening secret from staff members, to make it more interesting. We planned to hold the event somewhere away from the town, but not too far from Tapraya. There had been many warnings issued recently by UNBRO, advising foreigners to be off the roads by evening, due to the many bandit attacks in the area.

The following weekend, we set off on a drive around the villages to choose a suitable place to hold this celebration. We searched all day and had almost given up when we came across just what we had been seeking; a picturesque setting close to one of the villages about twenty kilometres from Tapraya. It contained a small pond, surrounded by trees, set among the rice fields, an ideal setting with plenty of room for people to move around, plus space for cars. Just what was needed for a relaxing start to the evening.

We drove to the nearby village to request authorization from the local people to use this site. We were directed to a group of farmers sitting together in the town centre. Dorcas, who spoke Thai fluently, was soon chatting away to these locals, telling them of our tentative plans for the party. She asked about the possibility of hiring buffalo and carts, for use as transport from the village for partygoers. The local farmers thought this a great joke. They couldn't understand why we would want to hold the party out there in the fields and use buffalo when we could use cars. Their spokesman, a farmer in his seventies, consulted the others, before coming back to say that they would need time to discuss these unusual requests, asking us to come back in a week's time for the answer. We had allowed plenty of time before the event, so we agreed, knowing we could not push these things with the villagers.

The same group of farmers was waiting for us on our return, along with about fifty onlookers. They all gathered around when we arrived, so they would not miss anything regarding this important event in the town, where foreigners were rarely seen. Dorcas and I were motioned to sit down beside the leader to hear the town's decision. After formalities had taken place, the spokesman told us that the local farmers had decided to grant approval to use this location, but no decision had yet been reached over the buffalo carts. We learned later that buffalo were not allowed on the roads at night, because they posed too much danger to other road users. In the typical Thai way, the farmers did not want to say an outright 'no'. That was okay. We would find other means of transport to make the party more interesting. Next, we would have to find somewhere to hold the rest of the evening's entertainment.

Not far outside the town was quite a large restaurant that appeared to be suitable, although we knew that it was also used as a brothel. It would certainly be an interesting place, but would it be the right place to bring our group, including nuns and priests? We would check it out before making a final decision. Next day we made an appointment to talk with the owners.

We were a bit daunted when we arrived at the restaurant to be faced with a notice out the front in Thai and English, requesting clients to leave all guns, grenades and other weapons at the counter. We explained to the owners about the party and what we wanted and they assured us that it would be all right, agreeing to close the restaurant to outsiders so that we could have the place to ourselves for the night. They promised to supply food and a band. It sounded good so we agreed and booked the venue.

As time for the party drew near, people were getting their heads together regarding outfits for the big event. It would be no easy job to acquire formal wear in this remote area. By now, about forty people had shown an interest in attending the function. Speculation as to the location was high among the workers, some guesses being Aranyaprathet, KID, Site 2 and even across the border in Cambodia. I don't know how they thought we could work that!

Drinks, other than the local Singha beer, were hard to come by in this town and we thought the celebration called for something more fancy; like champagne! Unprocurable in this part of Thailand, we had heard that a Russian 'champagne' was available at the market in Poipet, a Cambodian town just over the border. We decided to try to make it across the border illegally to purchase supplies for the big event.

Dorcas and I arrived at the border early next morning. Poipet was an important trading spot for Thai business people, many of whom came from Bangkok regularly, to pick up bargains at the large market where they could buy goods at duty-free prices, take them back to the city to sell for a profit of 100% or more.

Day passes were issued on the border to Thai citizens, but foreigners were strictly prohibited from entering. When we arrived, hundreds of Thai people were lined up waiting to secure passes at the military checkpoint, so we joined them. Officials were busy issuing documents at two tables set across the entrance to the bridge linking Thailand with Cambodia. When we reached the table the official looked up, then shook his head, pointing to the sign above the desk in both English and Thai, reading: NO FOREIGNERS ALLOWED.

We looked up at the sign, then Dorcas asked in Thai if we could be allowed in to the market for just one hour. The answer came straight back, a firm 'No'. Undaunted, we made our way to the second table, hoping for a sympathetic ear there. After waiting for a couple of minutes, I noticed that both officials had their heads down, busily filling out passes, so I pushed Dorcas through, following close behind. We quickly lost ourselves in the crowds rushing into the market. No shouts followed us, so we knew we had overcome the first hurdle, but now we had to get past both Thai and Cambodian military guards manning each end of the bridge. We kept to the middle of the crowd, with our heads down, kramas covering our hair and as much of our faces as was possible while approaching the checkpoint. Thai soldiers were busy scrutinizing passes and checking the bags of people filing through. We opened our bags for inspection, then keeping our heads down, we kept walking. No one stopped us and we congratulated ourselves on another obstacle overcome. Now for the Cambodian soldiers. We had no idea what faced us in this new territory, it could be a tough one. As we neared the end of the bridge where the Cambodian checkpoint was located, we could see the soldiers lined up waiting to check people before they stepped onto Cambodian soil. We realized there would be no chance of sneaking through here.

We walked up to the soldiers at their station, gave them the traditional greeting of clasped hands to foreheads, and addressed them in Khmer with "Choum re-ep sau" (good day). The soldiers looked at us in surprise, and smiled as they returned the greeting. It seemed that there would be no problems here, as they all gathered around, happy at the unusual sight of Westerners coming into their country. We were plied with questions: What is your nationality? Why are you here? Where did you come from? When we told them that we worked in Site 2, they were really interested, and it seemed all of them knew someone there. It was turning out to be much easier than we expected. Eventually we were able to continue on, promising to stop on the way back and collect written messages to be distributed to family and friends in the camp.

As we made our way in, we could see broken-down buildings everywhere with bullet holes and chips from shell fragments still visible, and gaping holes where windows had been. These ruins were now occupied by squatters. Open drains, full of rotting scraps and garbage lined the road, while emaciated dogs scavenged through. The smell was terrible. As we approached the roundabout from which the road led into town, we were besieged by beggars in rags. There were handicapped ex-soldiers, women with babies in their laps, small children and old people, all with hands outstretched toward us, begging for a few baht. It was a dismal scene and a sad introduction to Cambodia.

Bicycle taxis with a seat on the front were lined up waiting to take people to the market. These 'cyclos', as well as carrying passengers, were used for carting all manner of goods and materials. Some, their cargo piled so high that the driver could not see over the top, but they still pedalled along, periodically peering around the side of their load to see where they were going.

We headed to the taxi stand where a cyclo was waiting. Our rider was a wiry old man in a ragged shirt and shorts, his legs very muscly from pushing heavy loads from dawn to dusk. He was happy to be carrying foreigners, and enjoyed the attention he attracted along the way.

He told us that he rode the cyclo all day, sometimes only earning seventy-five cents after he had paid for hire of the bicycle, making it very difficult to support his family of eight.

It had been raining heavily and the market area was a mud patch. We stumbled over pools of water, slipping and sliding, first making our way to the shoe stall, where we each purchased a pair of wellington boots. With our new foot attire, the going was a lot easier, and we set out to check the surroundings. It was a surprise to see so many different things for sale in Cambodia. Stalls selling electrical goods, cameras, furniture, jewellery, chinaware, clothing, shoes, bags, food and drinks. We even saw live tiger cubs for sale at 20,000 baht each, (close to AUD$1,000). I could not see any Cambodians buying them for that price, but we were told that Thai traders were only too willing to part with that amount for these rare animals.

We were followed everywhere by groups of curious children, who had not seen foreigners before. Heavily armed government soldiers could be seen in the streets and market. I asked one of the soldiers if I could have a photo taken with him. He was happy to oblige, first combing his hair, replacing his hat, then proudly displaying his gun for the camera.

After wandering around for an hour, we found a coffee shop and stopped for a welcome drink. Groups of men sitting around, stopped talking to look and listen to us. Eventually, one of them struck up the courage to come over to speak. He had already heard by 'bush telegraph' that these two foreign women worked in Site 2, and he wanted to know if we knew his cousin. I thought, 'Oh yes, out of more than 200,000 people, I'm sure to know him!'

The man said, "My cousin's name is So Sayornn." I couldn't believe it; So Sayornn, my friend, was in the camp. He was very excited when I told him that I did know his cousin. He promptly sat down to write a letter to Sayornn. I knew it would be a big thrill for Sayornn's family to receive news from relatives inside Cambodia, for all contact with them had been cut off years ago. By now, more men had come over and were asking if we knew their friends and relatives, while others were busy writing letters for us to take back. It would be no easy matter to trace all these people and deliver the letters, but we promised to do our best when we returned.

At one of the stalls, I purchased some ornate cloth which I figured would be suitable for costumes for the dance and drama teams, knowing how thrilled they would be that it was bought in Cambodia. It was getting close to closing time so we went looking for the champagne. We bought eight bottles off Russian champagne. We had no idea what it would taste like but would take the chance; after all, it was champagne! At the same shop, I saw a bottle of drink in a fancy bamboo holder with the picture of a gecko on the label. It looked interesting, so I bought that as well. It wasn't till I got it home and had a closer look that I found it contained two full-sized pickled geckos. When I took it into camp and asked Chenda to translate the writing on the label for me, I found that it was used as an aphrodisiac!

It was now four o'clock, so we headed back to the border gates, hoping to get through without any problems. At the first checkpoint, the Cambodian soldiers came out, interested to view our purchases. They laughed when they saw the bottles of Russian champagne and still more when they saw the gecko bottle. After picking up notes written for camp people, we continued on, receiving quite a send off.

Now we had to make it past the Thai guards, who were not known for their friendliness. We waited until a few people were going through, and with lowered heads, positioned ourselves in the middle of the group. We had gone past them and were heading for the gate when we heard, "Hey you," shouted behind us. We did not look around, just walked faster, barely making it to the gate when the call was repeated, then we hurried across the border. There were no thumping footsteps behind, no shots fired, so we knew we had made it with our important cargo.

Party time was getting closer and prospective partygoers were still looking for suitable outfits for the night. Everyone wanted to get into the spirit of things, then someone remembered a box of clothes that had been donated for the camp people by one of the embassies in Bangkok. Camp workers and Cambodian staff gathered around while the box was opened. Out came beautiful evening gowns, cocktail dresses with frills, flounces, lace, embroidery and fancy beading, totally unsuitable for the Cambodians, who wore only sarongs and blouses, but great for our party! There was much hilarity, as dresses were donned and paraded, seeming so bizarre here in this remote border camp.

Dorcas chose a black taffeta dress, off the shoulder, with big wide frills around the neck and hemline. Ingrid decked herself out in a red and black shiny suit, Pam chose a purple lace top with a black skirt, Agnes went for a short, tight-fitting red silk dress and Leanne squeezed herself into a slinky, black gown with elaborate lace trimmings. Everyone was getting into the party spirit, it was going to be a fun night.

Dorcas and I made another visit to the restaurant to check on the preparations and take white tablecloths, flowers, candlesticks and other decorations to brighten up the dreary setting. We chose a selection of Thai dishes from their menu, hoping they would prove popular. All seemed to be under control there.

Our plans were gradually falling into place. Only one problem still to solve. Some alternative transport for the night to make it more interesting. We were mulling over this, the day before the party, when we were amazed to see two elephants with baby in tow, being led into Tapraya. We couldn't believe our luck. This was an unprecedented event in this town, maybe it was meant for us; after all, what could be more different than arriving by elephant! On consultation with the owners, we were disappointed to learn that they were on their way to Surin in the north and would be leaving Tapraya on the morning before the party. We told them about the event and our desire to use the elephants for transport, and after much haggling, they agreed to put off their departure for another day. We asked if they could keep the elephants out of sight, and with their approval, lead them to a field outside the town. Great, this would certainly be a big surprise!

We had been in touch with Michael, a US lawyer, who had previously worked in Site 2 and was now stationed in Bangkok, asking him to act as champagne waiter but to keep his presence a secret. Dorcas, Agnes and I, were in the house when he arrived by taxi. The sight of Michael emerging, towel covering his head to avoid being recognized, brought forth peals of laughter.

The day of the party dawned. Some of the workers had arranged to wear traditional Cambodian outfits, so they headed for the camp to be dressed by Cambodian friends, others assembled at Fr John's house that had been set up for beauty treatment. The local beauticians we had hired set to work giving manicures, pedicures, shampooing and setting hair and organizing face packs. There was much hilarity, as co-workers sat with hair tied back, face packs on, while sitting with their hands and feet in buckets of water waiting for manicures and pedicures.

Soon, it was time for everyone to get dressed for the evening's entertainment. As they arrived back at the house, there were cries of surprise at the assortment of clothes people had managed to acquire for the party. Some of the men had found suits and ties, others like Ken, were fully attired in Cambodian outfits. Ken wore a fancy gold brocade coat over an orange satin shirt and knicker-like pants in gold lame. These pants were made from three metres of cloth, meticulously folded and tucked into the waist. Ordinarily this outfit was worn by the groom for part of the wedding ceremony and he created quite a lot of speculation when leaving Site 2, camp people convinced he was preparing for his own wedding. Fr Alfonso, resplendent in a fancy silk jacket with matching silk tie, Stephen, a Canadian and Kevin from USA, were decked out in traditional Cham costumes, complete with baggy pants, brightly coloured shirts and little round black hats. Liz Uphoff, Ann and Edie had been dressed in the camp and wore satin and brocade, Cambodian wedding outfits. These featured tight-fitting long dresses, with an array of gold jewellery around their necks, up their arms and in their hair. Lud came out in 'forties' gear she had put together herself. The costume featured a tight, short, black skirt made from a cut off T-shirt; silk, sleeveless top; high-heeled shoes (retrieved from the embassy box); black, gangster hat, and a long cigarette holder. Ingrid, our Italian bombshell, had made a matching pillbox hat to go with her shiny satin suit. Everyone was really into the spirit of things.

By seven o'clock partygoers had all arrived at Fr John's house ready for the evening. They were waiting outside, still wondering where they were going and what the night held for them, when someone spotted the two elephants, complete with seats, being led up the street towards us. They couldn't believe their eyes, as the elephants stopped outside the house and people were motioned to climb aboard. To reach the elephants' backs they had to climb on to the back of a utility then on to the seat from there. There was a lot of laughter, as the girls tried to climb aboard with their tight skirts and high heels. The elephants made many trips before guests were all transported to another house on the road out of town. Here, the elephants were taken close to the second floor balcony, so that people could get off. While all this was going on, local people had lined the streets of Tapraya to watch the strange sight of the foreigners in their elaborate dress, riding on the elephants. They would never cease to be amazed at the strange behaviour of these foreigners!

Partygoers now got in the cars and we set off, everyone excited, still trying to guess where we could be headed. At first, we took the road towards Cambodia, then we turned onto the road to Aranyaprathet, branching off three kilometres from Tapraya. We followed this road for fifteen kilometres, driving through small villages, past farms and rice fields before arriving at our destination

Michael and Agnes had gone ahead to prepare the venue. It was now dark and as we approached the setting, everyone gasped at the sight that met their eyes. Michael had placed lighted candles in paper bags around the pond. The reflection on the still water made a beautiful picture. Under the trees next to the pond, tables were set up with candles, flowers, champagne glasses and bottles. Michael, looking the part in a black suit with bow tie, white cloth draped over his arm, presented a glass of champagne to each arrival, while Agnes greeted the ladies with a red rose. It was quite a sight to see all these well-dressed people, drinking champagne out here in the rice fields. It was not long before villagers ventured out to see what was going on, staying to gape at the scene that met their eyes.

Everyone was enjoying themselves. Though I must admit there were a few grimaces when people had their first sip of Russian champagne, it was pretty awful! While people were sipping champagne and chatting, Michael slipped over to the other side of the pool and set off the fireworks. This was quite a sight, as rockets flew, and bursts of stars hit the sky. It looked fantastic with the reflections over the water. Guests were settling in, as they thought this was the party place, but that was not to be. After the champagne, people were directed back to the cars for the next part of the night's entertainment.

We took a different route back, through small villages and over very bad roads, finally approaching our destination from another direction, everyone still pondering as to where we would finish. At first, nobody realized where we were when we pulled up at the restaurant, then someone recognized the 'No Weapons' sign.

The decorations looked great, with the tables set up beautifully, streamers and balloons everywhere. The band played soft music; very unusual for Thais, but that was what we had instructed, while we sat down to a tasty meal. By now, people were in a real party mood.

After dinner, the band played dance music we had requested and all guests were soon on the floor. It happened to be Pam's birthday and she declared it the best birthday party ever. She celebrated by putting on a lone dance performance in the middle of the floor. Leanne, accompanied by Malcolm on his guitar, entertained us with a number of songs. Leanne's beautiful voice had guests mesmerized with her rendition of 'Blue Moon', 'Streets of London' and other songs, finishing off with a duet with Malcolm, of a farewell song they had written especially for Dorcas. This was followed by an address by Fr Alfonso, thanking Dorcas for the good work she had done and letting her know how much she would be missed by her workmates. Dorcas followed up with her emotional farewell speech, thanking everyone for the great send-off. It was sad to be losing such a vital member of our team.

Dancing carried on until the early hours of the morning and would have continued, but for the restaurant owners, who were waiting at the door to wave us off. It had been a great opportunity for workers to let their hair down and enjoy themselves. The party continued at our house, finally breaking up at 3am, an unheard of hour for this sleepy little town.

This had been a night to remember and was talked about for years after, always being referred to as the 'elephant party'.

A Dangerous Mission

I had met up with a young married couple Sarawath and Tola, both friends of Tim. Sarawath, 21 years old, had lived in one of the Site 2 orphanages before joining the KPNLF forces as a soldier. He had been told that if he joined the military, after one year's training, he would become an officer, then he could come back to the camp and his studies.

Sarawath now had only two months left before completing his military training, which took place at Klang Dong camp, about twenty kilometres away inside Thailand. The training was very hard, recruits being drilled seven days a week and sometimes at night, with only six days off every three months. They slept in hammocks out in the open, with only a sheet of plastic over them when it rained. Food was short, their rations consisting of rice and morning glory plant that they had to cook themselves. He was really looking forward to the completion of his training so he could continue his studies and spend more time with his wife, who was now pregnant. I came to know Sarawath well as he often accompanied me on my way around the camp, enjoying my company and the opportunity to practice his English. Tola was kept busy working at a clothing stall in the market each day.

When his training was finished, Sarawath requested the promised return to Site 2, to study, only to be told that he was now being sent on a dangerous mission into Cambodia. He had been granted a three-day leave before setting forth on this assignment. He was not happy with this development, coming to the office to voice his concern, but knowing he must do as instructed by his superiors.

Two weeks later, a very thin, distressed Sarawath came to see me, telling me that he had just returned from the mission, and related a horror story to me.

The aim of the mission was to distribute radios, sarongs and other gifts to villagers in order to win favour for the KPNLF. A general accompanied them, employing more than a hundred armed soldiers for his own protection, using Sarawath and thirty-nine other soldiers as porters. They followed tracks over the mountains, weighed down by twelve-kilogram backpacks, while the general rode in an oxcart. The soldiers had no water and only uncocked rice to eat for nearly two days, while the general had a plentiful supply of soft drinks, alcohol and food for himself.

When they neared the villages, the general went ahead with a heavily armed escort to protect him, instructing Sarawath's group to stay where they were and wait until someone came back with permission for them to proceed with the goods. They were left in a dangerous area, with only eight guns between them.

They waited for one day and one night, then their leader decided to go ahead because he was afraid they would be robbed of the goods they were carrying. They had only been on the move for a couple of hours, when they encountered Cambodian government soldiers, who opened fire on them. Other KPNLF soldiers in the area, came to their assistance and an explosive encounter followed. KPNLF troops eventually gained the upper hand, causing the government soldiers to retreat, luckily resulting in no casualties to their side. Not long after this battle, one of the Sarawath's group stepped on a landmine, blowing off his leg. Sarawath and another soldier made a stretcher from a hammock, then carried him for three kilometres to the nearest village, leaving him in the care of villagers before heading back to join the others. In one part of the forest, they encountered a heavily mined area. They had to find their way around the landmines, measuring each footstep, never sure if the next would be their last. Sarawath told me that as he was making his way through the minefield, his heavy backpack made him lose balance and the pack fell onto a mine. He stood transfixed, but luckily, the mine did not explode. He carefully hooked the bag back with his gun.

By now, they were very thirsty and went searching for water. At each of the three water holes they found the bodies of men, women and children, some newly dead, others that had been there for a while, all killed by landmines. He saw the body of a baby that had died of starvation when its mother had stepped on a mine, and bodies of soldiers in sitting positions, held there by their backpacks and looking quite eerie. An overpowering smell of rotting flesh hung over the area. Finally, the group received a message from the general to come down to the village. They spent the next five days waiting while the goods were distributed in four villages, before heading back on the dangerous journey.

After arriving back in the camp three days later, the general held a big party for himself and other officers. He sent out $1 to each of the soldiers, who accompanied him. Sarawath and others were disgusted, saying, "Not much for a life!" Now Sarawath wanted to resign from the army, but was afraid they would not accept his resignation after he had signed on for six years. He was adamant that he would not go back.

A very distressed Tola came to see me a week later, telling me that KPNLF soldiers had come to their house and arrested Sarawath, taking him back to Klang Dong. She heard that he had been thrown in the prison there. It was not until later, when he came back to Site 2, that we learned what had happened.

Because he had gone AWOL, he was sentenced to ten days' imprisonment. He told me, "I was stripped and forced to lay on hot stones in the sun for an hour each day, then put into cold water for one hour each night. Other training students were brought out to watch me, and the officers encouraged them to jeer at me, and make an example of me because I had deserted." He was given no dry clothes, but made to sleep on the ground outside with no mosquito net. The rest of the day he worked chopping wood, often beaten with lumps of bamboo. He continued, "I was only given a half plate of rice with salt twice a day and was always hungry. One time, after I ate my food, they said that now I would have to 'give it back'. They rolled me around on the ground until I threw up and finally lost consciousness." After nine days of this treatment he collapsed and was sent to hospital.

After his prison term and hospitalization, he was returned to the military training school, but it was very difficult for him as his teachers continually pointed him out as an example of a 'bad student'.

This is the story he told us when he returned to Site 2, showing me the scars on his back from the beatings. He applied for leave to stay with Tola until their baby was born. For the next month he heard nothing, then was visited three times at his home by KPNLF personnel, who asked when he was coming back to Klang Dong. Each time he explained that his wife was soon to deliver and he needed to be with her. Two days after the baby was born, Sarawath was forcibly picked up and returned to the army camp. He escaped three days later, making his way back to Site 2, where he headed for the office to seek my help.

He hid in the office during daylight hours for the next few days, staying with friends at night, while I tried all means to have him transferred to another camp. During this time KPNLF personnel repeatedly visited his house looking for him. After two weeks of efforts on the part of another COERR worker, Mary and myself, we received word from the ICRC that they would transfer him and his family to Ban That camp where he would no longer be under the control of the KPNLF. They were thrilled with this news. They wanted to leave Site 2 as soon as possible, and began packing their belongings immediately.

They soon settled into Ban That, Sarawath finding work at the English school. I would often visit them there where they were much happier, telling me they were no longer afraid now that the KPNLF could not reach them.

CHAPTER 7

Heavy and close shelling woke me at five o'clock one morning in March. It was so close that the whole house shook. I took my tape recorder onto the balcony to record the sounds of battle, then made my way to our office to find out what was happening. Most of the staff was already there. I was met with the news that the camp was closed with a strong likelihood that we may have to evacuate Tapraya due to the shelling being close to the town.

The fighting was between KPNLF and Vietnamese troops, with KPNLF soldiers capturing many strategic strongholds only twenty kilometres from the Thai border. There was also fighting very close to Site 2, causing us all to fear for the people there, who had nowhere to go should the camp be attacked.

A group of us went up the hill at the back of the town, where we could look over into Cambodia. From there, we could see the smoke from the guns and explosions where shells landed, hearing the delayed booms later. Fr John was able to tell us what calibre guns were firing, how far they could reach and what ammunition they were using. We all thought Fr John had missed his vocation and should have been a soldier instead of a priest; he even looked like a military man with his crew cut hair and combat style of clothes. He spent hours talking to the KPNLF officers in the camp about military manoeuvres and tactics. Now he was about to go into the camp to check out the situation.

We all waited nervously for his return.

A few hours later, he was back, telling us that the people were terribly frightened, many lying in their bunkers clutching their bags of belongings, others packed and waiting to run if the camp was shelled. He could see the shells in the air as they went over the camp.

Meanwhile, aid workers in Tapraya were instructed to familiarize themselves with the evacuation route mapped out for them. All agency vehicles were directed to follow a UN vehicle, leading the way. I joined the COERR team in the convoy.

It transpired to be a circuitous route, taking nearly two hours to go through small villages over very bad roads, finishing up in a town fifty kilometres from Aranyaprathet on the road to Bangkok. This route was planned to keep the main road from Tapraya free for the transport of troops and tanks, if the need arose.

Evacuation

The threat of a major attack on the camp was a distinct possibility. UNBRO officers were in a quandary about what course to take. An area, called 'Site 3', for want of a better name, had already been set aside some ten kilometres further into Thailand, between Site 2 and Tapraya, for just such an emergency. Temporary roads had been built, bush cleared and water tanks set up. The problem was to know when the move should be made. Would they evacuate the more helpless people to the safer place now, or stay put, and hope an attack on the camp would not eventuate?

It was a big decision to make, for it would take a major effort to transport and set up shelter for so many people. Lists of highly vulnerable people, who could be an encumbrance in a sudden evacuation, had already been prepared by camp leaders. These people were classed as 'Category 4' and comprised the sick, elderly, blind, handicapped and women more than eight months pregnant. UN officials were holding many meetings but no decision had been made on when or if to make the big move.

COERR was concerned about their expensive equipment in Site 2, which could be damaged by shelling or looted. A meeting for leaders of all programmes was held to determine the best course to take. Finally, a decision was made to hire trucks to bring out as much of the equipment and as many supplies as possible. These would be stored in a house in Tapraya rented for this purpose. One truck was allocated to my programme and I would accompany it in, if permission was granted by UNBRO. In the meantime, I was able to get a message in to the fine arts people to have their gear ready for removal.

Permission was granted, two days later. The trucks arrived in Tapraya and we made our way into the camp. The first stop was at Ampil fine arts centre, as they had the most equipment. While they were loading this, I went over to see how the boys were at the office. Phoeuy came running out, really pleased to see me. He told me that they were very frightened over the close shelling and they could now hear the tanks rumbling into position inside Cambodia.

UNBRO had now made the decision to move category 4 people to Site 3 and I could see people lined up at the administration offices waiting for the trucks to transport them. It was a sad sight: handicapped in wheelchairs or on crutches, elderly, together with very pregnant women, many clutching small children to them, all holding on to the few possessions they were permitted to carry.

By the time I arrived back, Ampil fine arts workers had loaded their equipment, not leaving much room for the other groups. Next I made my way to Nam Yun and Nong Chan sections where workers were standing by the roadside with their gear. While waiting for the loading, I called in to visit the family of So Sayornn. His wife, mother and sister told me they were very afraid at the nearby shelling. It was difficult to leave, knowing I was going back to a safe place and they had no option but to stay here, not knowing when the camp may be attacked. I finally took my leave, unable to find words of reassurance for them.

The truck had now been loaded and we were preparing for departure, when Mao Kosal from the agricultural programme came running up. He begged me to take the books for his project, which he had already packed. I couldn't refuse, when he looked so desperate, so I gave him the nod and he hoisted them aboard.

By this time, the truck was full and time was running out. I asked the driver to make one more stop for the Obok group, who had promised to have their gear waiting on the side of the road. He refused, stating that the truck could not take any more weight. Neither would he stop, so I could tell them, for by this time, the shelling was closer and he was very frightened. All I could do was make a futile gesture when the truck passed the group waiting with the equipment. I felt really bad when I saw the look of dismay, then disappointment and disbelief, on Chenda's face as the truck passed, leaving him stranded on the side of the road.

A few days later, Fr John brought me a letter written by Pen Chenda.

March 11th, 1989

Dear Mother Margot,

Please go!!! to help me to bring the art materials to Aran!!! I think my mother doesn't give me the snack when I call for the bread.
Mother, why you bring the materials from Ampil FAS and leave every art here, as you carry a strong son and leave the small child to walk himself.
I had never seen a mother close the eyes to see his son crying, so I do hope that you will be able to help me.
Please, let me know even a word of letter.
Very very very very sad!!!

Pen Chenda

It really upset me to receive this letter and know that I could do nothing about it. The shelling had got worse and we were banned from the camp. Now the shells were landing in Thailand; three in the village of Kok Prasart only five kilometres from Tapraya, on the road to Site 2. Luckily, there were no casualties, but it sparked retaliation from Thailand. We could hear the shells being fired out of the Thai military stronghold near Tapraya, along with those coming in from Cambodia.

The UN was calling for volunteers to help with the thousands of category 4 people, who were arriving at Site 3 by the truckload. All COERR workers volunteered and we made our way immediately to the new holding area about fifteen kilometres from our village where we witnessed an incredible scene. Trucks, their trays packed with people, were pulling up every few minutes. People, all of whom were handicapped in some way, were trying to get down whatever way they could, while in the background huge marquees were being erected to serve as hospital and delivery rooms. People in wheelchairs were trying to push through the sand. Heavily pregnant women, the elderly and the sick, with armfuls of belongings wandered around aimlessly.

We headed for the arrival area to help, lifting down pregnant women, children, amputees, wheelchairs, elderly men and women. Chickens, dogs, ducks and pigs were emerging from under shirts or from belongings, people afraid to leave them behind lest they be stolen. Behind us, a double amputee was sitting on the ground in front of a fire he had lit, holding over it a large snake he had just caught, his mouth watering and those of the people around too, from the smell of roasting meat wafting in the air. It was a bizarre scene!

Truckloads of people continued to arrive. As people left the arrival area, they were given a small supply of bamboo and plastic sheeting to erect their own shelter for the night. As there was plenty of willing hands to assist the people dismounting from the trucks, I made my way over to help the elderly carry their belongings and ensure that they received the materials to build a shelter.

It was sad to see old people gathering handfuls of leaves to make beds and attempting to make a shelter for the approaching night, with only a piece of plastic. One old couple had stopped to rest. The woman, in her eighties, was exhausted, lying on the hard ground while her husband cradled her head in his lap, really concerned for her welfare. They had received no materials and were too frail to build their own shelter, anyway. The sight of these two helpless people sitting in the dirt not knowing where to go or what to do, moved me to tears. Here in the twilight of their lives, when they should be relaxing, they were face to face with all this danger and insurmountable problems.

I went to the UNBRO distribution centre to find materials for a shelter, only to be told that supplies had run out. I begged for something that would make a cover for the old couple for the night and was finally given the only piece of plastic sheeting they had left. I took this back, then arranged with people nearby, to make a covering for them.

Meanwhile, Ken was attempting to build a shelter for a handicapped man, but without success. Every time he put it up, the frame would collapse, prompting another handicapped man to come and take over from this useless foreigner, erecting a sturdy shelter in no time. Ken saw the humour of it and joined in a laugh with onlookers. He decided that he would help elsewhere, satisfied this was not where his skills lay.

One man with no legs was sitting on the ground trying to cut down a tree with a tomahawk, his four little children with him. By now, pregnant women and sick people had been moved to the hospital tents, a few hundred metres from the main settlement.

Just before dark, a UN convoy arrived with more building materials and a couple of big marquees that were erected for those people, who could not find shelter. It would be very crowded, but it was a relief to know that no one would be without cover for the night. We heard that 2,500 people had already been moved from Site 2 that day.

Volags were instructed to leave, as it was now dark. I arrived home at 10pm, falling into bed; arms, legs, back, all aching, exhausted after a tiring and stressful day, only to be awakened a couple of hours later by the sounds of heavy shelling close by. I could only hope that it was not near the people in Site 3, they had enough to worry about for the present.

Volunteers were called for again and we made our way back to the site at eight am. As we approached, we could see thousands of people sheltering under bright blue plastic sheets, held up by whatever they could find. They were spread out over a large sandy area bulldozed out of bushland. Even now, it was very hot and clouds of dust hung in the air. More truckloads of people were already arriving.

Today, our job would be to distribute rice cards. We handed them out to the people already lined up waiting, and were continually asked when the rice would come, everyone complaining of hunger. It transpired that no one had eaten since the morning before, when they left Site 2. We found later that they did not eat that day either; the rice arrived next morning.

After the rice card distribution, I wandered around the settlement to see where I could help. I met Phally, a handicapped man I knew from the camp, his six-year-old son with him. He had been looking for his wife, Mom, who was due to have her baby any day. He told me that Mom, together with their small daughter, had been taken in a different truck, and he was very concerned for her.

I promised I would try to track her down, so I headed for the hospital area, searching through the tents looking for Mom, but had no luck. I spent time looking through the lists, but her name was not on them. A nurse suggested that I try KID, where some of the women had been transported. I left, promising Phally that I would go to KID at the first opportunity and see if I could locate his wife and child.

There was still no entry to Site 2, for we were told the shelling was much heavier. More than a hundred shells had already landed in the area, though there were no reports of shells landing inside the camp, yet. We heard that many people had moved to the western part of the camp, the Thai side, ready to run if there was an attack. I could picture the fear of the people crouching in their bunkers, never knowing where the next shell would land.

Access to the Site 3 was now limited to UN workers, medical staff and half a dozen fluent Khmer speakers. This left me out, so I headed for KID to see if I could locate Mom and catch up with Sarouen and Yan.

I found Mom with about 200 other pregnant women from Site 2; some living in a big warehouse, others in tents. She and her daughter were sleeping on mats on the cement floor of the warehouse, one end curtained off for use as delivery rooms. She begged me to get her to Site 3 so the family could be together, but I convinced her that she was better off here until the baby was born. It would have been impossible to move her at that stage. She wrote a letter for her husband that I promised to deliver.

Volunteers were sought again for Site 3, so a group of us headed there next morning. Agnes and I made our way towards the big marquees housing many of the elderly, to see if we could help there. It was so hot under the plastic covering, it was like walking into an oven. Elderly men and women were lying in rows on the ground. We had brought bowls, water, soap and towels, so set to work washing the people who were too weak to help themselves. Included in this group were a number of blind people, along with some of the elderly too frail to even sit up. These people lived in an extended family set-up in the camp, and were powerless when taken out of that situation. Agnes and I spent the morning bathing people, washing clothes, cleaning, fetching water and food. We found a stretcher and took one sick, elderly, lady to the hospital tent. People were complaining of the cold at night, begging for blankets. I made enquiries at the UN centre, only to be told there were none available. I promised I would try to bring some the next day.

That night there was a huge storm with heavy rain lasting for hours. Next morning, our office received an emergency call from the UN asking for helpers in Site 3. We left early, with the rain still pouring down, carrying supplies of cord, rope, picks and shovels. It was a miserable sight that met our eyes. The whole compound was a sea of mud, many of the plastic canopies ripped to shreds, shelters flooded, leaving people wet and cold and their belongings soaked. The men set to work digging ditches around the marquees and shelters, while we assisted by handing out rope and helping to secure the plastic covers.

The UN had given out one cotton blanket to be shared by three people. Of course, this was not enough to keep them warm. Sr Ath had packed her car full of blankets to distribute and I had brought a bag of secondhand clothes to give out here and there to needy persons. I opened the bag to give a shirt to an elderly man, when I was mobbed. People crowded around me, grabbing clothes, fighting over them, ripping holes in the bag I was holding. I couldn't control them and within seconds all the clothes were gone. Blanket distribution was conducted from the back of Sr Ath's utility. No sooner had it got under way than the same thing happened there. Shivering people surrounded the vehicle, grabbing blankets out of our hands and from the back of the truck. By the time we calmed them down, all the blankets had gone, leaving many of the elderly, who really needed them, shivering and in tears. It was a desperate situation.

We received a UN message that volunteers were no longer required at Site 3. With Site 2 still closed, COERR workers in Tapraya decided to make the most of the video machines from the camp which were stored in a house nearby. This would be a great opportunity for us as we had no access to TV or videos in our village. We settled ourselves on top of the stacked supplies and sat back to enjoy 'Casablanca.' A second video was just under way when there was a huge explosion close by, causing us all to run outside to find out what was happening. Neighbours gathered in the street told us that a shell had landed behind the pagoda, about five hundred metres away. UNBRO vehicles were driving through the streets waving the Situation 3 flag, urging us to find shelter and prepare for evacuation. There was nothing we could do at that time, so we went back to watch the rest of the video.

Shelling eased off later in the day and the all clear was given, so an evacuation of the village was unnecessary that time.

Liz came over that night to tell me a Cambodian man had stopped her and John Henderson in the street that morning saying that one of their soldiers was in trouble and required assistance. He had sought their help, being too frightened to approach a Thai. John borrowed a COERR car and the man directed them out of town along a bush track and into a field, where they found a badly injured soldier lying under a tree. They were told that at 5pm the previous day, the 22-year-old man had stepped on a landmine inside Cambodia, blowing off his leg; four others with him had been killed.

After applying elementary first aid, two soldiers had carried him all night, coming across the border in the early hours, but were afraid of being caught by Thai authorities. They were so relieved to have help, lifting the still-conscious man into the back of the utility, bidding him farewell before heading back across the border. John then drove the injured man to KID hospital.

There was another big storm that night with more heavy rain and squalls, making us hopeful that this would stop the fighting. I could not help but think of all those people in Site 3, living under temporary shelters of plastic sheeting and how miserable it must be for them.

A KPNLF officer visiting Tapraya told us that their forces had run out of ammunition and had been ordered to retreat. The fighting we could hear now was between Government forces and Thai military. Gradually, over the next few days the shelling eased and we were allowed access to Site 2 again.

It was great to enter the camp to check on our friends, and find they were all right. It was also a big relief for the camp people when the foreigners returned to work. By this, they knew the immediate danger was over, making them feel much safer for the time being, anyway.

Thirteen days after the first people were taken to Site 3, category 4 people were moved back to the camp. Over this period in Site 3 settlement, many babies had been born, three people had died and many came back ill. It was a costly exercise and one of the most upsetting experiences I was to encounter whilst working on the border.

New Year Celebrations

In a short time, we were all back at work and on the surface, things were back to normal. However, you could feel or sense a general restlessness in the camp. Both Phoeuy and Saren came at different times to tell me they were depressed, Phoeuy saying that he missed Bangkok and wanted to go back, and Saren wanting to make the dangerous trip into Cambodia to look for relatives. Khmer New Year was approaching, so I hoped this might cheer them up.

Even here, in this remote displaced persons' camp, New Year was a time for celebration with games, fairs, stage shows, dancing, feasts and family gatherings, lasting for three or four days from April 13th. Dance and drama groups were busy practicing for their stage performances. Food drink and games stands were being set up in the pagoda grounds, women were hard at work cooking, while in the markets, people were busy shopping for new clothes for the special occasion.

Some of the COERR workers expressed a desire to put on a dance performance themselves, to entertain the Cambodians for New Year. They chose to perform the Cambodian 'coconut shell' dance and were busy rehearsing. Hundreds of people lined the outside walls, peeping through the cracks while the foreigners were practicing. They laughed uproariously at their clumsiness, after having seen the small children effortlessly performing the same steps. But after weeks of practice they certainly improved, before putting on a number of credible performances, both on the stage and at New Year parties. Judging by the applause, the Cambodian audience really appreciated their efforts.

My friend Marie in Australia, had sent a tape of the 'bird dance', which we decided to perform for a bit of fun. When the group presented this dance outdoors, in Nong Chan camp, there was dead silence at first; the crowds not knowing if they were supposed to be serious and too afraid of hurting our feelings if they laughed. We soon pulled some of them up to join us and it was not long before they all entered into the spirit of it, flapping their arms and wobbling backsides with the rest of us, the audience by now laughing.

I had applied to the DPPU to stay over for two nights in the camp for New Year and waited anxiously for their reply. I was really happy when I heard that permission had been granted, for this was hard to obtain. I would stay one night with Chenda and one with the family of So Sayornn.

On my first night in the camp, over New Year, I made the rounds with Chenda. We first stopped to see the drama being performed by his group on the stage, then made our way to watch the dancing. I took to the floor to participate in the 'romvong' - a traditional Cambodian dance performed in a circle, and one involving intricate hand movements I could never quite master. However, I evoked plenty of amusement when I tried.

Single Cambodian women and men do not socialize together under traditional rules, with the exception being at New Year. At this special time, the girls dress in their fancy blouses and embroidered sarongs, the more modern ones in 'short' below-the-knee skirts, while the boys try to look 'cool' in their sunglasses, smart shirts and jeans. The dance floors were filled with young men dancing, while the girls stood shyly by, enjoying being onlookers, with only an occasional daring girl having the courage to take part.

It was great to see the people having such fun, after the harshness of camp life. They were so pleased to see a foreigner in camp, and many asked if I was enjoying myself, which I assured them, I certainly was! By the time we made our way back to Chenda's house at 10pm, all was quiet in the camp, only the distant sounds of shelling and machine-gun fire.

Next morning, I was woken early by the sounds of camp activity. I was treated to a great breakfast of omelette, coffee and rolls especially made for the occasion by Chenda's wife, Mony. After this, we made our way to the pagoda to watch the games. The children thoroughly enjoyed this playtime, while parents urged them on, the successful ones being rewarded with small prizes. Adult games being held were similar to ours in many ways; throwing a ring over a bottle, chocolate wheel, betting on numbers and many others, letting themselves go this one time, when there was an exemption from the strict gambling rules.

When other foreigners had left the camp, I went to So Sayornn's house where all the family, including aunts, uncles and cousins were gathered. They were awaiting my arrival, intending to include me in the traditional 'washing' ceremony, regarding me as part of their family now. This ritual, performed at New Year, is undertaken to demonstrate respect and gratitude to elders and to purify them symbolically.

The ladies took me inside, giving me a sarong to don while they prepared a bench outside. Sayornn's mother, aunt, and myself, took our places on the bench while family members gathered around with buckets of water to perform this cleansing ceremony. First, our feet were washed, each family member taking a turn, then legs, arms, shoulders and hair, while each member expressed their appreciation for kind deeds and begged forgiveness for wrongdoings. I felt very honoured that they had seen fit to include me in this family ceremony. The washing ritual lasted for about an hour, starting off a very serious observance and everyone intent on the task. However, as the ceremony progressed, the fun surfaced, turning it into a water fight at the end, where everyone joined, delighting in this light-hearted finish to a serious ceremony.

Now it was time for the big feast the women had prepared, some of them up half the night cooking on two little clay pot stoves. Many interesting traditional dishes with fish, chicken and beef were placed before us, followed by banana dessert and rice cakes. After we had eaten, it was time for siesta, to prepare everyone for the evening's entertainment.

As darkness fell, we made our way to the pagoda, to watch the stage show to be presented by So Sayornn's drama group. Already, hundreds of people were sitting on the hard ground waiting for the performance to begin. We climbed the bamboo ladder leaning against the building and went backstage. I enjoy seeing behind the scene before any performance, where there is always plenty of activity, and this was no different. Actors were applying layers of makeup, others dressing in the elaborate costumes, wrapping themselves in metres of cloth, the band preparing their instruments, microphones and lights being set up and the roar of a generator above it all. We stayed backstage to watch the beginning of the drama, then made our way down to join the audience below. The crowds, appreciative of these performances, applauding loudly at the end of every scene.

After the stage presentation, we headed to the pagoda area where music was blaring, people danced, generators roared and the chatter of hundreds of voices added to the din.

I was sitting talking to So Sayornn, when my friend, Sarawath came running up, puffing and in a bath of perspiration, gasping, "Mother, you leave now. There is shelling in Rithysen. I radio for a car to take you out." There was so much noise we hadn't heard a thing! I thanked Sarawath for making the effort to find me and let me know, but telling him that I was all right, I would stay. He was very relieved that I was not afraid, relaxing and joining in the celebrations with us for the rest of the evening. No more shells landed that night and luckily only minor damage was caused by the attack.

Meanwhile Phoeuy was still feeling down. Word had filtered back to his family in a small village in Cambodia, that he had been located in Site 2. He came to tell me that he had just received word from his aged father; the first contact he had had for many years. He had sent Phoeuy a piece of cloth with a tracing of the outline of his hands and feet, which Phoeuy described as 'a poor man's photograph'. He was most touched by this gesture. Phoeuy was concerned about his father's very poor health and was still trying to work out how to help his father, when a guide from Cambodia arrived in the camp seeking him out. He told Phoeuy that his father had sent him from their village, to bring his two youngest children to be placed in Phoeuy's care. However, he would not hand them over until the outstanding amount of two thousand baht was paid.

It was a Sunday, therefore no foreigners were in the camp, so Phoeuy scouted around borrowing money from Viseth and others. It took him a few hours before he raised the full amount, then handed it over, waiting while the guide went off to get the children.

He eventually returned with Phoeuy's thirteen-year-old sister, Khun and his little ten-year-old brother Khin, neither of whom could remember their big brother, being only babies when Phoeuy left home. Khun produced a letter from their father, saying that his sight was failing and he was ill, unable to look after them and entrusting them to Phoeuy's care, as he wanted a good life and an education for the two. Suddenly Phoeuy, the young guy who liked to go out with the boys, flirt with the girls and have fun, had big responsibilities.

I arrived for work next day to be greeted by Phoeuy with his two siblings in tow. Khun, a beautiful young girl with a lovely smile, and Khin a small boy with a cheeky face, both still clad in the ragged clothes they had worn for the five day journey. First up, we went through the supply of clothes I always kept for emergencies, finding a suitable outfit for each of them before heading to the KWA office to get blankets and mosquito nets.

Phoeuy was taking this extra responsibility very seriously, telling me of his plans to build a room for Khun onto the house he shared with the other boys and enrol them at the camp school. I arranged with Phoeuy, to take them to the restaurant for a meal the following day. This would be a special treat for Khun and Khin as they had never been to a restaurant before.

When the time came, I borrowed one of the cars, and we all piled in and took off for our luncheon. We had not gone far when I saw everyone in front of us falling to the ground and crawling off the road. I stopped the car and Phoeuy asked someone what was happening. They said that a shell had just gone overhead. We had not heard it above the noise of the motor. I waited a couple of minutes and nothing further happened, so I continued on my way, only to see everyone dropping their bicycles and heading for ditches again, their faces contorted with fear. By this time, Phoeuy, Khun and Khin were crouched down in the car, arms wrapped around their heads. We could now hear the whine as more shells went over our heads. I turned around and headed back to the office. I will never forget the look of terror on the face of a small boy we passed, perched on the pillion of his mother's bicycle, his hands over his ears, screaming with fear as his mother pedalled furiously home.

It was a relief to get back to the office and see familiar faces. Though, I realized later that I should not have taken the risk of driving back, but should have dived for the roadside ditches that afforded some safety from flying shrapnel.

COERR had now moved into a new, much bigger office, but there had been no time to dig bunkers, so staff members crowded around in one room with radios on to pick up any news. The UN protection officer on duty, sent out a Situation 4 call to all workers, telling them to get into bunkers or seek shelter and stay where they were until further notice. Meantime, we could hear more shells landing. This was the closest I had been to the war and for the first time, I was afraid.

I looked around at the COERR workers clustered in our lunchroom, everyone finding different ways of coping with their fears. Marie-Claude couldn't stop eating. Another worker, Margaret Fong, was busy bargaining with one of the traders for a carving. Agnes Dupré la Tour, with a look of terror on her face, was clinging to one of the bamboo poles, David was talking nonstop. Sr Ath just sat there with a calm look on her face. It was a fearful time, not knowing when or where the next shell may land.

Phoeuy and his siblings had disappeared, the rest of the boys had joined us, all looking scared, though pretending it was all 'cool'. After ten minutes silence, the Situation 3 call came over the radio, telling all volags to proceed to the nearest vehicle and leave the camp immediately, continuing on to the designated meeting place. No sooner had the message finished than another two shells landed in quick succession, and the message was quickly changed back to Situation 4.

It was another hour before the all clear was given and we were instructed to leave the camp immediately. Meantime, stories of the shelling were filtering in. We heard that one shell had landed two metres from a man in Rithysen camp, bounced twenty metres, then stopped without exploding; another going through a building in San Ro, ripping through the mosquito net over a sleeping baby, exploding in an open area two hundred metres away. Two landed in Rithysen and five went over the camp. Amazingly, in this overcrowded place, there were no casualties.

We had to take a roundabout route back to Tapraya, escorted by a truck full of armed DPPU soldiers, because we were taking a little used road over the mountain that was known for bandits. This route took us past rice fields, small villages, around lakes and through bushland, a much longer trip than usual.

Back in Tapraya, we clustered around the radio seeking further news of the situation, but by now the attack was over. It was another week before we were granted access to the camp.

Search for a Missing Brother

One of Phoeuy's older brothers, Sopheap, with his wife and child, had recently transferred from Sok Sann camp in the south of Thailand to Site 2. Phoeuy was really happy to discover that his brother was still alive and to have him living close by. His father and two sisters, Sophuat and Soki, were living in their village of Khok Prey in Cambodia, so all family members but one older brother, Sophet, were now accounted for. Phoeuy made many enquiries but no one knew Sophet's whereabouts. Then, one day, a man came from his village to tell Phoeuy he had heard that Sophet was living in a pagoda in the town of Trat in the south of Thailand.

Phoeuy was delighted to receive this news. He was now determined to find Sophet and would go down to Trat to start the search. If he did this, he would be on the run as an illegal immigrant again. I tried to make him see reason as to the folly of this venture, but he would not listen. Then I had an idea.

In a couple of weeks time I planned to take a group of dance teachers to Sok Sann camp, which was not far from Trat, so I decided to put Phoeuy's name on the list. Saren was still very unsettled, so I included him as well. I approached David to accompany us and he happily accepted.

I would take the eight dancing teachers, leave them at the camp, then with Phoeuy and Saren go on to Trat, from where we would conduct a search for Sophet while waiting to pick up the fine arts teachers. This would be highly illegal but a good chance for Phoeuy to look for his brother and for Saren to see what lay beyond the barbed wire.

We left early in the morning, taking the van with a Thai driver, Lek, ten dancers, Phoeuy, Saren, David and myself. Everyone was very excited to be leaving the confines of the camp and to see new scenery. We drove through beautiful countryside, through mountains, past rubber plantations, orchards and thick jungle. The lush, green fields were such a contrast from the barren countryside around Site 2. As we travelled further south, the rain came down in torrents but this did not dampen the spirits of the passengers who were laughing, singing and enjoying every minute of their new-found freedom.

I had crossed Phoeuy and Saren off the list of names on the pass to enter the camp, so I asked Lek to drop me off with them in the town of Khlung, about ten kilometres from Sok Sann. He and David would then drive on, leave the dancers at Sok Sann camp, returning to pick us up later. We had lunch at one of the small street restaurants before heading off to look around the markets. Phoeuy had gone off on his own, but Saren was too frightened to leave my side, freezing every time he saw someone in uniform.

The van did not return to pick us up until 5pm, by this time, I was getting quite anxious. David told us that the roads into the camp were just mud tracks and everyone had to get out and push, even the women in their best clothes. By the time they entered the camp, all were covered from head to toe in thick brown mud.

We took off for Trat. Along the way we passed a wat (pagoda), Phoeuy imploring us to stop so he could check if Sophet was there. We did this with no luck, stopping at another two wats with the same result. Trat was like a small city. Saren gazed in wonderment at all the buildings, shops and traffic. We booked into a hotel in town, Saren and Phoeuy sharing a room. After unpacking our bags, David and I went down to see how they were faring. Saren couldn't leave the light switches alone, turning them off and on, turning on taps and picking up the telephone to hear the dial tone. These things were all new to him.

We took Phoeuy and Saren to dinner at the Hotel Trat restaurant. We had almost finished eating, when in walked two women, Jean and Nora, who worked for UNBRO in Aranyaprathet. I froze! Here we were with two people illegally out of the camp, now faced by UN officers. They saw us and headed for our table. I was so nervous and I'm sure my face must have shown the strain as they stood by my side and chatted. I did not introduce the boys, but as they were leaving, Jean turned to Phoeuy and said in Khmer, "Do you work for COERR?" Phoeuy did not answer. I was sure that she knew they were out illegally, but luckily, she did not pursue the matter. We finished our meal and left as soon as possible.

Next morning, we took them on a tour of the town, Saren, overawed by everything he saw, Phoeuy acting very nonchalant, for he had seen it all before in Bangkok. We went into a department store where Saren saw his first elevator, at first too frightened to climb aboard, but enjoying it when he finally stepped on and was borne upwards. He would certainly have some stories to tell his friends when he returned!

We continued our search for Sophet, trying at eight different wats. At the last one, set in beautiful surroundings, with fruit trees and flowers filling the grounds, we asked about Khmer monks. The head monk told us that they did have one Cambodian monk, sending someone to find him. Phouey waited with bated breath to see if it was Sophet, only to be disappointed when the monk returned with an unknown man.

Saren had told us that he had never seen the ocean, so next morning we headed for the port of Laem Gnop. When he caught his first glimpse of the sea, he just stood still, exclaiming, "I can't believe it, I never imagined it would be so big; it goes on forever!" We spent a few hours at the end of the pier, watching the fishermen unloading their day's catch, folding their nets and cleaning up for the next day's expedition.

Soon it was time to head back to Sok Sann camp to pick up the dancers. We arrived at the gates, leaving Phoeuy and Saren with Lek the driver, while David and I took the van in. We were told that the Site 2 dancers were putting on a performance for the people of Sok Sann; so we went to the outdoor stage where the presentation was being held. Hundreds of people were crowded into the compound, loudly applauding each dance and delighting in the show.

We finally left the camp at one o'clock, barely giving us time to get the people back to Site 2 before closing time. The dancers told us they had really appreciated their sojourn in another camp, and enjoyed the trip back, singing and laughing all the way. This experience certainly lifted Saren out of his depression. Phoeuy also appreciated the trip but was disappointed that he had not found his brother. He imagined that Sophet would be at the first wat we visited, having no idea just how large a town Trat was and the number of temples in the area.

Boomerangs and a Sad Farewell

I still made regular visits to the boarding school boys, who had now moved to Site 2 South, not far from our new office. On my last visit home, I had bought a number of boomerangs for them. Fr Vincent's brother, Fr Charles, was visiting from Belgium and his eyes lit up when he saw the boomerangs. He knew all about them, much more than the Australians did, so I was to find out. He came with me when I took them over for the boys to try out.

Fr Charles gave a demonstration of how to hold and throw a boomerang and soon all the boys were having a go, with boomerangs flying everywhere. In a short time, dozens of small boys appeared, appointing themselves the task of retrieving the ones that did not come back. It was a dangerous activity but luckily no one was hit. It was not long before some of the young men had mastered the art and the boomerangs. were returning. Soon, the only casualties were the boomerangs, and one by one they broke up after hitting the hard ground. Fr Charles promised he would help them to make their own. We ordered supplies of plywood, glue, fretsaws and sandpaper and they set up their own workshop. Soon after they enjoyed flying their homemade boomerangs, this new activity drawing crowds of laughing spectators.

John Henderson was leaving to go back to the US and the boys from the boarding school were feeling very sad. They had thoroughly enjoyed their involvement with him, due to his bright and cheerful disposition, the jokes he cracked, and the cheer he brought to their lives. The boys had arranged a party for his farewell in one of their classrooms and had been busy decorating with homemade streamers and balloons. Their cook had prepared a nice meal for this special occasion. After the meal, the boys organized entertainment for their guests, all taking turns to play the guitar or sing a song. It was a great send off, but the boys were extremely sad when it came time to say goodbye to their favourite teacher. I realized that I would also miss his cheerful presence.

John's departure left Ken without housemates, so Marie-Claude and I moved in to share the much more comfortable dwelling. It was a typical Thai house, brick downstairs and wood upstairs, with a balcony that overlooked the rice fields. This was a good move, Ken being an easy person to share with and we were to spend many happy hours together in our new home.

The past few weeks had been very trying for the camp people and aid workers too. There had been three Situation 4 calls when we had to leave the camp because of shells landing, while the frightened camp people were forced to remain. Numerous grenade attacks, DPPU crimes against the camp people were escalating, and domestic violence was on the increase. It was a very stressful time.

Sr Joan, one of the Australian nuns, had organized a 'reflection' evening to be held in her house each week, for the purpose of easing the stress of workers. The meeting would start with a prayer, soft music playing in the background, while each person related their problems and trials of the week. These would be discussed at length by the group, if necessary. This proved to be good therapy for many workers, however, not the right formula for dealing with everyone's stress.

Some of us discovered our own particular way of easing this strain. We called it 'Friday night beers'. Every Friday night a group gathered on our balcony, each bringing their own drinks, usually the popular Thai beer 'Singha', and we supplied snacks. We sat around talking, laughing and sharing anecdotes. They were pleasant evenings, sitting outside in the balmy night air looking out on a peaceful setting. Okay, we constantly slapped at mosquitoes, but a good supply of 'Rid' mosquito repellent on hand, helped. Australian staff members, Leanne and Malcolm, entertained us with singing and guitar playing. Some nights there was the steady 'boom, boom' in the distance as the war raged not far away over the border, but we learnt to overlook this background noise. Many topics were debated on that balcony. Camp problems never seemed so bad in this setting, and we could often find something to laugh about.

Visitors sometimes asked, "How do you cope with all the stress?"

My answer was always "Friday night beers. They help a lot!" Friday night get-togethers were to continue for years, proving to be a worthwhile distraction from the daily rigour of our lives.

About May every year, when the rainy season started, there was an outbreak of dengue fever amongst the foreigners working on the border. This was an illness passed on by a mosquito . Nineteen eighty-nine was a particularly bad year for dengue, with most of our staff coming down with it. After four years in the area, I finally succumbed to dengue fever. As well as a very high temperature, the sufferer is affected by a bad headache, inability to eat, a rash all over the body and aching bones, prompting the locals to call it 'break-bone disease'. Although the actual fever only lasts for six days, it has a debilitating effect on those infected. I was laid low with this affliction, never leaving my bed for days, too weak to even reach out for a drink beside my bed. I did learn the daily antics of the daddy longlegs spiders on my ceiling. All I had the energy to do, while lying on my back until the fever subsided, was watch them.

By the time I recovered enough to return to camp two weeks later, the fine arts programme was in a mess and worse still I found Phoeuy in hospital with a very bad case of hepatitis. It took another week to sort out the programme and get the workers in line again, meantime Phoeuy was very ill. I went to visit him in the hospital each day, and because he was not eating, tried to tempt him with food from the market. But to no avail, for he told me he had no appetite and was very depressed, saying he wished he had never come back to Site 2. By now, his eyes were bright yellow; he had a high fever and an abscess on the liver. He spent the next two weeks in hospital before being pronounced well enough to return home. It took a long time before he was back on his feet again and out of his depressed state.

There were many reports coming in around this time, about atrocities being committed by DPPU soldiers. A sixteen-year-old girl had been raped while collecting firewood outside the fence. Thai soldiers, searching houses for hand grenades or guns, were robbing people of their valuables at the same time. A nineteen-year-old Cambodian man had been shot and killed on the road outside the camp. Survivors of this shooting told the UN that they were caught taking a bamboo roadblock set up by DPPU. They were taken into the forest, where they were forced to squat down and beg for their lives. Fearing for their lives, they ran, prompting the soldiers to fire, killing the young man with a shot to the head. Two soldiers were arrested and put into Tapraya prison, but no one felt confident that they would go to trial. Too often, these matters were left until the furore died down, then the accused were released. It seemed Cambodian lives were not important to the Thais.

UNBRO held a meeting for all volags, to see what could be done about the increasing harassment by DPPU members. Strict guidelines that had been laid down, were not being adhered to. DPPU soldiers were not permitted within the confines of the camp, unless for a designated purpose and never while armed. However, these rules were forever being broken. UN officers promised to ensure that guidelines were enforced and soldiers breaking those rules were punished in accordance. We would see!

I had applied to COERR for a vehicle for my programme and work which took me from one end of the camp to the other, long distances when covered by bicycle. A few months later, I was pleased to hear that I had been allocated Fr Pierre's old utility, while he received an upgraded model. It was a bit of a bomb but I didn't care, it would be better than pedalling in the hot sun. This vehicle certainly had a few problems. It left me stuck in the morning, many times, for an hour or so, before I could get it started, only to break down just as often on the way to camp. But it was great to have wheels.

There was much fighting along the border at this time. Site 8 had been shelled two days in a row, killing eight people and injuring a further twenty-eight, causing 36,000 people to flee to a village nearby. Very close shelling near Site 2 every day had the people in constant fear.

I was in the market with Phoeuy one day when I heard the 'Stalin organ' firing - a frightening sound. The Stalin organ, mounted on the back of a truck, consisted of forty long barrels firing one after another, completely devastating the targeted area for miles around and with no escape for anyone caught in the middle. The Cambodians along the border were going through another tough time.

An Illegal Boat Trip

It was still almost impossible for any foreigner to enter Cambodia. Only a few workers were permitted and their movements were strictly controlled by the Government. I met up with a US journalist, Nate Thayer, who covered Cambodian stories for the overseas press, a guy who liked to get right to the front line, regardless of danger. He told me he had just made a trip into Cambodia illegally, taking a boat from the southern Thai village of Klong Yai. I asked him what my chance would be of making it through, receiving the answer, "No problem, the Cambodians would welcome you."

In 1990, after five years of working with the people in the camp and hearing so much about their country, it would be great to go in and really see for myself if the trees really were full of fruit just for the picking, if there was such an abundance of fish that you could hear them rubbing together, and if the rice did grow twice as high! This was a good time to make the attempt, as the Vietnamese, after ten years of occupation, were due to make the final withdrawal of their troops from Cambodia about this time.

That night, I contacted David to see if he would be prepared to make an illegal trip to a southern Cambodian town with me. He jumped at the opportunity. We talked it over and decided we needed a third person in case something went wrong and we were held in Cambodia.

We went over the list of COERR employees, to find someone likely to have a go and who would keep it a secret. We decided to ask Liz, who was fluent in Khmer and spoke some Thai. The plan was that David and I would hire a boat and make the attempt while Liz stayed behind to report if we did not arrive back by a certain time.

We invited Liz over for dinner that night and told her of our plan, asking if she would be interested in taking part. She told us that she was happy to participate, but said, "There is only one thing - I want to go into Cambodia too." We realized that we could not leave her out and her language skills were a decided advantage, so we agreed. Now we needed to find another person as a backup. We asked Fr John, our adventurous priest, who readily agreed. His only regret being that he could not accompany us. We set a date for twelve days ahead, when we would make our attempt, promising to ring him as soon as we returned. If he had not heard from us three days after that, he was to alert the authorities.

We left in my old car, hoping it would make the distance without breaking down. We drove to Klong Yai; the last part of the journey taking us along a road with the ocean on one side, a mountain range marking the.border with Cambodia on the other.

What we planned to do was strictly illegal, so we were trying to keep a low profile. However, we were soon in the spotlight when I drove the car, with 'COERR' emblazoned on the side in both English and Thai, the wrong way up a one-way street. People appeared from everywhere.

We found a hotel a little way out of town where we could leave our belongings, and the car, when we made our attempt, then headed for the harbour to see if we could book a boat for the next morning, to take us to a Cambodian port.

At the end of the pier, we met a Thai man, who invited us into his home and introduced us to his family. We sat down, chatted with them and told them of our plan. The man said we should have no problem getting into Cambodia, that his son had a boat and would take us the next day. We arranged a price and left promising to be back at seven the following morning. Not too difficult ... so far!

Back at the hotel we discussed plans, deciding to take a small backpack each with a change of clothes and mosquito net, hoping that we would be able to stay for one or two days.

We arrived at the pier next morning to find the son already waiting in a boat tied up to the jetty; a long, narrow craft with a pole at the back for steering. We clambered in, the fisherman pushed off, and amid cries of farewell from the family gathered there, we headed for the open sea and Cambodia. Happy and excited to be on our way, we congratulated ourselves that it had been so easy.

We travelled south, about three hundred metres out from the shore, on a flat ocean with only small fishing boats for company. Twenty minutes along the way, the boatman pointed to the Cambodian shoreline in the distance. We were all excited to see how close we were and know that we would soon be landing on these shores. Then ahead, between us and our goal, we spotted a small flotilla of boats. This, we decided, must be a floating market where Thai and Cambodian traders met to exchange goods. But as we drew closer, we could see that one boat among the fishing trawlers, was full of armed Thai soldiers. They ordered us to stop, and when we came alongside, one of the soldiers jumped aboard our craft. He did not look very friendly, asking us in broken English "What you doing here?" We told him that we were going to Cambodia. There was a chorus from the soldiers: "No, you can't go there, too dangerous," putting fingers to their foreheads and saying, "Bang, Bang!" We assured them that we were not frightened and still wanted to go. They conferred together, then another soldier jumped aboard our boat and the others took off for the shore, telling us they would speak to their commander. We sat out there in the hot sun, under the gaze of many curious onlookers, awaiting their return, hopeful that the required permission would be granted.

Ten minutes later, the boat with the soldiers returned. They pulled alongside and one of the men told us that their superior said, "No," that we must turn back. He said, "Subai, subai," so we smiled back, repeating

"Subai, subai," which in Thai means 'happy/comfortable'. After repeating it several times, we could see that he was getting quite irate. Then Liz realized that he was saying we were, 'spies', Thais unable to say 'sp'. This was the reason we were not allowed to proceed. We tried appealing, even with a monetary bribe, but all failed and we had to reluctantly turn back, right within sight of our goal. It was a very disappointed trio, who arrived back at the pier a short time later.

We asked the fisherman if we could make another attempt the following day but he was afraid to risk it again. His father suggested we try by road to the next village that was right on the border, and from where it would be easier to avoid the military checkpoint. That night we discussed our next approach, deciding on the road trip as the most viable. We went to bed, full of confidence that tomorrow we would make it.

We left by car for the fishing village of Had Leg, about twenty kilometres away, early next morning. We drove along a terrible road full of potholes, in the pouring rain, our spirits still high. After about thirty minutes, we came to a Thai army checkpoint, where we were halted by a barrier across the road. A soldier came over to the car, telling us we must turn back. We told him we would just like to go to the next village, pleading to be let through, but receiving a definite, "No." More soldiers with stern faces appeared around the car, all saying we could not proceed. We reluctantly turned back and headed back to Klong Yai. Failed again!

It was only mid morning by this time, so we called into a coffee shop to discuss our next move. We decided that we could not fail after coming all this way and getting so close; we would give it one last try. We headed down to the fishing boat anchorage, where we came upon a fishermen cleaning his boat. After hearing our story, he said he would be willing to take us, for a price. We agreed, knowing this could be our last chance. The plan was made to leave at three o'clock in the afternoon. The fisherman said the military patrol boat should have returned to base by that time.

At the appointed time, we returned with our bags, and were taken out on a small jetty, followed by a group of interested local people, all offering advice; some saying, "Don't go; too dangerous," others maintaining there would be no problem. We looked at our guide. He was full of confidence, so we were satisfied it was all right. As the boat pushed off, we received a great farewell from the crowd that had swelled to about thirty, completely filling the pier. They waved and called out good wishes until we were out of sight, all enjoying this small involvement in our adventure.

As we passed the village of Had Leg, off shore, our guide advised us to crouch down in the bottom of the boat in case a lookout was posted at the military base. We did so, covering ourselves with plastic rain capes, staying there until the boatman gave us the okay when we had passed the Cambodian border and were safe from the Thai military. As we sat up and looked over, we were thrilled to see the mangrove swamp and forest shores of Cambodia.

The boat had been moving along at a reasonable pace, when suddenly the motor coughed a few times, then died. Try as he might, the owner could not get it going. Meantime, we were drifting closer and closer to the mangroves. We couldn't believe our luck, within the boundaries of Cambodia, and now it looked like we would not make it. The boatman desperately tried to restart the motor. It would cough, start, then cut out. This happened a few times, while we drifted closer to the shore. When we were only about twenty metres away, the motor suddenly sprang into life. We let out a concerted cheer as the boat headed back on course. By this time, the sky had darkened and it had started to rain but this didn't worry us, as our goal was in sight.

We continued, following the tree-lined coast then rounded a point to be met with the first signs of civilization. A large ship was at anchor in the harbour, and in the background could be seen the houses of the village of Pak Klong. We headed for a small jetty, where dozens of fishing boats were tied, all very excited as we approached this pier. However, our pleasure was short-lived when we looked up to see many unsmiling faces glaring down at us, including a number of stern looking policemen.

We gathered our bags and climbed up to the jetty, where we were immediately surrounded by officials, who motioned for us to follow them. They escorted us to the police/immigration office at the end of the quay. This office consisted of a desk, four chairs and a table with a typewriter that must have come out of the ark. It was a rusty old machine that would have been at least fifty years old. Above the desk was an opening, now occupied by dozens of curious onlookers, all crowding there to get a look at the unusual sight of foreigners in their village.

One of the policemen, who spoke a few words of English, asked for our passports. We had not brought them, so we handed over the only identification we had. Mine was my Thai driving licence; Liz's, a photocopy of her passport, and David's, his Australian driving licence. The officers studied these documents carefully, but we could tell they did not understand a thing on them. Liz had decided it best not to divulge her knowledge of the language, so she could listen to what they were saying. They asked us for our cameras, which we handed over, then they wrote down our names. After talking together, the guy in charge, in his broken English, said they would allow us to stay until 6pm; it was then 4.30pm. We asked for longer, but were told, "No hotels." I said we did not need a hotel, informing them that we had brought our mosquito nets and were willing to sleep anywhere. They had a conversation in Khmer, after which I asked again. The policeman said, "Yes."

I was busy thanking them, when I looked over at Liz who was trying to suppress her laughter. She whispered to me that she had been listening to their conversation, the policeman saying, "I don't understand a word she said!"

We were told that we could walk around the streets but must return to the office by the designated time. We thanked them and set off. As we made our way along the main street, everyone came out of their shops and houses to see the three foreigners, but there were no smiles as we had expected from Cambodian people. An open market was our first stop, where we all bought souvenirs to keep as a memento of our trip; mine being a brass bell in the shape of an apsara dancer.

We walked through the market and schoolgrounds before coming to the residential area. The wooden houses here were built on stilts on ground that was very marshy and would surely flood in the rainy season.

As we were wandering along the street taking in everything, a lady appeared at the door of one of the houses and invited us in. We agreed that it would be good to meet some of the people and find out what life was like in Cambodia under Vietnamese rule, so we accepted the invitation, climbed the steps and entered the house. We were invited to sit on mats on the floor, where the whole family was gathered. They plied us with questions: Where you come from? Why you come here? What you think of Cambodia? Liz answered them in Khmer telling them of our trip here and our work in the camp.

We had only been there about five minutes, when two young policemen came to find us. They said that their boss told them that they must stay with us and that we must go with them now. We reluctantly said our goodbyes to the family, hoping they would not be in trouble for inviting us in, though they did not appear unduly concerned.

The young policemen took us back through the market, past the police station, along wooden walkways on stilts to a new market built over the swamp. We now had three guards with us, two 22-year-olds and an older man. The younger ones both spoke a little English, which, they told us, they had learnt in Phnom Penh and were anxious to improve their language skills. Liz was enjoying listening to their comments in Khmer when they discussed English grammar and how great it was to practice at last with English speakers.

By now, we were very thirsty for it was very hot, so our guards directed us to a restaurant, where we ordered Coca Colas. People around were much more relaxed now; I guess the word had spread around the town that we were not 'Soviets' - what they called the Russians - who were the only white people they had seen to date. They were now smiling and happily accepting us.

Liz then decided to let them know she spoke their language, realizing it would be good to find out something about their lives. When she spoke in Khmer, they were really surprised and happy to talk to her. They said their homes were in Phnom Penh but they had been sent to work in this town. They missed the city life, but were making the most of it. The weekly dance held from 7pm to 2am was the highlight of their week and was on tonight. They were really sorry we could not stay and join them for it.

When asked her nationality, Liz told them, "I am an American."

Back came the quick reply from the young man, "Oh! I have brother in California." It sounded so weird coming from someone in this remote part of Cambodia.

It was nearly six o'clock and another policeman arrived to tell us we must report to the police station. As we were heading back, one of the young men told us how much they had enjoyed having us there, saying it was like a dream come true!

On arrival back at the police office, our cameras were returned and officials gathered to escort us back to the jetty. By this time, about fifteen people, all smiling and friendly were in the party accompanying us, enjoying the scene. We arrived at the jetty to find a boat already waiting to 'deport' us. As the boat pulled out with us aboard, we looked up to see all the officials smiling, waving and calling out, "Come back for visit, but bring visas next time."

We congratulated each other on our success. Even if it was only for such a short time, it was great to have had the experience of seeing this part of Cambodia.

When we told our boatman that we wished to return to Klong Yai, he told us that he was only going as far as Had Leg, and no amount of coaxing would make him change his mind - that was his home and that was as far as he would take us.

It was dark by the time we arrived at his village where he left us on the shore. We asked some locals how we could get to Klong Yai and were told that there were four cars in the town - good news, until we found that they had no keys for three of them and the fourth was in another village. We had no choice but to wait, the car finally arriving one and a half hours later. We were taken back to Klong Yai, arriving at our hotel at nine o'clock, exhilarated by our adventure.

Our first job on return was to ring Fr John to tell him of our return and reassure him that all was well. He was delighted to hear about our adventures, and relieved to know we were safe, as he'd just started to get anxious as to our whereabouts.

CHAPTER 8

By 1990, the situation in Cambodia was very grim. Constant shelling, fighting by resistance forces and government troops and shortage of food was causing hundreds of families to flee over the Thai border. Stories of the brutality of Thai guards had filtered through to Cambodia, forcing many of these desperate people seeking shelter in Site 2, to hide out in the forest until they felt it safe to proceed. Some would take the chance and venture in at 6pm, when the soldiers left their guardposts briefly unattended while they had their evening meal, others choosing to wait until nightfall, before making their attempt. With so many people pouring in, UNBRO's resources were being severely tested, resulting in the pagodas being used to house newcomers temporarily.

I heard that a big group had arrived the night before, so Phoeuy and I made our way over, taking a bag of clothes intended for the needy. I was not prepared for the sight that met my eyes! More than two hundred people were crowded in this small area, taking up every available space, hammocks strung over the top of those lying on the floor, others walking around trying to find a space. Everyone tired, dirty, hungry, looking dazed and bewildered. I realized that the few clothes I had brought would not suffice, as everyone needed them. Better not to give any out.

We stopped to talk to an old man, who appeared to be the leader of the group. He told me about the situation in their small village of Sala Kram. "There was constant shelling and most of our houses were burnt down and our crops and animals destroyed. We were all very frightened, so the village leaders called a meeting. The decision was made that all villagers would leave and make the long trek to Site 2. There, we could find food and shelter and we would be safe from the shelling."

The people gathered together a few possessions and set out on foot on the journey through heavily mined areas, which was to take them eight days. The man went on to tell us, "We experienced more shelling on the way here and three of our group were killed, and another five injured. We had to leave the injured in one of the villages, just hoping that when they recover, they will find their way to Site 2." With tears in his eyes, he told us how sad he felt to leave his land.

Nearby, a white-haired lady was sitting on the floor attempting to patch a tear in her sarong but having great difficulty with eyesight that was very poor. I asked her age and she told me that she was more than eighty years old. She spoke about the shelling in her village and how frightened she was. In a quavering voice she told me. "The shelling was really heavy, and I ran to a bunker for shelter, but when I got there I found the bodies of four neighbours lying inside. I wanted to get out, but there was nowhere to go." She felt that she was too old to leave her village and was prepared to stay alone, but the village leaders would not allow it, so here she was. I wished her luck, just hoping that it would work out well for her. I took her photograph and somehow she managed a smile for the camera. The courage shown by these people in the face of such adversity, was amazing.

Assisting New Arrivals

Noeurn was now back and living with his wife on the outskirts of the camp, close to one of the frequently used entry points. He would see many of the new arrivals trudging past his house at night in groups of twenty or more, mostly women and children. By the time they reached this point they would be weary from the long walk; frightened, confused and hungry, often with no possessions, only the clothes on their backs.

Phoeuy, Noeurn and I put our heads together and devised a plan to help these needy people. Noeurn and his wife would set up a distribution centre outside their house, providing each new arrival with a small supply of rice and an article of clothing on arrival. The food would be particularly useful as it would be more than a day before UNBRO registered each person and issued them with a food card, then another day before their ration could be claimed.

I approached Fr Pierre, who willingly contributed money for rice, and together with secondhand clothes from my office, we had enough supplies to start the project. I left my camera with Phoeuy for he or Noeurn to record the allocation of food and clothing to the people when they entered the camp.

Next day I went over to see if they had taken photographs of the distribution, but they had none. Apparently, the night before, they had gone to the border track with the camera. The border was determined by a deep ditch, commonly known as the 'tank ditch'. This trench was dug by the Thais in 1979 when there were fears that the Vietnamese may push their way over the border in armoured carriers. It had now been abandoned and was overgrown with weeds. Paths leading from Cambodia traversed this ditch.

People coming in would follow tracks through the forest on the Cambodian side, making their way down the tank ditch, along paths through some small bushland, before coming to a road that was the border of the camp. When they reached this road, they were in full view of the DPPU checkpoint, about 500 metres along the road to the south.

Phoeuy and Noeurn were waiting with the camera when a group of 25-30 people arrived and attempted to cross the road. At the same time, a truck with four DPPU soldiers was approaching from the south. The soldiers saw the new arrivals and pulled up, ordering the people to stop, firing around their feet when some did not immediately obey. The people were terrified; just coming from a war zone to what they considered would be a safe haven, then to be confronted with this! The soldiers started slapping, kicking and beating the people. One man had his head split open when he was hit with the butt of a gun. Some started to run, but were forced back, rounded up and made to form a circle, by the Thais.

Phoeuy and Noeurn, were hiding behind bushes observing all this, as did other camp residents, but were too afraid to intervene. They could not take photographs because the camera flash would have alerted the soldiers. Meanwhile, the soldiers were enjoying themselves by showing their dominance over these terrified people. They ordered all the newcomers to strip, while one DPPU guy stood in the middle of the circle, then commanded the group, which was made up of men, women and children, to crawl around on their hands and knees while the other soldiers stood by and laughed. After they had finished their fun, they stole two bicycles and all the people's belongings before sending them on their way.

We went over to where the incident had occurred the night before, finding a group of residents gathered together talking about the night's happenings. All were horrified, frightened by what they had witnessed. I told Phoeuy it was important to report incidents of this kind to the UN, but he was reluctant to do so for fear of repercussions, saying, "It's all right for you foreigners, you can leave the camp before nightfall, but we have to stay here and suffer the consequences." After some persuasion and assurances that it may save others from the same humiliation, he reluctantly agreed to accompany me to the UN protection office.

The protection officer, with whom we spoke, took down details of the incident, promising to investigate. He visited the area where the incident had taken place, going to all houses in the vicinity to get statements, but no one would talk, saying they knew nothing. His trip to the hospital to find the man with the head injury, also proved fruitless, the man obviously being too frightened to seek medical help.

I spoke to Noeurn in the hope that he would go to the UN to back up

Phoeuy's story, but he was too afraid. By this time, Phoeuy was also feeling the pressure, saying to me, "Okay, story finished; it is too dangerous for us!" I respected his wishes.

Because the story could not be verified, no complaint could be lodged with the DPPU, so the soldiers remained unpunished.

Left to Die

I would often come over to the border if I had some spare time. Many people were now sneaking over in the day and it was always safer for them if a foreigner was present. I would call into Noeurn's place to replenish stocks of clothes and check on how many people were still coming through.

Tim and I were at the top of the tank ditch at 1.30pm one day when Noeurn came over to tell us that a woman had been injured by a landmine three or four kilometres from the camp that morning, and was still out there. A man collecting firewood told him that he had heard her call for help and with others, had gone over to see if they could assist. He climbed a tree to locate the victim and could see there were mines all around her. No one was prepared to tackle the minefield to get her out. The men returned to camp, doing nothing more about it. We asked people coming in, if the woman was still there, and they said she was. They could still hear her calls for help, but now they were very weak.

I went to the UNBRO office to advise them of this terrible dilemma. None of the protection staff were on duty, so I went to see Mr Lay Khek, who was then the camp administrator. As soon as he heard the story, he contacted Keo Lundi, administrator of the camp close to that part of the border, who assured me that he would send someone to help immediately. I went back to the border and waited, questioning everyone who came in. We heard that a man had also been injured in a separate mine explosion about 9am. By now, no one knew if the two victims were still alive. While we were waiting, we heard another landmine explode in the distance. Could there now be a third victim?

We waited at the border for another thirty minutes, expecting a team of rescuers to go in, but no one appeared. A Cambodian policeman came along so we used his radio to get through to Keo Lundi to find what was happening. The answer came back that after contacting DPPU, they were told that they were unauthorized to send a team to the victim's assistance, as it had happened more than 300 metres from the camp. This was, supposedly, outside the territory where camp people were permitted. It was also unbelievable. Didn't anyone care about these poor people? It was now 5pm and we had to leave the camp. I drove back to Tapraya feeling helpless and depressed. I could not get these people out of mind, thinking of them out there in the forest, slowly bleeding to death, with no one willing to go in and help.

I went straight to the border next morning, to be told the news that the man had been rescued and taken to KID hospital. The woman, who had gone out to collect reeds to make new thatch for her hut, was still in the same place but she had died during the night. I was to learn later that the man lost both his legs, but he would survive. Even so, soon after this tragedy there was still a steady stream of people making their way out into the forest to collect wood and thatch, apparently undaunted by the dangers they faced with every step.

I contacted the UN to see if better means could be used, should this situation re-occur but was made to feel that it was my fault that the woman had died, because I did not leave it in the hands of UNBRO staff. It took me a long time before I could come to grips with this tragedy and lose my feelings of guilt.

About this time, a trader from Cambodia arrived in Site 2 with a message for Phoeuy, from his older sister. He learnt that his father was very sick, not expected to live long and was asking to see Phoeuy before he died. Phoeuy decided to make the dangerous journey, taking his little brother with him, hoping to arrive in time to see his father. He planned to bring the remaining members of his family back to the camp with him.

Phoeuy and Khin left at first light, walking for many kilometres along bush tracks, passing through a number villages that had been razed to the ground by the shelling. On arrival in his village, he found it deserted and devastation greeted them; most buildings were destroyed, including his father's house. They searched everywhere for the villagers, eventually finding them living in bunkers out in the rice fields, the only place they felt safe from the constant shelling the town had experienced.

He finally located family members, only to be told the sad news that his father had died three days before and the cremation had already taken place. He was devastated. There was no reason for him to stay now, so he made plans to leave next morning. His attempts to get his sisters and their families to accompany him were unsuccessful. They chose to remain in their village, feeling tied to this land of their ancestors, afraid of losing it should they leave. At the last minute, his older sister, Sophuat, decided to join him. She was anxious to trace their missing brother, Sophet. A villager had recently returned with the news that he had seen Sophet in KID, where he was reportedly receiving treatment for a head injury. After searching for this brother for years, it was the first positive news they had received for a long time as to his whereabouts, so Sophuat was determined to follow it up.

A Long-Lost Brother Found

A few days later, they were back in the camp and Phoeuy brought his sister to meet me. She was a small woman, about thirty-five years old, very strong and tenacious, the unofficial head of the family, now that her father was gone and her brothers all in Thailand. She was determined to bring the family together, to fulfil her father's dying wish. After hearing the latest news of her missing brother, I offered to follow up the lead in KID, as it would be impossible for them to gain admittance.

I went to the KID hospital the following day. I spoke to the nurses and medics, checking the ward boards with patient's names but could find no one by the name of Men Sophet. Hospital staff advised me to try the TMC (Traditional Medicine Centre) as head-injured patients often ended up at the mental health section.

I introduced myself to the German doctor in charge, relating the story to him. He knew of no patient by that name but passed me on to the office, suggesting that I go through their register. I found the name Men Savouen, cited as having a head injury and psychosis. It looked like I was on the right track. One of the nurses offered to find this man, while I waited anxiously to meet him. The patient he brought back bore no resemblance to Phoeuy's family, but I did not rule him out. After asking a few questions and mentioning family names he showed no response, so I realized that this could not be the person I was looking for. Next, I approached the Cambodian medics, asking if they had any recollection of a patient by that name. They did not. I was told that many patients were absent at this time but would be back in the morning, so I planned to return later and try again. I had to go back to Site 2 to tell Phoeuy and Sophuat that my search had been unsuccessful. Their disappointment was obvious, as they thought he would be easily found.

A few days later, I had time to spare and made my way back to the TMC to continue the search. The medics, who by this time knew of my quest, were keen to help, sending two patients out to meet me. I showed them family photographs but there was no sign of recognition from either. I was just preparing to leave when a man walked past, looked over at me and smiled. I saw the family resemblance immediately, calling him over. The medic said this could not be the man I was seeking, as this man's name was Wichai and he had no family.

However I was sure, for to me, the family likeness was so apparent. When I showed him the photograph of family members, a big smile came on his face and he pointed to Sopheap, saying his name. It was certainly the right person.

He was very excited when I told him that his family had sent me to find him, repeating their names over and over. The medics and patients, who had gathered around, were as pleased as I to have found this missing person. I could see that Sophet, who was on a heavy dose of drugs, was becoming quite confused, so I promised that I would report the good news to his brothers and sisters and return for a visit the following day.

The family were thrilled when I told them I had located their brother, but concerned about his health and very anxious to meet him. Every day an ICRC truck left Site 2 for KID, taking patients for treatment and returning with other patients. I took Sophuat to ICRC, explaining the story and requesting permission for family members to visit Sophet in KID. Permission was granted for five people to go the following day on the afternoon transport. I planned to meet them in KID and take them to catch up with their long-lost brother.

However, Sophet was nowhere to be found. Patients told us that he had gone visiting and pointed in the direction he had taken. I set off with family members Sophuat, Sopheap and his little daughter, Khun and Khin, to search for him. We were walking between the houses when suddenly we came face to face with Sophet. There were cries of joy from his siblings, Sophuat throwing herself into his arms sobbing, everyone else close to tears. It was a joyful and emotional occasion for all.

Sophet was thrilled to be back with his family, hugging them all in turn, looking carefully at the youngest family members, Khun and Khin, whom he had not seen since they were babies. It was a happy group that headed back to the TMC, Khun holding fast to Sophet's hand and everyone talking nonstop. Permission was granted for family members to stay for a few days to become re-acquainted with their brother.

I came back for a visit two days later, first going to talk to the doctor in charge. He told me that there had been a marked improvement in Sophet's condition since he had been re-united with his family. I found the group and learnt they were staying with Sopheap's in-laws in KID.

They told me Sophet's story since they had seen him last. He had been living in Sok Sann camp. One night he left the camp, going illegally into the town of Borai where he secured a job in the gem mines, changing to the Thai name of Wichai. For two years he worked in this mine, and saved a large amount of money from his earnings. He met a

Thai girl and married her. They were living a comfortable life with her family, until neighbours became jealous of his wealth, planning to have him robbed and killed.

As he was returning from work one night, he was attacked, hit over the head repeatedly, then left for dead. He was found next morning, unconscious with serious head injuries and taken to hospital. When he regained consciousness he had lost his memory, babbling in Khmer and Thai, only remembering his Thai name, Wichai. Police, figuring he could be Cambodian, sent him to KID camp. He showed us a huge dent in the back of his skull where part of the bone was missing and which was still causing him many problems.

It would be a few weeks before Sophet was pronounced well enough to leave KID to live with Sopheap and his family in Site 2. Sophuat, now satisfied that he would be in safe hands, returned to her family in Cambodia. Sophet's treatment would be ongoing, he being one of the first patients to receive treatment in the new mental health service.

This service, called the KPDR (Khmer Peoples Depression Relief), was the brainchild of one of our employees, Mary-Beth, who had been helping depressed people in the camp by listening to their problems over a cup of tea. As more and more people sought her help, she realized there was a desperate need for a treatment centre in Site 2. At that time, all people with mental problems were sent to KID where they were kept, sometimes for years, away from their families.

A request was made for COERR to set up a treatment centre in Site 2. After receiving permission from UNBRO, the first mental health centre, KPDR, was established in Rithysen camp. Initially, the programme was staffed by an Australian psychologist, Sr Mary, and a Cambodian couple, Phally and Soeurn. As the number of patients seeking treatment grew, psychiatric nurses, Lud, Peter and Helle were recruited, together with social workers; Sr Joan, Megan and Leanne, followed later by the appointment of Dan, a psychiatrist from the USA. It was not long before more than 400 patients with all degrees of mental problems were attending this centre. Later, another centre, MHTH (Mental Health and Traditional Healing), was opened in Site 2 North, to cope with the growing numbers.

A curriculum was developed to train Khmer staff as counsellors, a completely new concept for them, as similar programmes were unheard of in Cambodia. These counsellors were trained over a three-year period, achieving a high standard of mental health education by the time they graduated. One of these workers, Nee, showed outstanding skills when dealing with patients. By the time he commenced his mental health training, he already held teaching, medical assistant and management diplomas, gained in the camp. Later, he was sent to Chiang Mai in Thailand for a course in psychiatry. On his return, he trained Cambodian staff and it was not long before they were coming up with their own excellent and innovative ideas.

The KPDR centre was set in an enclosure off one of the busy roads in Site 2 South. Coming through the centre's gate was like walking into another world. There were beautiful gardens all around, hanging baskets with trails of flowers, cane furniture, pergolas and fruit trees, all contributing to a peaceful setting for patients receiving treatment. Also within this compound was the Traditional Healing Centre. Camp people with numerous complaints, both physical and emotional, visited the Krou Khmer (traditional healers) to be treated with traditional medicine derived from the roots and leaves of plants and herbs collected in the forest.

These traditional healers were older men, known for their wisdom; their training passed down from generation to generation. The Krou Khmer at this centre had been included in the first level of the mental health course, so whenever they suspected a mental problem, they referred the patient to KPDR/MHTH where they would be treated with a combination of western and traditional treatment. In addition to treating mental problems, the traditional healing methods proved very successful in the treatment of skin disease and coughs, restoring breast milk, and assisting recovery after delivery or illness. Traditional massage and steam baths being used widely in their treatments.

One of the nurses, Lud, was most impressed with the treatment and recovery of one of her patients treated by the Krou Khmer. The patient, a young woman, was admitted to a camp hospital with a severe and very painful skin problem, big blisters and skin peeling off in sheets. All treatment applied by Western doctors had failed and the woman had become very depressed.

At this stage, Lud was called in to arrange counselling for her. After observing the woman's distress, Lud went back to the healing centre and requested help from the traditional healers. One of the Krou Khmer agreed to treat the woman, on condition that approval was granted by the hospital. Doctors reluctantly gave their go ahead for the traditional treatment to be applied, for they were baffled by her condition and at a loss to know what to do next. The first thing the traditional healer advised was to place the patient on banana leaves, so that sarongs that lay under and over her would not stick to the skin. Next, he treated her with the juice of a coconut in which was dissolved a diuretic. The patient was directed to drink half the mixture and apply the other half to the skin. In a short time the skin disease was cured.

The Site 2 mental health project really proved its worth and was to continue until the camp closed. During the years of operation, this programme helped many depressed and mentally disturbed people regain some meaning to their lives. However, for some who were on full-time medication it was to prove disastrous when they returned to their country, where there was no mental health follow-up. Aware that this may happen, a weaning process was introduced to gradually sever patients' dependence on these drugs, but this method failed to help in the long run. Many of these, including Sophet, had huge problems when they returned, making it very difficult for both patients and families back in Cambodia.

Among the hordes of people tracking across the border, were large numbers of Vietnamese. As Malcolm was returning home from the camp one day, he was flagged down by a group of people, three men and one woman, limping along the road. One of the men, who spoke a little English, told him that they had come from Vietnam, leaving there eighteen days before.

On reaching Cambodia, they had paid a local guide, who promised to take them to Phanat Nikhom camp, but instead robbed them of everything, then abandoned them before they reached the Thai/ Cambodian border. Since then they had walked nonstop for three days. They had crossed over the Thai border that morning, and having no idea where they were, followed a road they had found. Exhausted, they decided to stop the next car , which happened to be a lucky choice.

Malcolm took them to his house, where they had their first bath for weeks, washed their hair and clothes, soaking their blistered feet in bowls of warm water, before having a meal. They slept in his house that night and in the morning he contacted UNHCR for their advice.

Later that day, a UN representative was sent to interview the new arrivals. At this time, the Thai government had a new policy, whereby, Vietnamese arrivals were kept in local police stations, before being transferred to Phanat Nikhom camp. Previously they had all been sent to Site 2 where they would languish, many times for years.

After the UN interview, Thai authorities were notified and the four people were taken to the prison attached to the police station in Tapraya. They were not locked up but permitted to sleep in an open hut in the grounds, with facilities provided for them to cook their own meals. They were allowed a fair amount of freedom, with visitors permitted in at any time. After assessment, they were moved on to Phanat Nikhom camp.

A couple of weeks after this incident, I was approached by a Vietnamese man I knew in Site 2. He told me that three of his relatives had arrived from Vietnam during the night, then asked if it would be possible for me to take them to Tapraya. He said that if they registered in Site 2 they would be stuck there, whereas, they could have a chance of gaining resettlement if they were sent to Phanat Nikhom. I said I would meet them and then decide.

He took me to his house, where I met three young men, two brothers and a cousin aged 19-20 years. They were very tired and hungry, having been without food for two days, so I took them first to the restaurant for a meal. They were ravenous, downing a couple of plates of fried rice each, before we could begin to talk. They told me that life in Vietnam was very harsh, the journey to the camp fraught with danger. Before crossing the border they had been accosted by Cambodian soldiers, who beat, then robbed them, finally releasing them, only to receive similar treatment from Thai soldiers when they reached the outskirts of the camp. I'm sure that if people in Vietnam knew how dangerous the trip was across Cambodia to the border, they would think twice before attempting it. We heard so many horror stories of happenings on the way, and we only heard accounts of the ones who made it!

On their arrival in the camp at midnight, the young men had found their way to the Vietnamese section and there made contact with their relative. After listening to the story of what they had been through to get this far, I decided I would attempt to take them out of the camp, knowing it would be risky.

First I contacted Ken, for his approval to take them to our house. He agreed, offering to accompany us when the attempt was made. While negotiations for their escape were taking place, the young men were made safe in one of the rooms in the COERR office, where I had left them with pens and paper to write down their history, required by UNHCR. I knew I would have to be very careful, for we were all aware that one of our Cambodian workers was an informer for the DPPU, reporting anything overheard in the office that he thought may be of interest to them. Because of this, I knew we would have to move fast to get the guys out. I swapped my car for a COERR twin-cab vehicle with tinted windows, figuring it would be easier to hide the occupants from the Thai guards in this. We decided to leave in mid-afternoon when there was not much traffic and the guards were less alert.

We put the three guys in the back seat, I was driving, with Ken in the passenger seat, from where he could hand our passes to the soldiers. When we arrived at the Site 2 gate, I stopped at the guardhouse and we signed out on the board provided. Another soldier came up to the car window, looking in, checking out the occupants. I thought, 'This is it, I am going to be caught this time, my luck can't last forever.' I sat waiting for the order for us to get out, but the soldier turned to Ken, indicating that he wanted a ride, then climbed into the back of the utility. We realized that he had only been checking to see if there was room for him. I looked in the rear-vision mirror at the three young men in the back. Their faces were white, as they sat, staring straight ahead, frozen in fear. I would have laughed, had it not been such a serious situation, for we still had the soldier in the back breathing down our necks and another checkpoint to get through.

At this checkpoint, vehicle registration and driver's pass numbers were given as we went through in the morning, then inspected again and crossed off on our return. By the time we reached this base, I was so nervous that I did not fully stop, my foot frozen on the clutch. The soldier checking had to run alongside the car to get the details. Ken was whispering to me to stop, but I couldn't. Luckily our DPPU passenger in the back had alighted and Ken had called out the required figures. This seemed to satisfy the guards and I took off, relieved that we had passed the last hurdle before Tapraya.

We took the three young men, Lam, Buu and Sung to our house. With the aid of a Vietnamese phrase book, we were able to communicate with them and learn a little about their lives. They told us that their parents had been imprisoned in Vietnam for speaking out against the government. Their Chinese teacher had also been arrested, and they feared they would be next. Relatives banded together to raise the money to send them to Thailand. So here they were!

They were very likeable young men, full of fun when they got over their initial nervousness, and very grateful to us for our efforts in getting them out of the camp. They stayed with us for three days before being interviewed by UNHCR, then transferred to the local prison. I would visit them there after work or they would call in when allowed out to go to the market. We got to know them very well in the five weeks before they were transferred to Phanat Nikhom camp. We corresponded regularly for the next year, but unfortunately for them they were assessed as ineligible for resettlement and transferred to another camp in Thailand, Si Khieu. I lost touch with them after that, but fear that their dream of resettlement did not eventuate, because most people from this camp were later returned to Vietnam.

A French organization, 'Enfants du Mekong', had been arranging scholarships in France for high school graduates from the camp. Fr Vincent, together with high school teachers, held interviews and examinations to determine who would be eligible for these six bursaries. This was the second year these awards were offered, as six students had already completed a year's study in France. All the boarding school boys, who had graduated, applied for a scholarship and were taken through a series of interviews and tests. They were now anxiously awaiting the results.

The successful applicants were announced a couple of weeks later. I was delighted to hear that Saren was one of those selected, together with Vily, another of the boarders. They were both very excited when they received this news, but nervous at the prospect of living and studying in a Western country. Arrangements were set in motion to obtain passports and visas. Because these documents would have to be processed inside Cambodia, it would take some time.

The transition from Site 2 to French society would not be easy for them, so Agnes and I arranged to take Saren and Vily to lunch in the camp restaurant to teach them some Western etiquette. First, they would need to learn to use a knife and fork, as all meals here were eaten with a spoon or with the hands. They were used to plates of food being placed in the centre of the table, everyone diving in to them with their own spoon. We explained that this was not accepted in other societies and they would have to use the utensils provided, and they could not throw chicken bones, tissues and empty bottles on the floor, as they were accustomed to doing here. They looked at me in amazement when they heard these things, not understanding our 'strange' foreign ways. I told them that spitting was not acceptable in other countries, and was considered a dirty habit. Neither should boys hold hands, like they did in the camp. Saren looked at me in astonishment when I told him this, asking, "But what if he is my friend?"

It would be another five months before all papers were finalized and it was time for the six young men to leave the camp, the only home they had known for years, for the journey of their lifetime to France. Fr Vincent would accompany them on the trip. On the day they were to leave, crowds of friends, family members and students assembled to bid them farewell when they boarded the buses to take them to Bangkok. It was a happy, yet, sad occasion, as goodbyes were called, well-wishers waving, calling out, some in tears, as the buses bore the young men out of the camp on the way to their new life.

I took the bus from Aranyaprathet next day, after arranging to meet them in Bangkok to assist Fr Vincent with their shopping. There, I met a very excited and nervous group. We took them to Central Plaza, a huge shopping complex, where they were in a complete daze, so overawed by the vastness of the city, the volume of traffic and size of the shops. We helped them buy clothes for the journey, shoes, and presents for the families with whom they would be billeted in France. Then we headed for the airport. I was very happy for them to have this opportunity of further education but sad to see them go, realizing I may never see them again. Saren and Vily promised to keep in touch, which we do to this day.

Fr Vincent told me later that it was a nightmare trip with visa problems, none of the boys sleeping and all of them airsick.

A couple of weeks later I received this letter from Vily:

Dear Mother Margot,

Now I'm here in France. How are you?
I'm fine but I've had a very bad experience.
It happened in the bathroom. Normally, the French people take a bath in a so-called 'baigneur' (basin). They don't tell me how to do. So I took a bath outside the baigneur. The water climb up! I tried to find the hole but I couldn't find. So I and some French boys have to take aways the water and make dry the room.
The French food is terrible to me. At the first time, I couldn't eat at all. I was hungry. I tried to eat and eat and now it is better.
I think in 1 or 2 months, it goes automatically.
I feel sleepy the whole day. I'm lost! I'm like a stupid boy.

Goodbye! Good luck!
Friendship

Vily

I had a good laugh when I read this letter, realizing our lessons should have included a segment on bathroom etiquette.

I was sitting in my office one morning when Sarath's wife, looking very upset, came to see me. I sat her down and through her tears she told me that Sarath had been injured by a hand grenade and was in KID hospital. Families were not permitted to visit so she begged me to call on him. I headed there next day.

When I finally found him, it was a sorry sight that met my eyes. His face was cut and swollen; he could barely talk. He had sustained a broken jaw, badly cut lip, leg injuries, and had lost his two front teeth. He told me, through swollen lips, "I recently opened a video room in the camp. A drunken KPNLF soldier came in and was screaming out and causing a disturbance, so I ordered him out. He got very angry and returned the next day. He stood in the doorway and threw a grenade into the room."

Two women and a man, as well as Sarath, were injured. It would be two weeks before Sarath returned to Site 2 and a few months before he recovered from his injuries. After this incident he closed the video theatre.

By 1990, the population behind the barbed wire fence of Site 2 had grown to around 200,000, making it the most populous Cambodian city after Phnom Penh. At this time, approximately 360 foreign workers were employed in camp programmes.

COERR now had a large number of education and social service programmes operating in Site 2, including English and French Language, Law, Engineering, Teacher Training, Family Services, Mental Health, Youth Services, Fine Arts, Alcoholic Centre, Handicapped Workshops, Agriculture, Silk Farm and Postal Service. To cope with all these new projects and the expanding established services, many more staff members had been recruited. It was a real multinational group, with workers from twenty-two countries employed by COERR.

Most of the people, who came to work in the border camps were in their thirties and early forties, with a small number in their twenties and a few older people. I really admired the young people, who came to work here, leaving home comforts, friends, family and social life, to work in such a stressful situation in this dirty, dusty camp in unbelievably hot conditions, many times for little or no pay. However, it proved to be a real character-building exercise, and what they learned by working there, would stand them in good stead for the rest of their lives.

When I read in the papers back home about vandalism, car stealing, assaults and crimes committed by young people, obviously bored with life and with nothing better to do, I could not help but think how beneficial it would be for them to spend some time up here or working in the Cambodian villages with the really poor people. To witness and take part in the hard physical work and observe the struggle these people endure to survive another day, should make these young people appreciate their relatively easy and uncomplicated lives back home.

COERR workers were awarded more freedom in the camp than members of other agencies that enforced much stricter rules on their staff. Many organizations would not allow their workers to budge outside their workplace without a radio, whereas COERR workers were given the choice. There were never enough radios to go around, anyway. This angered UNBRO officials, prompting them to label COERR workers the 'unguided missiles'. Our staff members could be seen roaming all over the camp, walking, riding their bicycles, or a few driving agency cars.

Ken, confined to the classroom for his work as a teacher, envied the freedom my job afforded me and the experiences I had while roaming the camp. He loved to listen to the stories of my day's exploits, when I arrived home. Most days there was some interesting story to relate

The house next to ours in Tapraya was now occupied by a multinational, fun-loving group - Michael from USA, Australian David, Agnes who hailed from France, and a Scottish girl, Dorcas - and we spent many happy evenings in their company. Ken and Agnes had now formed a relationship, difficult here in such a small community. They spent much of their free time together, but it was very hard to have any privacy in this situation. Their romance was to continue for a year before they broke up and Agnes left to work in Cambodia. However, she kept in touch, returning to Tapraya a number of times to visit, before returning to France a year later.

In this remote part of the world, we had to invent our own entertainment. We had discovered a large reservoir about ten kilometres from Tapraya where we could swim, often going there after a long, hot day in the camp. It was so refreshing to swim in the clean water, the men wearing shorts and women in sarongs, our bathing suits being too brief for here. We sometimes took drinks, made a floating table of a car tube with a laundry basin in the middle and sat in the cool water drinking local beer and eating potato chips. Thai people gazed open-mouthed at the crazy foreigners sitting up to their necks in the water having a party!

Thai food was delicious and cheap, so most times the foreigners ate out at one of the many restaurants in town. In spite of the tasty food here, we did miss our Western food. When there was a group together, we would often talk about the food we missed most - good bread, cheese, chocolate, mashed potato, items we take for granted at home, but cherished here because they were unobtainable. Staff members going home on holidays came back laden with supplies of chocolate, wine and cheese that would be shared around and enjoyed by our small foreign community.

Education had taken top priority for many Cambodians. They now realized, since life had settled down, that it was important to work towards preserving their culture and to do this they required knowledge. The first group of teachers had now graduated from the teacher training school, significantly improving the standard of education in schools set up around the camp. Three high schools now operated with many more choices for further education on graduation. Word had filtered back to Cambodia regarding education opportunities in Site 2 and many young people were making their way to the camp to take advantage of the free instruction.

Talk of repatriation was in the air and word had spread in Cambodian villages near the border that UNHCR would be giving returnees many benefits. Registration time was drawing near and this prompted many of the villagers to head for the camp, hoping to register as refugees, and cash in on these rewards. It was a difficult situation for UNHCR, for it could not turn the people away. However, it made their job so much harder. Already, the number of Cambodian refugees inside Thailand numbered around 360,000. Nobody envied them the mammoth task ahead.

Repatriation information centres had been set up all over the camp where people could go with their queries. UNHCR were planning to start repatriation early in 1992, with the aim to have all Cambodians back in their country in time for the elections in May 1993.

In spite of all this hype about repatriation, the news seemed to have little impact on the population of Site 2. They were aware that when they returned, civil war would probably await them, as fighting still continued between Government and the feared Khmer Rouge. It was a real dilemma for people, who did not want to spend the rest of their lives in a camp on foreign soil, either.

I had been feeling quite homesick and was seriously considering resigning, as I was missing my family, when Tim, who had found it hard to settle back in Australia, returned, hoping to find work in Site 2. It was great to have a family member with me again, partly filling the void, and he was happy to be back in the camp that had never been far from his mind in the two years since he left. At first, he stayed in Tapraya, where we could be close to each other. Before long, he had secured a job with the IRC (International Rescue Committee), working on their newly established landmine awareness programme, then he moved to Aranyaprathet to live.

This new programme, LMAP (Landmine Awareness Programme), was designed to draw camp people's awareness to the ever-constant threat of landmines. The latest figures showing that there were 1,000 people maimed by landmines along the border and inside Cambodia each month. This country was fast becoming a nation of one-legged and legless people. With repatriation now close, it was important for all to be aware of this danger when they returned to their country. This also applied to the forest near the camp, where so many people ventured out to collect wood, bamboo shoots and reeds each day. Tim's job was to create materials in the form of posters, leaflets, silk screens, T-shirts, games and booklets with a landmine awareness theme, to be used in all the border camps in the education programme. This worthwhile project was later taken over by the UN and continued until repatriation.

There had been many grenade and mine incidents in the camp and the rumour was that grenades could be purchased from only sixty cents at the market. When Phoeuy and I were wandering through the market one day, I decided to prove if this rumour was true, and hand grenades were readily available at such a low cost. I asked Phoeuy to enquire at one of the market stalls if we could buy a hand grenade. He looked at me in surprise, then took me aside, whispering, "I can get you a hand grenade if you need one!" I tried to explain that I only wanted to prove the validity of the rumour, that I did not really want a hand grenade, but he couldn't understand the strange ways of the foreigners.

Phoeuy and the other boys had now moved from the COERR office and had their own house in another part of the camp. While visiting one day, Phoeuy's friend, Sokha, arrived. He had just returned from his daily trip into the forest where he collected landmines for scrap metal. Between himself and three guys working for him, they collected up to a hundred mines each day. Sokha would remove the detonators and explosives, then sell them to Thai scrap metal dealers who came to the camp market daily.

Sokha asked me if I wanted to see a mine, producing one from his pocket. It was a round object about the width of a saucer, coloured green with a brown cross on the top; the most common mine found in this area. He said they were not dangerous if you knew how to handle them, then started to pull it to pieces, saying, "This is how I defuse them." I quickly stopped him, saying that I didn't want to watch and was not interested in how it was done.

Two weeks after this encounter, Phoeuy told me that Sokha's eight-year-old son had been killed and two little friends seriously injured, while playing with one of the landmines at home.

Saving Lives

While visiting the hospital one day, a man rushed in with the body of a six-year-old child, recovered from a nearby reservoir. Medics worked desperately to revive the child but it was too late. Only the day before, two 12-year-old girls had lost their lives in another waterhole near our office. Hospital staff told me there were around forty drownings in Site 2 each year, mostly of children swimming in these water catchments. It was terrible to hear of this needless waste of young lives.

Over the next few days, I thought a lot about this problem, weighing up in my mind what I could do. After all, I had been a swimming, water safety and resuscitation teacher for twenty-five years, so there must be some way I could apply these methods here.

Slowly a plan began to form. The same procedures could be used as those undertaken by surf-lifesavers at home, with lifeguards placed around the reservoirs where the children played and swam. I could train the recruits in rescue and resuscitation procedures, upgrading their swimming proficiency where necessary.

With this idea in mind, I approached Joe Hegenuar, Child Protection Officer for UNBRO, with my idea for this project. After outlining my plan, his answer was, "It can't be done." These were fighting words for me, making me more determined to show that it really could be undertaken, if certain procedures were followed.

I went home and wrote up a proposal, outlining how the programme could be made to work and stressed the beneficial results, arranging to meet Joe when my draft was finished.

We met in Aranyaprathet a week later, where I presented him with the proposal, explaining how it could work here in this camp. Recruits would be selected and I would train them in rescue and resuscitation procedures, while lifeguard towers were being erected at all reservoirs. When lifeguards finished their training, they would be on duty at these stations from early morning till dusk while people were swimming. By the time I had finished presenting my ideas and plans for this project, I had won Joe over. But he would still need approval from his superiors before this new programme could be introduced.

My next task would be to approach Fr Alfonso, head of COERR projects team, presenting the idea to him, so that the programme could operate under the umbrella of COERR Social Services. Usually a hard man to convince, Fr Alfonso was quite receptive to this new scheme, saying he was all for it if it would save lives. The only problem being that COERR had no budget for new programmes, and would not supply funding. I assured him that it would be possible to run the project with assistance from the UN and donations, without any cost to COERR.

Meanwhile, Joe was having some problems getting approval from tough UN members, who initially said a definite 'No' to the project. Then, after he walked out of the meeting, saying, "Okay, then, you will have any future drownings on your conscience," they changed their tactics, saying that though the UN was not willing to accept it as a project, they would be willing to support the programme by supplying rice for the workers. The ration they would receive was in addition to their weekly handout, allowing them to sell or trade this extra subsidy. Great, now that the UN had agreed to an involvement, I knew the programme could go ahead.

A few days later, Joe called to tell me that two girls, nine and ten years old, had drowned that morning. It was now April and the hottest time of the year, with large numbers of children playing in the reservoirs daily, making it imperative to get the scheme underway as soon as possible. Joe had seconded Vuth, a reliable worker from his office, to run this new programme, so together, we sat down to devise a strategy to set the project up.

We decided that an inspection of the camp reservoirs would be the first job. Vuth recruited two of his friends, Remo and Seng, to conduct this survey. They rode all over the camp by bicycle, taking notes, recording numbers of swimmers, seeking out danger spots and checking drowning statistics. After studying their findings, we came to the conclusion that it would be essential to set up lifeguard stations at all nine reservoirs. Each one had its danger spots and all were being used by swimmers.

Approval for this project would be required from camp administrators, so Vuth and I met with these camp officials to present the idea and explain how we intended to run the programme. They were all very impressed with this new concept and agreed that it would be a good project, for they were also concerned about the needless loss of life due to drowning. They agreed to assist with recruitment of staff from their respective camps.

We envisaged that fifty lifeguards would be required to man all stations. Notices were soon displayed in each section of the camp, calling for applications for the position of lifeguard (something unheard of here), though we received plenty of applications, regardless. The only requirement requested was that the applicant be a strong swimmer. Job candidates were advised to meet at the big reservoir in Rithysen camp in a week's time with their swimming gear.

April 24 was registration and swimming-trial day for lifeguards. Vuth, Remo, Seng and I, made our way to the meeting place, already busy with children swimming, men filling buckets and carting water, women and girls washing clothes and scraping their cooking pots. The first applicants, twenty-six men and three women arrived. They displayed an interesting array of swimming gear; shorts, underpants, jeans, the girls planning to swim fully clothed in shirts and sarongs.

First, the applicants registered names and details with Remo and Seng, and then came the swimming test. We chose a shallow part of the reservoir to send swimmers, one at a time, from one corner to another, a distance of about five metres, to check if they were capable swimmers. The water in these catchments was like pea soup, no visibility at all, so it was sensible to try shallow water first.

The first two made it all right then it was time for the third, a seventeen-year-old girl. She jumped into the water from the muddy side and headed straight out towards the deep water in the middle. She was a weak swimmer, and I could see trouble coming up. Worse still, she did not heed our calls to change direction. After about ten strokes she stopped, then went under. Other swimmers converged, but just watched as she came up, then went down again.

I was standing on the side, screaming, "Grab her, grab her!" in English, which no one understood. I was just preparing to go in myself when, on her third appearance, someone grasped hold of her. She was pulled to the side where she struggled up the slippery slope and hid herself, too embarrassed to come out. After this fright, I made sure that everyone swam over the short course I had planned for safety.

As a result of these trials, we chose twenty applicants, who would be strong enough swimmers to enrol for the training, to take place before the final selection was made. Twenty-two hopefuls turned up for the next intake and we had a repeat of the swimming trials and by this time, with plenty of curious onlookers. We chose another fourteen to undergo instruction, agreeing that this would be enough to commence the training programme. The training consisted of three hours at the reservoir each day for three weeks, learning water safety and rescue techniques. Recruits needed to strengthen their swimming, for it was obvious that though they could swim reasonably well, they had very little stamina over a distance. Also, their swimming styles were atrocious. Resuscitation techniques would be taught for two hours each day, in a building in a UN compound, which had been allocated to our programme.

I had recently met members of the ANZ (Australian & New Zealand)

Phoeuy with young brother, Khin, and sister, Khun, when they first arrived from Cambodia

Photo: Margot

Mine Awareness poster designed by Tim. Photo: Tim Grant

Unexploded shell which landed in the camp. Photo: Margot Grant

Crowds gather for weekly dramas on outdoor stage. Photo: Tim Grant

Actors in full traditional drama costumes. Photo: Margot Grant

Evacuation to Site 3. Helping the elderly. Photos: Margot Grant

Lam, a friend, Buu,& Sung. Vietnamese men I spirited out of Site 2.

Swimming area at camp reservoir. Photo: Margot Grant

Lifeguards practising rescues. Photo: Margot Grant

Camp children collecting rainwater. Photo: Tim Grant

A sad Khun at her wedding. Photo: Margot Grant

Street children sailing their homemade craft. Photo: Margot Grant

Handicapped child having fun with his friends. Photo: Tim Grant

A minefield I went through close to the camp. Photo: Margot Grant

Prisoners behind bamboo bars. Photo: Margot Grant

With my good friend, Saroeun, a triple amputee. Photo: Bruce Horgan

A rare chance for aid workers to dress up. Ingrid, Leanne, Pam, Dorcas, & Runyaporn at the 'elephant party'.

Photos: Margot Grant

Picking through the embers after a devastating fire in the camp.

Peace walk through Cambodian countryside. Photo: Margot Grant

Government troops retreating during the peace walk. Photo: Margot Grant

Women's group in Bangkok, who had offered to donate any materials required for my work. I wrote to them requesting T-shirts, shorts, caps and whistles for the lifeguards. A reply came back immediately, agreeing to fulfil this request and telling me that their members were already scouting around the markets to find these articles.

In the meantime, I had rung my friend and fellow swimming teacher, Marie, in Australia, with a request for swimming and water safety certificates for the lifeguards. These would give the trainees something to strive for; Cambodians have a love of certificates and presentation ceremonies. She promised to contact the Western Australian Education Department swimming office, enquiring as to the availability of these certificates, along with any posters, books or leaflets they may like to donate to the programme.

Word about the programme had now spread around the camp and more people were turning up each day to apply for the lifeguard positions. New applicants were tested for swimming ability and another twenty-five names placed on the waiting list for the next training course.

Before the first training sessions commenced, Joe visited the centre to talk to the new recruits and describe the programme, as something like this was completely alien to them. Joe, a very impressive person, blonde hair, blue eyes, stood nearly two metres tall, and looked especially big here among the shorter Cambodians, most of whom barely reached his shoulder. There was dead silence when he entered the classroom, stooping to get under the doorway, then many gasps as he straightened up and they saw his size. The recruits listened attentively to his description, we could only hope that they really understood what their role would be.

We took the lifeguard trainees around to all the reservoirs, pointing out danger areas, showing them safer swimming places and choosing, with their help, where to place the towers. Vuth and I took the first group to the big reservoir to start their rescue training. They were like a class of mischievous schoolchildren, laughing, playing, ducking each other and generally enjoying themselves. They were taught how to make many different rescues, how to lift and carry a patient out of the water, a very difficult task here, as the edges were muddy and slippery. Most of all they loved performing the 'hair rescue'.

In this particular rescue, the lifesaver first turned the patient on his back then grabbed a handful of hair above the forehead, pulling him along this way. All rescuers and onlookers would be in fits of laughter when this rescue was performed. They really enjoyed these training sessions and the ride there in the back of the utility, another novelty for them. They would laugh, sing and call out to passers-by while we drove through the camp to the reservoirs. I think they learnt some rescue work as well!

Water in camp reservoirs was like mud with no visibility more than two centimetres below the surface, so teaching trainees to dive to locate a body was almost impossible, but they made the most of it, diving again and again to complete the task. We used a rock wrapped in a shirt to represent the body for which they searched, losing three shirts in the process!

After a few days of water training, I realized that they needed to improve their stamina, considerably, if they were going to make rescues. Although the men had strong looking, muscular bodies, they could only manage a very small distance in the water, I guess this was the result of their meagre diet of rice and tinned fish.

A plan was made to start each day with a distance swim, beginning with about twenty metres and hopefully building it up to two hundred metres or more by the end of the training. This, I thought would be their limit. As for their swimming technique, forget it! It would take months of dedicated work to improve their styles, if ever. As long as they were making the distance and conducting the rescues successfully that would be okay by me. Gradually, over the following weeks, their stamina improved, as did their rescue and water safety techniques and I could see they were starting to understand what it was all about. Resuscitation was another matter. They could not comprehend why they had to blow air into someone's mouth; they had never seen or heard of this before!

About this time a parcel of books, posters, videos and certificates arrived, donated by the West Australian Education Department and sent by Marie. We put books out and posters around the walls of our training centre to give them an idea of what was required. We borrowed a video machine and I showed the trainees a film of rescues taking place in a pool in Australia. I could not understand why they all burst out laughing when the rescues began, then I realized that they were laughing at their first sight of clean, clear, pool water.

Two large boxes came from the ANZ women's group with a hundred shirts, shorts, caps and whistles. This was a great donation, which was really appreciated by trainees, who were quite excited about starting their job decked out in a new outfit. We had the shirts printed with a red cross and 'LIFEGUARD' in Khmer. It was hard for them to translate this, as there is no word close to it in their language. The nearest they could get to it, being 'person who helps others in the water'.

The UN had a large construction team responsible for the erection of public buildings in Site 2. Now that UNBRO had recognized this new programme, it was time to make a request for the construction of lifeguard towers. We held a meeting with the Khmer building manager, where plans were discussed to erect towers at each of the nine reservoirs. Some of the larger reservoirs would need three stations, others requiring two, while the smaller ones could make do with just one tower, a total of seventeen altogether. The lifeguards' jobs would be to man these towers, keeping swimmers together in front of them, using whistles to draw swimmer's attention if they strayed from the group.

The first group of recruits was progressing well with their training and a second group was starting the course. Towers were in place at the reservoirs and the first lot of the worker rations had been given out, the regular weekly UN worker ration consisting of three and a half kilos of rice and three small tins of fish. Joe was urging us to get the programme started, as another child had drowned in one of the water catchments.

It was the middle of May, still very hot, with many swimmers using the reservoirs each day, when we put the first group to work. The lifeguards worked six-hour shifts, seven days a week, one group doing the morning shift and another taking over from them in the afternoon. Their training was still incomplete, so they worked in the morning, and attended training sessions in the afternoon or vice versa. Supervisors were appointed, their job being to ride bicycles around to monitor each of the lifeguard stations.

Initially, the programme was not without its problems. On my first tour around to see how it was progressing, I found two of the lifeguards asleep in their hammocks strung up in the towers. We had to ban hammocks and further stress the importance of their jobs and the responsibility they had to the swimmers. Another time, I came on one of the guards chasing the children away with a piece of bamboo. He had to be told that his job was to ensure their safety, not deter them from swimming. Apart from these instances, all seemed to be going well.

Lifeguard training was continuing, their swimming distance now up to a hundred metres for most and two hundred metres for the stronger swimmers. The public was beginning to understand the role of the lifeguards and purpose of the programme. Lifeguards had been approached by parents telling them they were so happy with this new programme, now feeling confident that their children could swim in safety at the reservoirs. This feedback was encouraging.

The guards looked very smart in their new T-shirts, hats and shorts. One of them, a man in his fifties, with no teeth and not very good looking, had even won himself a young wife on the strength of his outfit.

This young woman had seen him wearing the T-shirt with the red cross displayed on the back, thinking he was a medic (a very respected job) agreed to marry him, much to the amusement of the other guards.

Within a week of the project commencing, the first rescue was reported. A guard at a reservoir in Rithysen camp had pulled a seven-year-old girl from the water. A few days later another rescue was performed at the Dong Rek reservoir, which had been the scene of many drownings. The programme was beginning to prove its worth. At our weekly meeting, Vuth informed the gathering of the rescues, praising the lifeguards involved. Now they could understand what it was all about.

Training for the present lifeguards was finished, but training for new recruits would be ongoing. I was due to go home for a three-week break in June, but before I left I planned to hold examinations for the swimming certificates. I had attempted to do some correction on their swimming techniques before examination day, but it was very difficult to change long-established styles. I would have to waive the 'correct technique' part of the exam, concentrating on distance and stamina, if they had any semblance of the correct stroke.

On the appointed day, all turned up full of excitement at the prospect of gaining a swimming certificate. They would attempt the Junior Certificate, which comprised a ten-metre freestyle swim, ten-metre breaststroke, a dive and a surface dive. We mapped out a course for the swimmers and in groups of five they had a try for their certificate. They all made their swimming section. Diving proved to be the difficult part, due to a slippery slope on the side of the reservoir, so we had to make do with only the surface dive, which they all mastered. It was a happy group that returned, thrilled with the success.

All candidates fronted up again the following week, for their attempt at the next certificate, the Intermediate, for which they would have to swim fifty metres freestyle, fifty metres breaststroke, twenty-five metres backstroke and dives. This proved much harder, especially the backstroke. They had never encountered this stroke before, but they certainly came up with some ungainly renditions of it. Only about half of the group were successful in gaining passes this time. Those who had failed looked so downhearted that I promised I would give them all another try when I returned from my vacation.

A day was set for the presentation. Fr Alfonso, Joe, Ken and administration heads were invited to attend the ceremony to present the swimming certificates. The lifeguards sat in rows facing the microphone, all dressed in their outfits, anxiously awaiting their big moment. Joe spoke about the aims of the project, followed by Fr

Alfonso and Mr Lay Khek, before the presentation of certificates began. The lifeguards were thrilled to receive their colourful certificates, inscribed with their names, even though they could not understand a word on them, as they were all printed in English! A small party followed to mark this important occasion for them.

Whilst home in Australia, I contacted an acquaintance in the Cottesloe Surf Life Saving Club, telling him of my programme in the refugee camp. They were very impressed and offered to help in any way possible. I requested a manikin, to help the lifeguards with their EAR (expired air resuscitation) and CPR (cardio-pulmonary resuscitation) training. So far, resuscitation had not been necessary in any of the rescues performed by the lifeguards. It was so alien to their culture to have such close contact with another person that I was concerned they may not use it when the occasion arose. I hoped that the use of a manikin might overcome this cultural barrier. Before I left to return to Site 2, I received word that the Western Australian Surf Life Saving Association (WASLSA) would donate a full-size female manikin (Resusci-Annie) and a life-size baby. I was most grateful for these donations to the programme.

Now, I was faced with the problem of how to get the manikins into the camp. They were too big to hide and the rules were very strict at the time. I decided that it would be best to do it openly, so I sat Annie in the passenger seat of my car, with the baby in her lap, her left arm dangling out the window with my camp pass taped to her hand. I set off for the camp with my two 'passengers' hoping that the Thai guards would be in a receptive mood that day!

At the first checkpoint, the soldiers walked towards the passenger side of the car, then stopped in their tracks, looking in amazement; they had never seen anything like this before. They came over for a closer inspection, then burst out laughing, calling all their mates over to have a look. They were so busy touching Annie, poking their fingers into her and pointing at the baby in her lap that they did not notice that I was taking in illegal goods. At the next checkpoint, we had the same performance with all the guards enjoying the distraction, so I made it in with the two manikins without any problem. Wherever I stopped in the camp, a crowd gathered to look at this strange sight, making it a slow trip to the office, but creating plenty of interest along the way. Finally, I arrived at the lifeguard office with my special cargo.

Vuth and I, decided it would be wise to commence resuscitation training with the manikins immediately, for we didn't know when it may be required. After the first training session, the lifeguards were able to grasp the concept of actually blowing the air into the mouth and not just the pretence it had been with the live 'patient'. The look of realization on their faces told the story!

About ten days after we introduced this new resuscitation training with the manikins, one of our lifeguards reported the first use of EAR. He told us that he had pulled an unconscious six-year-old girl from the water, then, finding no sign of breathing; he had revived her after applying mouth-to-mouth resuscitation. It was great to hear that the training had paid off and a life had been saved.

We called the lifeguard forward at the weekly meeting, congratulating him on his successful rescue and revival of the patient, then asked him to demonstrate on the manikin just how he had gone about it. He did this, receiving a round of applause from the group. We reiterated the importance of their jobs and the responsibility they faced each day.

Seng, Remo and I, then paid a visit to the home of the rescued child. She had recovered and the parents were full of gratitude for the lifeguard, who had saved their daughter's life. They told us that she had gone to the reservoir with her sister, who was washing clothes, when the little girl slipped on the muddy bank and fell into deep water. The older girl alerted the lifeguard to her sister's predicament, but by the time he found her, she was floating face down. She was very lucky.

Not long after this, Seng came to tell me he was leaving the programme, planning to go to Bangkok, illegally, to find work, because he was having trouble with his two wives. He told me that he had left his first wife and two children, marrying his wife's sister. They now had a child. Both his wives lived in Site 2 and there was constant friction, so he decided to get out. He asked me to look out for his second wife and daughter until he returned, promising to send money for them when he found work. He was a reliable worker, and would be missed in the programme. Remo would now take over as head supervisor of lifeguards.

Vuth came to my office a few weeks later, to tell me that a ten-year-old boy had drowned in the reservoir in Nong Chan camp that morning. It was sad, as it was the first drowning that had happened during patrol hours, since the project started. On investigation, it was discovered that the guards on duty at this station had left their posts at midday to get lunch. When they returned a short time later, children told them that a little boy had disappeared, and the lifeguards were taken to the spot where he had gone down. The guards dived in this vicinity a few times before recovering the child's body. They were applying CPR when the victim's father came running up, grabbed the child by the ankles, put him over his shoulder and ran off. By the time he reached the hospital, the child was dead. We did not know if the child would have survived, anyway, but he may have had a chance if CPR had been allowed to continue.

The lifeguards, who had left their posts were in trouble with their manager, Vuth. He told me that the guards were going to be put in prison because they left their station during working hours, and were not doing their job properly. I remonstrated with him, saying that I thought the punishment too harsh. He then said that he would give them two choices; either three days in prison or cut their ration for two weeks. I had to leave it up to them, as the Cambodians were now running this programme. The lifeguards chose prison!

After this drowning tragedy, we decided that stricter rules were required, for the lifeguards were becoming careless. Hammocks were reappearing in the towers, some guards were not wearing their uniforms on the job and others not turning up for work. The new rules stated that anyone leaving their post or not appearing for work without prior notice would receive instant dismissal. Not wearing approved attire would result in a one-week ration cut. After this tightening of the rules, the guards' behaviour improved considerably.

This drowning and the previous rescue made me realize that the public also needed to understand the use of resuscitation and the role of the lifeguards. I approached the drama groups about conducting a short drama during the weekend performance on the outdoor stages. Together, we devised a story of a near drowning and how the lifeguards came to the rescue and applied resuscitation. We showed how it was considerably more successful than the old Cambodian method of shaking the child whilst holding it upside down. I could only hope that the message got through, to at least some of the audience attending.

As I was coming through the camp one morning, I saw a large crowd gathered at one of the reservoirs next to the main road. I could see Remo there, so I stopped to find out what was happening. He informed me that a seventeen-year-old girl had had a fight with her father the night before, had run away and jumped into the reservoir. No one had actually seen her go into the water but her shoes were at the side. The lifeguards were busy using the diving skills they had been taught, in an attempt to locate the body in the deep muddy water. They dived many times, but to no avail. Sadly, the girl's body surfaced the next morning.

The programme had been operating very successfully for some time, when I decided to give the lifeguards a refresher course to hone their skills. My plan was to take them to La Han Sai reservoir, about seventy kilometres from the camp, where they could train in the clean water, but first I would have to get permission from the DPPU headquarters. They would need to be taken in two groups so that one lot could still remain on duty, therefore the request would be for two separate day passes.

I wrote this letter explaining about the role of the lifeguards, stating how it would be beneficial to the programme for them to train in the clean water of this reservoir. I did not tell anyone in the programme about this request, as they were often refused, which would disappoint them. However, within a few days of applying, I received permission to take the groups out. They were delighted when they heard the news. Malcolm and Dorcas offered to come along to assist.

Twenty-five happy lifeguards, all in their work outfits, except the two women, who wore their best clothes, piled into the van on the appointed day, and we took off. As we drove through the Thai villages, our passengers were excitedly pointing out houses, animals, fruit trees and crops, everyday things they had not seen for years. There were gasps of surprise when they saw the size of the reservoir. It was about one kilometre wide and disappearing into the distance as far as the eye could see, and so clean, compared to Site 2 water!

We had hardly stopped, before all the lifeguards were out of the van and racing towards the water, all wanting to be first in. The two women in their best clothes and all their jewellery, started wading into the water too. I asked them if they had brought sarongs in which to swim but they said no. They preferred to swim fully clothed in their fancy blouses and good sarongs, still wearing jewellery, makeup and all; even performing their rescues wearing all this paraphernalia. With Dorcas and Malcolm's help, the morning was spent working on water safety and rescue techniques, the group enjoying themselves along the way.

Lunch was at eleven o'clock; their usual eating time. After this, they were given free time to do their own thing, some preferring to play water games with tyre tubes and balls, others wandering off to explore.

Dorcas, Malcolm and I, were sitting relaxing in the shade when there were loud shouts from further up the reservoir. We hurried over to see if there was a problem, only to find the guys happily collecting large, live snails they had found among the reeds; a great delicacy that they remembered from Cambodia. This set off a big snail hunt, lasting the rest of the afternoon, with all the lifeguards taking part. Every available receptacle was employed to bring these treasures back to the camp, where the snails would make a welcome change to their camp diet. By the time we were due to leave, everyone was exhausted from the day's activities, including Malcolm, Dorcas, and myself! We would have one day's rest before bringing the second group for a similar training session.

By now, Cambodian trainers were quite proficient and had taken over the instruction of new recruits themselves. They, and the lifeguards, were doing a great job, as Joe and I found when we took stock of the programme. Statistics showed that over the period this scheme was in operation, more than one hundred rescues had been successfully performed, with the drowning average only three or four a year compared to 35-40 in previous years.

This programme was to continue very successfully, keeping up the good record until the start of repatriation, when the UN cut worker rations for lifeguards, classing it as a non-essential service.

I felt proud and happy to have been involved in this very important, worthwhile and successful project, classing it as the most rewarding job I undertook while working on the border.

CHAPTER 9

Sister Ath, a French/Cambodian nun, who had come from France to work with COERR two years before, had set up a centre for families in crisis in the camp. People seeking assistance at this Family Service Centre were first assessed for the skills they could offer. These skills included cooking, dressmaking, weaving, mat-making, furniture and building construction, and the aim was to encourage them to use their expertise to help themselves. Support was on hand to set up small businesses; training was also available at the centre for handicraft work. Banana trees and vegetable seeds were supplied to poor families to encourage them to become self-sufficient. Sr Ath did not believe in giving handouts, saying to her people: "Let us have no more begging. Stand up and act like men and women. We have lost everything else, let us not lose our dignity, too."

This programme was highly successful and Sr Ath worked tirelessly to deal with the many problems encountered by poor families in the camp.

Her proficiency in dealing with these difficulties was well known. This prompted Joe, from UN Child Protection, to approach her for assistance with the growing dilemma of street children in Site 2. It had recently come to the notice of UN officers that there were many children living on the streets by night, begging and stealing in the markets in the day. They were at a loss to know how to handle this huge problem.

Sr Ath consulted with Fr Alfonso and it was agreed that COERR would set up a street children's centre in the camp. The biggest problem would be to round up these children, who had an ingrained distrust of authority. Police, being the only ones allowed out after 8pm, were directed to look out for these homeless children and bring them to the UN office.

Phoeuy told me that there was a group of about ten or eleven children, some as young as five years old, sleeping in the street outside his house. They kept a lookout for the police and would run and hide whenever they approached. He would often go out to talk to them, gradually winning their confidence, and they told him many sad stories.

He learnt that some of them were orphans, some had parents in the camp, who had thrown them out, others had left because they were beaten, another boy ran away because his parents were always drunk and there was no food for the children. A seven-year-old boy told Phoeuy that his father was imprisoned in Cambodia and his mother had gone back, leaving him in the care of an uncle. His uncle beat him and made him scavenge for his food, so he ran away.

They went begging in the streets, stole from the market stalls or went through the bins for food to survive, washed in the reservoirs and slept wherever they could. It was a hard life that kept them constantly on the run from the police and DPPU. They had formed their own small groups, each one having an older child as their leader. This was as close to a family as many of them had ever had.

Phoeuy was woken by the sound of shouting outside his house one night. He looked out just in time to see Khmer police grabbing the sleeping children, beating and kicking them, before dragging them off screaming. Some children escaped, while those captured spent the night in prison before being taken to the UN office in the morning. When UN officials heard about the treatment meted out by the police, they were quick to point out that this was not the way they expected them to act.

Sr Ath's Street Children Centre opened a few weeks later, with fourteen children who had agreed to give the centre a try. It was very difficult to encourage more street kids to join in, as apart from not trusting anyone, they were reluctant to relinquish their freedom. But gradually they were persuaded by the children already there, who told them that the centre was good, there was no pressure on them, they could have a bed to sleep on, regular meals and go to school. The idea of attending school won most of them over, as this was the main desire of all camp children. It took time, some of the children only coming for meals at first, checking out the place, ready to run if need be, but eventually they realized that they would not be kept against their will and they learned to trust the staff.

Staff members from the centre now scoured the markets, outdoor stages and community buildings at night, to locate homeless children, giving them the option of attending the centre. It was not long before more than forty children, mostly boys, were living full time at the home.

Books, coloured pencils, blackboards, games and toys were purchased, classrooms set up and teachers employed. These children had never so much as held a pencil in their hands before, so it was a completely new experience for them.

Not long after the centre was established, Sr Ath left to work in Cambodia and Ingrid, a volatile Italian girl, was put in charge. She was a familiar figure as she cycled around the camp streets, a large Vietnamese hat perched on her head, colourful bag over her shoulder and two-way radio tucked in her belt. Cambodian leaders changed several times while Ingrid was overseeing the centre, owing to explosive encounters over treatment of the children by the staff. She loved her little charges, working tirelessly to improve their conditions and along the way making life interesting and exciting for them.

Many of the foreigners working in the camp called in to the centre to assist with the children's activities and watch their progress. The children loved these visits and a chance to show off their handiwork. One of our English teachers, Tom Luongo, and I, called in one day not long after the centre had been established. As soon as we stepped inside the enclosure, we were surrounded by kids of all sizes pulling at our hands for attention, all chattering at once. Some of the older boys escorted us through the compound, proudly showing off their sleeping quarters, dining area and then to the school, finishing up at their classroom. There were ten children in this class, nine boys and one girl, ages ranging from nine to thirteen years.

Tom and I decided that we would like to do something for them. We promised to come back the next day after lessons, to take them for a drive around the camp. What a shock when we arrived, to see a group of seventeen excited small boys waiting expectantly for their ride.

What could we do? We couldn't disappoint them, but where would they all fit? I had brought my old utility with a high cover over the back. Amazingly, they all squeezed in, not caring about the crowded conditions as long as they got their ride. We drove through the camp streets, the children shouting, waving and singing, then we headed for the outskirts of the camp where a Thai farm adjoined.

Most of these children had either been born in the camp or had left Cambodia as babies, so had no memories of farmland. We stopped to show them rice growing in the fields. One little boy, his eyes wide with wonder, said, "I didn't know that rice grew in the ground, how does it get into the bags?" They all listened intently while we gave them a rundown on the growing-to-bagging process. Meanwhile, each of them had broken off an ear of rice to show their teachers and friends back at the centre. After buying drinks for them, we headed back.

The car was immediately surrounded by children wanting to know where we had been and what we had done. We left them all chattering excitedly and showing off their rice stalks, while relating the story of their rice field excursion.

Tom was now taking a group of children from the centre one afternoon a week for different activities, but he was soon to leave, so he asked if I would take over his class. I agreed, but first I would sit in, to observe. Tom showed the children a video of the sea and marine life. This was all so new to them and they sat entranced. After the video, he handed out coloured pencils and paper, requesting them to draw a picture of what they liked most in the video. After sitting and thinking for awhile, they set to work, coming up with some great drawings. Tom took their artwork home and framed each one with coloured paper, returning them a week later. The children really treasured these as something of their own; for many, their only possession.

The following week, Tom and I bought packets of toothpicks, glue, and sheets of polystyrene of different thicknesses, from which we cut bases for boats and pieces in many shapes and sizes for the children to make models. It was great to see the concentration they exerted on their own creation, bringing some surprising results. When their work was finished, we loaded them into utility and took off for the reservoir, the boys all cradling their treasured boats so as not to damage them.

Nong Chan reservoir was quite shallow, so the children waded in and floated their boats without any danger. They spent a happy hour sailing their homemade craft, racing them one against the other and screaming with delight when they took off in the wind.

Tom left the following week to take up a teaching position in Bangkok. Now, this group of eleven boys and one girl would be my responsibility for one day every week. I planned a variety of activities, both educational and enjoyable.

Street Children's Excursions

The camp had been operational for more than five years by this time and new systems for procuring water, together with improvements in distribution, had been made. The first expedition I planned was to observe the different methods employed and see for themselves the work and organization that went in to supplying water for the camp population.

I picked the children up and they all crowded into the back of my utility. Our first stop was at the big reservoir at the back of the camp. The workers were great, taking time off to show the children the different processes through which the muddy reservoir water was taken, before being purified. Here, the reservoir water was pumped into a big flat tank on ground level. In this tank, the muddy water was treated with chemicals before filtering over rocks into another tank. The process was repeated twice more to cleanse and treat the water before the now clear water was deposited into a huge above-ground tank. The children were amazed at the transformation of the muddy reservoir water into pure, clear drinking water. From the large container, the cleansed water was pumped through large pipes into street tanks. This purification process was very slow, and only enough water to supply the population of Nong Chan and Ampil camps could be provided by this method.

Our next stop was at another reservoir closer to the foot of the mountain, where a different method of water collection was used. To fill this reservoir, fresh rainwater was piped down from the mountain at the back of the camp, then treated with chemicals before being pumped into waiting tankers. These trucks then delivered the water to the remaining street tanks. The children enjoyed watching the water tankers being loaded from big hoses. One of the drivers invited a number of children to sit in the cab of his truck while it was being filled, which was a great treat for them. Everyone was thirsty by this time, so out came the watermelons I had bought at the market that morning. They all dived in, thoroughly enjoying this unexpected treat.

Wells had by now been dug in two of the camps. This was a difficult process, with ten metres of hard clay to be dug before water could be reached. We located these wells in Obok and Rithysen camps. Operators on duty there were only too pleased to explain to the boys how the water was pumped from the ground. The children were very attentive and interested in everything they were shown. It was an education for me, too, as I had never considered how they acquired these hundreds of thousands of litres of water needed every day for the camp people. By the time we had finished this tour, the children were very hot and sticky, so it was off to the reservoir for a swim, an activity they loved. After they had splashed around in the water and cooled off, we headed back to the classroom so they could put on paper their impressions of the day's outing. They enjoyed these drawing sessions, concentrating hard before commencing their portrayal of the day's activities. On this day, their biggest inspiration came from the water trucks, featuring them prominently in their drawings.

For the next outing, we went to the usual classroom to view a video of the Grand Canyon. They watched intently, overwhelmed by the size of the mountains shown, having before seen only the small mountain at the back of the camp. Afterwards, I took them to an area just outside the camp where the clay soil had been eroded by years of wind and water. What was left, looked like small rugged mountains ranging in height from two to five metres. I let them loose to run around and use their imagination, playing in their own 'grand canyon'. This was doubly exciting, for we had left the confines of the camp with the permission of the guards on duty at the entrance, something they had not done before.

The children played for an hour, getting the feel of space and freedom, climbing, 'shooting', hiding and generally having fun. This was followed by a treasure hunt to find small gifts I had hidden around the area. It was a treat for them to uncover their little treasure, something they could call their own. By now, our return was always heralded by a waiting crowd of children, anxious to hear where they had been and what had taken place on their weekly venture.

Repatriation was now being planned. However, many camp people had only a vague recollection of their country, the children none. For the next activity, I asked the children to draw pictures of how they visualized Cambodia. The drawings they produced, depicted noticeably soldiers, tanks, guns, explosions, skulls, bones and spirits floating. Altogether, a very distorted view of their country. I realized that they could certainly do with some education about their homeland before they returned.

I had acquired a video made by an Australian television crew that had recently returned from Cambodia. This video depicted daily life in the villages, markets, festivals, city streets, traditional dancing and temples, shown together with interviews with families inside Cambodia. A good view of daily life as it was at that time, both in the villages and cities. This video would give them an idea of what to expect when they returned to their country, over the next year.

The children sat through the video entranced, asking many questions: Why were the houses built on stilts? Could you pick the fruit off the trees in the forest? Would the soldiers shoot you? Could they go to school there? Would Sr Ath's centre also be in Phnom Penh? Chenda and I did our best to answer all their questions. This was followed by another drawing session. The drawings they produced this time were quite different, showing coconut palms, temples and pictures of the forests and lakes. The one little girl in the class drew a picture of a house, flowers in the garden, and her mother wearing beads and earrings, surrounded by her smiling family; obviously, the happy family for which she yearned. It was a good exercise, as the children, who had been fearful before, now seemed more relaxed and happy at the prospect of returning to the country that was home, though unknown to them.

Cambodia is predominantly a farming country and most of the children would be going back to these rural areas. I remembered how ignorant they were of the rice farming process when I took them to look at crops before. I planned to take them out of the camp so they could learn something about rural life. It was rice harvest time, so a good opportunity to put my plan into operation. The first step would be to get approval from DPPU officials for permission to leave the camp, to see the rice harvest in Thai farms nearby. Passes to take people out of the camp had to be applied for a month before and were only issued if there was a very good reason. That would be too late for us;.by then the rice would be harvested. I would try, anyway!

The children were already in the utility when I approached the DPPU office. I explained why I wanted to take the children out to see a rice farm, and how important it was for them to have some knowledge of this, before they returned to Cambodia. After being passed from one official to another, I finally met with the commander, who granted the permission I had been seeking. The conditions imposed were that a DPPU officer be assigned to accompany us, with a time limit of two hours.

A young woman, Dang, was the officer chosen to escort us. She did not speak English or Khmer but, because he spoke Thai well, Chenda was able to translate.

The children were chattering excitedly when they realized we were leaving the confines of the camp. We drove about two kilometres into the countryside, where groups of farmers were cutting the rice with big hand scythes and throwing it into piles. The children gathered around to watch them at work. One of the men came over to talk to us, interested to know where we were from. I told him the children were from Site 2 and had never seen rice harvested before. From then on, he took charge, ushering them over, giving them a first hand demonstration, then allowing each of the youngsters to have a try. After all had had a turn, we directed them back to the vehicle for their next lesson. By now the children had recovered from their first fear of the DPPU guide and were chattering away to her. She was a lovely girl, friendly, and kind to the children.

We followed a track leading to another farm where a huge mechanical thresher was working. These would not be seen in Cambodia, where all this work was done by hand, but the children did not know this. They were enthralled as they watched the workers hurling sheaves of rice stalks into one end of the machine, to be followed by rice seeds spewing out the back into sacks. The workers here were great, allowing the kids to help throw the rice sheaves into the machine. We stayed there for an hour, the children running around, interested in everything.

On our way back, we passed a Thai school with children playing in the grounds. It would be good for my charges to see a 'real' school, after their bamboo and thatch huts, so I asked permission from our guard for a short stop. Dang agreed, accompanying me in to explain to the principal, why we were there. He was only too happy to take us on a tour of inspection. The children were taken into the library, where they looked around in wonder at the shelves of books, wooden desks and chairs. One little boy stood transfixed, remarking: "It's so beautiful." They sat down and were given illustrated storybooks to look through, then listened, as a story was read to them in Thai, translated into Khmer by Chenda.

Next, we were taken into a classroom where lessons were in progress. The group were introduced to the children in the class and invited to sit down with them. However, they were too shy to do this and remained standing, looking on with interest. Our guard was getting restless, so we prepared to leave. We thanked the principal, said our farewells to the teachers and students, and took off.

It was now past midday and I knew that the children would be hungry as they had missed their lunch, which was their first meal of the day. I asked permission to stop for a meal at a roadside restaurant. Never before had these children been in a restaurant, and they looked around in awe. We ordered, and they tucked into a meal of fried beef with rice, savouring their first ever taste of meat.

A Thai man sitting at the next table struck up a conversation. He said he was from Bangkok and wanted to know where the boys came from. When we told him they were Cambodian children from the camp, on their first excursion outside, he insisted on buying them all drinks and cakes; another great treat. Soon it was time to leave, so we headed for the camp with twelve excited youngsters, all anxious to get back and relate their experiences to teachers and friends.

Every Tuesday, my little charges would be waiting for me. I always gave them each a big hug when I arrived. Sometimes I'd miss one, but it wasn't long before the child would sidle up to me, waiting until he received his cuddle. It was the only closeness many of them had received in their lives, and they loved it.

Cambodia is one of the most heavily mined countries in the world, so landmines would be a daily hazard for the people when they returned to their villages. I decided that the next tour would take in some landmine training, so the children could be made aware of the dangers facing them when they returned their country.

Arrangements were made for a UN landmine awareness teacher to educate the children about the dangers of landmines and unexploded ordnance. Charts were used with pictures to identify different shells, rockets and mines used in Cambodia, showing where landmines could be planted, how they could be detected and what to do if they found a mine or unexploded ordnance. It was impressed on the children never to touch any of these if found. As part of this training, they were shown how to find their way safely out of a minefield, and how to leave signs for others, to indicate that there were mines in the area. They listened attentively as these messages were relayed to them.

At the conclusion of this session, we continued on to visit one of the hospitals in the camp. Landmine victims were brought in here for immediate treatment, before being transferred to the hospital at KID. These children, like most camp people, had already witnessed mine victims being carried in, so understood a little about the horrors of these injuries. At the hospital, medics explained how landmine injuries are not confined to one area, due to pieces of shrapnel being sprayed out and causing lacerations all over the body, though the leg area is invariably the most affected. It is not a pretty sight. They finished up with a brief lesson on emergency treatment for landmine victims.

Our next stop was at the rehabilitation centre near the hospital. Here recent amputees were being taught to make their own prosthesis. Handicapped men were hard at work shaping their own artificial legs, double amputees nearby were occupied making their wheelchairs from bamboo and wood. They showed us around the workshop, explaining to the children, the different stages of construction.

At the end of the building, ramps with double sets of handrails had been built. The men practising walking on their new artificial legs, invited us over. I explained to them why I was here with the children, and they all agreed it was a good idea. One of them, an older man, explained to the children how he had lost his leg when he went out into the forest to collect wood. He did not see the mine that was under the grass and warned them to be very careful, for it could happen to them. This was a good lesson for the children, coming straight from a mine victim, and they listened intently. We watched the men practicing walking on their new prosthesis. I could see that it was a difficult and painful exercise and I was amazed at their perseverance. Again and again they finished their walk up the ramp and came back to try once more. Some were holding on to the rails, others walking without aid, all laughing and joking but also supporting each other during their efforts. It was a good lesson for the children as most would be returning to the countryside.

Next, the children watched a video of the 'Great Wall of China' that had been dubbed in the Cambodian language. They learned about the time taken and the ensuing struggle to complete this immense structure. At the completion of the story, I took them to the foot of the mountain at the back of Site 2 where rocks of all shapes and sizes were strewn about. Here they would build their own 'Great Wall of Site 2'. They set to work with gusto. It was not long before they had their own working system in place, sending smaller children off to collect rocks while bigger ones commenced the construction of their 'great wall'. Drinks and biscuits were consumed while they laboured on their building. They really enjoyed this exercise, which resulted in a wall about one metre high and five metres long. They stood around surveying their final achievement with pride. After all this hard work, they wanted to know just how it was possible to build one so long and so high in China! This had been hot work, so it was followed with a swim in the reservoir to cool down before they returned.

Over the weeks I had been taking this group, they were involved in a number of drama sessions. The children rated these sessions as their favourite activity so far. They asked if they could present a drama performance for the staff and students at their centre. We talked about the subject, finally deciding on a story about their lives on the streets. The children put their heads together, pooling ideas and experiences, and a week later, came up with their story. Another week of rehearsals and they were ready for their performance.

Centre staff members, Chenda and I, gathered to watch the play, not knowing what to expect. They came up with a great, though sad presentation of their daily lives. The children acted out their lifestyle - sleeping out; always on the lookout for police; stealing from the stalls at the market; being beaten by police and stallholders; crying when they were hungry; trying to find somewhere safe to sleep - finishing the story with their arrival at Sr Ath's centre and living happily ever after. Their rendition was excellent and they were very pleased with themselves and the applause they received.

They enjoyed this performance so much that I decided to give them a go at something more complicated. All these children had watched Cambodian drama on the outdoor stages, so they had an understanding of traditional stories. I suggested that they make up their own version. Chenda agreed to loan the costumes from his programme, offering to send his drama teachers to assist with their acting.

Within a week, the children had devised their own story and were busy rehearsing for the performance, which would be held at their centre and attended by staff members and other camp workers.

There was great excitement when they set eyes on the elaborate costumes they were to wear. Costumers from Chenda's centre arrived three hours before performance time, to dress them and apply heavy makeup. By the time this was completed, the children were barely recognizable. Now they were ready to act out their own version of Cambodian drama. The audience waited expectantly.

Their performance was brilliant; their story different, but including the usual degree of violence expected in Cambodian stories. The show lasted for one hour, the audience enjoying every minute of it, roaring with laughter at some parts of the story. The children showed real acting talent, amazing the crowd with their presentation. Word of their performance spread around the camp, soon followed by requests for the group to entertain at a number of ceremonies, functions and on the outdoor stages. They thoroughly enjoyed showing off their talents and the ensuing attention.

For the next activity, I decided to take the children on a camp tour so they could see firsthand, how justice was meted out in Site 2. I arranged to take them to the new, partly built prison near the entrance to the camp, then to the courthouse to sit in on a trial, followed by a visit to Rithysen prison. I went to the appropriate authorities for permission to do this tour, which was duly granted.

We took off for the new prison, which was still under construction. The Prison Director invited us in to his office, then personally escorted us around, while he told us the function of each building. The cell area was made of brick, unseen previously in this bamboo and thatch city. It was a big complex, planned to accommodate all the prisoners from the smaller prisons in the camp, as well as long-term prisoners from other camps along the border. When completed, it would be the most imposing group of buildings in Site 2.

The courthouse in Rithysen camp would be the next stop. Here, we planned to attend a court case for two young boys accused of robbery. It would be good for the children to see what the consequences of these actions could be. We fronted at the courthouse but were disappointed when told that the trial had been postponed to another date. However, we could still visit the prison.

I surmised that the police officers would take us around their office building and explain to the children their role, how the prison worked and that would be the end of the tour. However, after a quick tour of the office we were escorted over to a bamboo building in the yard where the guard proceeded to unlock the padlock on the door, then led us inside.

We found that we were in the prison cell housing short-term prisoners. This consisted of a large, long room with a bamboo bed along each wall. There were about seventy men and ten women, sitting on the beds or walking around. They told me that they were all caught outside the camp and brought back by Thai police, who handed them over to DPPU. They would be kept in there for six to ten days as punishment.

We were taken into an adjacent building where about sixty men and eight women were incarcerated. This was where long-term prisoners were held. What an eye-opener it turned out to be! The bamboo and thatch building was divided into two rooms about five metres long and two metres wide. All the sides were completely enclosed and the rooms were very dark. Each of these cells housed approximately thirty male prisoners. A long bamboo bed, where all the inmates slept and on which most of them were now sitting, took up one wall. Large buckets at the end held water for showering and drinking. Next to this were lavatories, comprised of holes dug in the ground with cement around. The stench from these open toilets and unwashed bodies was overpowering.

At the front of these cells was a long room only about two metres wide, where the women were housed. There was no privacy for them at all, as they were only separated from the men's cell by open bamboo bars and a padlocked door. Above the bed in this cell was a blackboard giving the statistics of prisoners. I read the following:

	Male	Female	Total
Murder	6	1	7
Robbery	24	1	25
Illegal use of weapons	8	1	9
Stealing	6	4	10
Rape	4	0	4
Assault	10	1	11
Other case	11	4	15
Arrested by DPPU	73	8	81

When we entered the building, prisoners in the men's section came rushing to the bamboo bars to get a closer look. It was such a novelty for them to have visitors, especially children and foreigners. The boys were a bit afraid to come over, but did so after they were called by the prisoners. I went over to the bars to talk to them, Chenda reluctantly following. I could see that he was very frightened.

On closer inspection, I could see that about a dozen of the men sitting on the bamboo bed, were chained together by the ankles, many of them with abrasions where the chains had cut into the flesh. I asked one of the men why some were manacled and others not. The reason was, he told me, that the chained prisoners had attempted escape at some time. They must sleep shackled like this, only being released to go to the toilet or for their weekly shower. Meals were eaten here on the bamboo beds. Some of the men told me that they had been in this prison for years, already. I could pick these prisoners out by the yellowish hue of their skin. I was horrified by the whole scene.

The prisoners complained about their conditions, lack of contact with families, shortage of food, but their main problem was the boredom. There was nothing for them to do all day long. Family members were only allowed to visit for about ten minutes once every two weeks. I asked if there was any way to ease their boredom and they begged me to get them some chess sets, storybooks and English language books. I assured them I would do my best but I would have to enquire if the prison rules would allow this.

Meanwhile, some of the men in the other cell were talking to the children. One of them called a small boy over. The child was afraid and very reluctant to go near the bars, but the other children pushed him forward. The prisoner said in a serious voice: "Kill, rape, rob and you, too, will end up here like us!" All the prisoners were laughing, but not the little boy, he was very frightened and came quickly over to stay by my side.

I sat down to talk to the women. Many of them had children in the camp and missed them very much. They told me how difficult it was for them, living so close to the male prisoners, having no privacy and having to listen to their taunts. I brought my camera from my bag and surprisingly the guard did not stop me, so I snapped a few shots of the prisoners in chains, the women and their dreary surroundings. The guard was now indicating that it was time to leave, so I bid them all farewell, saying that I would try to return for another visit, but I could make no promises.

When we boarded the car to take the children back to the centre, they were strangely quiet. This visit had made a huge impression on them. It was not until I saw them a week later that they told me how horrified they were to see chains on the prisoner's legs. They talked about this visit for weeks after, all vowing that they would not commit crimes that would lead them to prison.

As I drove home, I could not get the prison out of my mind. I thought of all those people crowded in together in that confined area and the smell that they had to live with twenty-four hours a day! Was that the way to treat human beings, even if they had committed crimes? I could not wait to tell Ken, who worked with the police and justice committee, about what I had seen that day. When told, he was disgusted, finding it hard to believe this was happening under his nose and he knew nothing about it, and promising to look into the matter. We both realized that it was a difficult situation as we were dealing with another culture that had different sets of values and concerns to Westerners.

Prison Visiting Service

I thought long and hard about what I could do for the detainees, finally coming up with the idea of a mobile library. But first, I would need to seek permission from the appropriate authorities. Next morning I went back to the prison office to talk to the officer in charge. I sat down in his office, thanking him for the tour. He was very proud of his position as head of the prison, telling me that he was pleased that I had found the tour interesting. I would have to be careful not to override his authority when I put my plan before him, so I started by saying that the prisoners seemed healthy and the prison very well run. He preened himself before my compliments. I went on to say there was only one thing I could see wrong at present, which was the prisoner's boredom. He agreed that it was so but what could he do about it. That was when I put forward a request for another visit, bringing chess sets and books, also promising to bring some for the prison officers as well. After giving it some thought, he agreed to my request.

I realized that it would take time to get this scheme under way. I would first have to find books printed in Khmer language and these were very hard to come by.

I went to see Fr Alfonso that night. I told him about my visit to the prison, of the conditions and how difficult it was for the inmates to fill in their days. I asked him if it would be possible for me to initiate a programme for the prisoners under the umbrella of COERR Social Services. I was met with a blast from this priest. He told me that it was none of my business, to keep right out of it and leave it to the appropriate authorities to address this situation. I knew the powers-that-be were doing nothing about it and had no intention of changing their policy. Too bad about Fr Alfonso and COERR, I would go ahead with my plan regardless. I would start my own project without the assistance of COERR or anyone else..

Permission to visit the four camp prisons regularly was given a few weeks later by the respective prison commanders, so I set to work to put a package together.

A few trusted prisoners were permitted to go with guards to another section of the compound to make furniture for the office. On one of my visits, I made my way over to watch them at work. A prisoner approached me with a request for materials for their workshop. I asked what they wanted and he said they needed hammers, saws and chisels. I was a bit taken aback by this, asking the guards if they were really required for their workshop. The answer came back, "Yes, they do need them." Before I left the camp, I asked the director and he agreed that I could bring them in, which I did a few days later. Ken loved to tell this story; about the time I brought hammers, saws and chisels in for the prisoners!

I already had some basic English books and dictionaries and was lucky enough to locate chess sets in the market in Aranyaprathet. The big problem would be to find books printed in the Cambodian language. Storybooks were in short supply, most of their printed works being textbooks. Through my efforts that week, I only managed to find two books; not much good for sixty prisoners! In town, I picked up a supply of Thai comic books. Although in another language, they contained plenty of pictures, which should suffice. It would be a start, anyway.

I was still trying to think what to buy for the women prisoners, with two days to go before my scheduled visit, when I came up with an idea. I would buy cloth in many colours, which they could cut into squares to make a curtain to hang around their beds to give them some privacy. Needles and thread would be supplied so that the women could all participate in the making of this patchwork curtain. This would occupy their time, with the end result being a much needed screen for them.

A few days later I headed back to Rithysen prison with my purchases. First, I gave chess sets, comic books and an English dictionary to the officer in charge, to distribute to the prison staff, hopefully this would stop them stealing from the prisoners. The inmates were delighted to see me, expecting that I would not return to visit them again.

Prisoners elected their own leader in each cell; usually the oldest person. Everything must be distributed through this appointed leader, who would make the allocation according to their rules. They were very excited when I brought out the chess sets and handed them over to their leader, who in turn, handed them out to different groups. They set the games out immediately, keen to get started. The books were also gratefully received, all prisoners crowding around to have a closer look.

One young man came over to the bars to speak to me. He did not look like the usual run-of-the-mill prisoner. He told me that his name was Sam Sojoeun and that he had been a musician at one of the pagodas before he was imprisoned for taking part in a robbery. He asked if it would be possible for me to bring in traditional musical instruments so that he could teach the prisoners how to play. I said I would ask permission before promising anything.

By now, I was on good terms with the prison commander. I told him of the prisoner's request, asking permission to bring in some instruments. He agreed that this would be a good idea to keep the inmates occupied. I approached Kike with my request and he was only too happy to oblige, promising some traditional musical instruments - tro-ou, tro-sao, (violin-like instruments) and khim - which were made in his workshop. I had some old instruments from my programme, so I would get them repaired, and along with two drums I bought, it would make quite a band.

There was great excitement when I arrived at the prison with the musical instruments a couple of weeks later. Sojoeun told me that he had chosen his pupils and they were all ready to start. He planned to start training them immediately. In no time, they had quite a band. It was great to go past the prison and hear the haunting Cambodian melodies issuing forth. The music brought happy faces to the prisoners as they sat for hours, beating time, while listening to their traditional music. It was a welcome respite from the boredom of their lives and they really appreciated it.

The next problem would be to locate books written in Khmer language. There was a printing programme in KID camp where storybooks were printed for the schoolchildren. I would try here. I introduced myself to Kurt, the American guy in charge, explaining to him why I required the books. When he heard the story he was very supportive, telling me to help myself. His Cambodian assistant took me to the storeroom where books were piled to the ceiling. I spent hours with him, choosing books I thought would be suitable for the prisoners, many of whom were illiterate and most, semi-literate. The books were Cambodian folk stories with illustrations, which should be easy to follow.

I left KID with the back of my utility filled with boxes of books. I would have to bring a few in every day in my bag, until I had enough to start a mobile library, for I had no pass. By this time, I had secured the assistance of an Australian social worker, Anne, to help me with this project. We set to work stamping and numbering the books and setting up a workable system. We devised a method whereby we would take turns in visiting the four prisons in Site 2, with boxes of books. Prisoners would choose their book, sign for it and change it the following week.

The women were now hard at work stitching patches together by hand, taking great pride in their work. The leader of this group was a woman in her fifties, who had been imprisoned for twelve years for the murder of her husband. She organized the women to work for a few hours every day on the curtain. When it was almost finished, I brought in bamboo and hooks to hang it. When finally the colourful curtain was hung, the women were thrilled with their new privacy.

There seemed to be no segregation of prisoners here. No matter the severity of their crime, they were put together into one of the two communal cells. Some of the inmates were anxious to tell me their stories. I heard tales of murder, robbery and sad stories of people wrongly imprisoned. I noticed over the years that I was involved with prisoners, both here and later in Cambodia, that only the obviously innocent ever asked for help, guilty ones accepting their fate.

On one of my visits, I found eleven girls in a bamboo cage, in the same room as the men prisoners. They were prostitutes, arrested for breaking the camp curfew. Two of them, aged seventeen and eighteen years, told me that they had just come from Cambodia with a guide, who had sold them to the brothel on arrival. I managed to secure their release and found someone to look after them till I could find them some work. I spoke to the other girls, asking if they would give up that life if I could arrange craft classes and homes for them. They all agreed. I went back next-day to let them know of my progress with the arrangements, only to find that they had been released and gone back to the brothels. No simple solutions here.

One good-looking young man in the main prison came over to talk to me in perfect English. I asked him how long he had been inside and he told me two years, then I asked how much longer he had to serve. His answer took me by surprise. "Twenty-three more years to go," he told me. I asked what crime he had committed, to warrant such a long sentence and was told that it was robbery. I thought this very severe until I found later that he had committed murder as well. After committing the robbery, he was seen leaving the house by a fourteen-year-old girl, who was a schoolmate of his. He killed her to prevent identification. Justice people I spoke to later, told me that he was a cold-blooded killer, who showed no remorse for his crime.

The justice system in the camp was not very reputable. If an accused had money and could pay out the judges or committee, he would not be brought to justice. If a prominent person wanted to destroy an opponent, he could accuse them of a crime. This person would then be incarcerated awaiting trial, which could take up to a year. There were plenty of camp people willing to become a witness for a price, so the trial could be a sham.

A few weeks later, we had prepared the books, set up a basic system and were ready to start our mobile library. The prisoners looked forward to every Thursday morning, when we would arrive with our boxes of books and they could make their choice. At first, it worked well, everyone waiting to return their books and sign up for the next. However, before long the books began to disappear. When asked about the missing books, we were told they did not remember where they were. First, it was the more expensive English books that went missing, followed by the storybooks. I guessed the prisoners had found a way of getting them out to be sold. We continued this programme with our dwindling supply of books, picking up more Cambodian books whenever we could. This programme, together with the music project, helped bring some release from the boredom of the prisoners' daily routine.

After watching one of the street children's drama performances, I had an idea. If permission could be granted, it would be great to hold a performance for the prisoners. I presented this idea to the prison chief in Rithysen. He said he would have to think about it and would let me know in a week's time. Nothing like this had ever been done before!

The following week I went back, fully expecting a definite 'No'. I was pleasantly surprised to find that he would allow it. The prisoners would not be permitted out of their cells, so we would have to find some place to present it, so all could get a view. I looked around at the cramped space and wondered how it could be managed, finally coming to the conclusion that the only place to hold the performance would be on one of the large bamboo beds in the women's cell. From there it would be possible for all prisoners to view the presentation if they came up to the bars. We arranged to present this performance in a week's time. Meanwhile, the street children worked on their own version of a Cambodian drama for this special day.

The children arrived at the fine arts centre three hours before the performance starting time a week later, to have makeup applied and to be dressed in the elaborate Cambodian costumes. On arrival at the prison, the inmates were waiting expectantly, all gathering at the bars to watch.

The story was presented and the prisoners loved it, laughing uproariously at different parts of the presentation. At one stage, the actors got a little rough with the only girl in the story, reducing her to tears. After the performance was over and the applause had died down, one of the prisoners called the little girl over to the bars, giving her five baht, all the money he had, saying he was sorry she had been treated so roughly. We finally left, amid cheers from the prisoners. It had been a great interlude for them. One of my workmates later asked me what had been going on at the prison that day. She was amazed, when driving past, to hear the sounds of loud laughter issuing forth. Not to be expected from a prison!

Conditions in the prison were so bad that I was amazed how people could survive living like this. However, requests to various bodies fell on deaf ears and I was virtually told to mind my own business. One of the prisoners told me he was very sick with TB and should be on continuous treatment. His wife brought his daily supply of medication from the hospital, leaving it at the prison office, from where it should have been passed on to him. It was now three weeks since he had received it. He was afraid that the guards were selling it.

I approached the prison director about this problem, being careful not to aggravate the situation or appear to be making accusations. He told me that he knew nothing about the case. I made a request for a nurse from the nearby Rithysen hospital to examine the man. He agreed, as he was concerned that the infection could spread to other inmates. The nurse made her visit and was horrified to see the conditions under which the prisoners were living and the state of health of many of them. Immediately, she put in a request to make weekly visits to monitor their health. This permission was granted by the prison commander.

UNBRO had appointed an Australian policeman, Barry, to train police and prison staff in the camp. While I had been visiting the prisons, Barry had been home on vacation, but now he had returned. Ann and I made an appointment to meet with him to discuss our work with the prisoners and to suggest the introduction of training programmes into the prison system. Prisoners were now being transferred to the new building so there would be plenty of room for this type of project.

On the appointed day, we fronted up at his office in the camp. We waited thirty minutes past the arranged time, before being ushered into Barry's office by his Cambodian assistant. Before we even had time to be seated, we were met by a tirade of abuse from Barry.

"Who gave you permission to go into the new prison?"

I told him that the officer in charge had invited me in and had escorted our group around. I was immediately sorry I had told him this, as he vowed to take this man to task for allowing myself and the children inside. I explained my reason for the visit, but he was too angry to listen.

Ann and I put forward our suggestion for the visiting service to continue in the new prison. We were met with more aggression and the question: "Why do you think these people are in prison? They have committed crimes and must be punished."

He would not listen to us. We got the same angry reaction when we suggested the training courses, followed by an hour of lecturing and aggression. This was to be the start of a stormy relationship between Barry and myself. Sometimes friendly bantering but more often, abusive and threatening. It didn't deter me, but I realized that I would have to be more careful. Ann was due to go home to Australia so I would soon be on my own to fight these battles with Barry.

By now, the prisoners had all been transferred to the new prison but I was banned from visiting. I enquired as to the whereabouts of the musical instruments but found that they had been taken from them. Enquiries as to their present location were fobbed off with, "I don't know" from all concerned, so I guessed they had been sold by prison staff.

Not to be deterred by the visit ban, I waited until Barry had gone away for a week, then made my way to the prison. I was escorted through a number of locked doors, then into the section where long-term prisoners were held - a second Alcatraz! It was built along Western prison lines, with a long corridor up the middle where prison officers patrolled, two-man cells each side, with bars from roof to floor in front of each cell.

When I arrived, all the prisoners rushed to the bars to greet me, so pleased to see a familiar face. I had brought Chenda with me, so was able to communicate freely. I was shocked at the appearance of the men I knew, all so much thinner now. They told me they hardly received any food and were always hungry. It was now very hot and they had no water in their cells. This was only brought in once a day and amounted to a cupful each. I went straight to the prison director to complain. He told me that they received enough rice but would see that they got more water.

Barry returned in a few days and I went to tell him of the situation with the prisoners. He was very angry with me for going in to the prison, but he did show concern over the food and water problem. A check on this, showed that the prison director and staff were stealing the prisoners' food. He was to sack this director later, for more dishonesty. The outcome of this was that I was banned from visiting the prison for all time! I would come back in, but that is another story.

I thoroughly enjoyed my sessions with my group of street children and they obviously did so too. I took them on a variety of excursions right up until repatriation commenced. When the time came for them to return, the UN placed children from the centre with family members, if they had any, or with other families, who offered to take them.

The family was given $25 (the standard fee given by the UN for each child) and a year's food ration. In return, the family agreed to give a home to the child when they returned to Cambodia. Sadly, in many cases, this was not to be. On return, many of these children were abandoned. When I went to Cambodia later, I met many of these children in Phnom Penh and Battambang, back on the streets or in street children centres. It was sad to see this, after all the promise shown by them at Sr Ath's Centre in Site 2.

Phoeuy had married his long-time girlfriend, Phally, while I was away in Australia and he was anxiously waiting to tell me the good news when I returned. He was very family conscious and often talked to me about his family in Cambodia and the village of Prey, where he was born. He had not been back there since his father had died, and was preparing to go again within a week. He had heard that his younger sister, Soki, was very sick, so he planned to take medicine for her that could not be bought in Cambodia. I told him that I would love to see his village, about which I had heard so much, and hoped to get there some day.

Phoeuy looked at me to see if I really meant it, saying, "Would you really like to go into Cambodia?" I reiterated that I would, maybe one day when peace came.

Next day, when I came to visit, he told me he had been talking to some guides, who took people over the border and they had offered to take me in with him, if I was prepared to pay an agreed price. I was taken by surprise and took some minutes to think about it. I knew this would be highly illegal, maybe dangerous, but it would be great to see village life in Cambodia and meet other members of Phoeuy's family. I agreed to meet with the guides next day and find out more details.

After discussing the trip with the two guides, I decided I would take the chance and the great opportunity to see what was happening on the other side of the border. We would go on motorbikes through the forest, traverse a number of Thai army checkpoints, cross the border, passing through Cambodian checkpoints, then on to the large village of Thmar Pouk. This would be the easier part of the journey, as the road from there to Prey was very dangerous, with many Khmer Rouge bases and regular fighting. We would not know until we arrived in Thmar Pouk if it was possible to continue on. They told me that I would have to go in disguise, as foreigners were forbidden to enter Cambodia.

I arrived in camp early on the appointed day and made my way to Phoeuy's house. I had told only Liz where I was going that day, as I did not want the word to circulate. Phoeuy and his wife dressed me as a KPNLF soldier, with a camouflage jacket, dark glasses and a krama over my head to cover my hair and nose, as they said foreigners can always be identified by their 'long' noses.

The plan would be for one motorbike with Phoeuy on the back, to go through the checkpoint first and pay to the soldiers on guard duty, the required bribe for four people. The second motorbike, with me on the back, would stay behind, driving slowly, then gather speed to follow the other after payment was made. I was to turn my head away as we passed through the checkpoint, to avoid detection. However, before this could be achieved, Phoeuy and I must make our way from the camp, through the forest, to be picked up by our guides further on.

We left on foot from the back of the camp, going through the tank ditch and along forest tracks. We had not gone far when we came on an illegal DPPU checkpoint, where soldiers were demanding money from all commuters. These were camp people, who daily risked a foray into the forest to collect wood, bamboo shoots or thatch, which they could sell for a few baht to supplement their living. Thai soldiers were really bleeding the very poor, leaving them with no alternative but to pay. People were too afraid to refuse, as they could be arrested, turned back or even shot, if they did not come up with the required fee.

As we approached, I could tell that Phoeuy was quite nervous at the prospect of an encounter with the DPPU soldiers, so we changed to another track about twenty metres away, hurrying as we approached the closest point. Luckily for us, a big group of people from Cambodia came through about the same time, engaging the soldier's attention long enough for us to slip past and avoid apprehension. I breathed a sigh of relief at this close shave, as it could have been the end of the trip before it started, if I had been discovered at this point. We walked on another kilometre before arriving at the arranged meeting place, where we sat down out of sight of the path, to wait for our guides.

A Wild Ride

After a half-hour wait, our transport arrived and we climbed aboard for our adventure into Cambodia. It was not the most comfortable journey through the forest, sitting on the hard pillion seat, as we dodged in and out between the bushes, over clay tracks full of potholes, down creek beds and through loose sand, sometimes having to get off and push where the sand was too deep. We passed many people on foot or riding bicycles over the tracks, heading in both directions. My driver spoke no English, so I could not ask where we were, and I was too busy hanging on precariously, anyway. We successfully traversed eight checkpoints, sticking to our plan, thus avoiding detection.

We came to our first checkpoint inside Cambodia, after about one hour's riding. Soldiers in government caps, baggy fatigues and carrying AK47s, stood by the bamboo huts at the roadside. We followed the same format as at other army bases, making it through another three Cambodian guardposts without mishap. I couldn't believe that I, a foreigner, could get through without detection, into a country that I had heard was inaccessible.

Now we were over the worst part, I could look around. Ahead of us, I observed wide, flat countryside. It was the dry season, fields harvested, now faded and empty and with clumps of ragged palms, the only green in sight being the huge mango trees that seemed to be everywhere. These trees heavy with the season's crop of ripe fruit, made a great display in the otherwise colourless surroundings. We came to the first village, the dwellings built on stilts to avoid seasonal flooding, with thatch roofs and wooden sides. Farm animals sheltered under the building or in the shade of nearby trees. A few villagers braved the midday sun, but mostly it was a quiet scene, until we reached the market of Thmar Pouk. We came on this suddenly, turning a bend in the road, and there it was, all hustle and bustle. Rows of stalls took up both sides of the street, all trading briskly.

It was now lunchtime and we were hungry and thirsty, so we sat down at one of the open-air restaurants for our midday meal. It was very hot and flies were everywhere, sitting on our backs, sticking in our eyes and all over the food. Never mind, we were hungry and I had learnt by now not to worry about small inconveniences like that. The food was passable, though not as tasty as Thai food. I was to learn over the years that Khmer food was very bland, without the spices and tasty sauces that made Thai food so delicious.

Many people were coming to the table to talk to us. It was hard to believe that I was inside Cambodia, it seemed only such a short distance from the camp, and here I was, conversing with Cambodians, who were free. People here did not realize how lucky they were to have the freedom and independence not afforded the camp people. Though poor, they seemed happy and content with their lives. I had to pinch myself to make sure this was really me, here in the town of Thmar Pouk, a place I had heard so much about from my Cambodian friends.

Our guides left to enquire about the road to Prey, promising to return with news soon, as time was passing fast. Phoeuy and I took the opportunity to look through the markets. Everywhere we went, people would stop us, wanting to know where we came from. Now and then there would be squeals of delight, as someone recognized me from Site 2. An open army vehicle full of Khmer Rouge soldiers passed us, some no more than eleven or twelve years old, with guns bigger than themselves, others carrying loaded rocket launchers.

We paused to watch a lady spinning silk at the front of her shop, and a group of women stopped their gossiping to watch us pass. By the time our tour of the market was over and we returned to the restaurant, the guides were back. They had been advised not to take the road to Prey, they told us, as it was too dangerous. There had been fighting there the night before and Khmer Rouge troops were heading that way now. That was disappointing, especially to Phoeuy, who was anxious to get the medicine to his sick sister, but he had to accept their advice. The motorbike riders told us that they would return to pick us up in about two hour's time, so that would give us time to talk more with the people and do some sightseeing.

In the centre of the town, were the ruins of an old temple, surrounded by a moat. We climbed over piles of rubble to have a look. We could see that it had once been a huge building, now all that remained were parts of the outer walls and foundations. Pieces of ancient carved stone were lying all over the ground mostly covered by weeds. We were told that this temple was probably built around the 14th century. What sacrilege to see this once beautiful building in such a sad state, with no chance of reconstruction. Our next stop was at the pagoda on a hill overlooking the town. Monks in their bright saffron robes were walking the grounds between more ancient pieces of carved stonework, some using these sculptures as seats. They told us that their old temple had been shelled and they were now raising money to build a new one. One of the monks pointed to the broken sculptures and with a wave of the hand, told us that they had to clean up, get rid of this rubbish and build something new! They had no appreciation or comprehension of the value of these ancient treasures scattered around their feet. They fired questions at us about where we had come from, how we got here, also wanting to know all about Australia. One young monk asking, "Do you have monks dressed like us in your home town?" After chatting for awhile, we headed off, as it was getting near time to leave. I left a donation with the monks for their new pagoda, which they were happy to receive, begging me to come back to see their new building some day.

Before we had reached the market, our guides came looking for us, anxious to move on, not knowing what problems may arise along the way. We hopped back on the bikes and headed off. At the first checkpoint out of town, there was a long conversation between the front bike rider and soldiers on duty. I could see that the guide was quite concerned. My driver and I followed on, stopping further up the road to find out if there was a problem. Phoeuy told us that the soldier on duty had warned them that word had spread about a foreigner being aboard one of the motorbikes and there could be trouble along the way. The riders conferred and decided it would be best to take a different route back.

This new course would take us along a sealed road to the army base of Ban Trakeoun, from where we would branch off to take bush tracks through to the camp. It would be much longer and more dangerous, but with less chance of detection. We took off, passing through Ban Trakeoun without any problems, stopping about a kilometre the other side at a small clearing, just off the main road. As I prepared to alight, Phoeuy screamed for me to stop. There next to me, partly concealed by bushes and weeds was an anti-tank mine. I would have stepped right on it had I not been warned. I gingerly stepped off the other side of the bike, thanking Phoeuy for his timely warning. He pointed to another mine on the opposite side of the track. This close encounter made me realize just how dangerous it was out here.

We stopped at this spot for awhile, while our guides had a cigarette and conferred on what route to take next. After a ten-minute stop, a decision was reached and we took off, driving through narrow bush tracks, sandy patches and along a cleared area where KPNLF had felled trees, in preparation for the construction of a new road. After about an hour's riding, the bikes came to halt in the middle of a narrow track. I was thankful for this respite. By now, my back was aching and my bottom sore from sitting for hours on the saddle while being bounced around as we manoeuvred these trails, bumped over rocks, dodged trees and overhanging branches. We were in an area of low scrub on both sides of the track with signs of a recent bushfire. Phoeuy came over and pointed out about fifty small wooden boxes lying on the ground. Some of them were broken, lids and sides flung in all directions. He told me these were PMD-6 landmines, commonly known as box mines. These boxes have a hinged lid that overlaps the sides; pressure placed on this lid will trigger an explosive device capable of killing or severely injuring a person. It was a real eye-opener for me. Here was this minefield, only about a kilometre from the Thai border, through which so many people came to escape from Cambodia or returned to visit families in their country. The risks they took to get to and from the camp were unbelievable. It was a bit unnerving getting back on the motorbike and knowing we must continue through this minefield and maybe more, before Site 2 was reached. The motorbike riders assured me that we would be all right if we kept to the tracks, barely a metre wide. I hoped they were right.

Further on, there was a completely cleared area, not a tree in sight, only stumps left. Rounding a bend, we found ourselves smack in the middle of a KPNLF army camp. We took the soldiers by surprise and were lucky not to be shot when two of them raised their guns, but were stopped by a shout from the leading guide, who knew them. They had not heard our approach above the roar of their saws working. All around the camp were piles of logs stacked ready for transport. The soldiers told us that Thai traders came in after nightfall to buy and collect these trees; a highly illegal, though profitable operation. It was sad, though, to see Cambodian forest gradually being decimated for profit. We stayed while our guides had another cigarette, then took off for the last part of the journey.

We had not gone far, when my rider indicated to me that we had crossed over the border into Thailand. I was relieved when the track ended and we drove onto a smooth dirt road, making the ride a lot more comfortable. We were now travelling parallel to the border.

After riding a few kilometres along this road, a Thai soldier suddenly stepped out in front of the lead bike, signalling it to stop. My rider held back, but the soldier gestured for us to come forward. As we came abreast of him, I turned my head away but he came over and asked me to get off the motorbike. I could see his look of surprise when he realized that they had a foreigner aboard and I just hoped there would be no trouble. Our guides had a long conversation to him, alternately pointing to me and the motorbike. Evidently, they had satisfied him, as he came over and said, "How are you" in English. I spoke a few words back, which delighted him. He pointed to the only chair, saying, "Please sit down," then settled down to practice his English on me. He would have kept us there for hours, as he was enjoying this opportunity to improve his language skills, but the guides told him we must be on our way. I found later that the guide had told him my car had broken down further up the road and they had picked me up and were taking me to Site 2. I don't know how he accounted for the army camouflages I was wearing.

We had to leave the road further along and take to the bush tracks, going around the back of the camp to avoid the legal entry. When only about 200 metres from Site 2, a DPPU soldier came out from the trees, stopping us and demanding that we pay him forty baht each. At first I refused, telling the soldier it was illegal, but changed my mind when he picked up his gun threateningly and asked me what I was doing there. We were both doing illegal things but he had the gun, so I handed over the 500-baht note; all the money I had. It seemed so ludicrous as I stood waiting for my change out there in the bush. Here was I, unauthorized to come in at this point, paying money for entry through an illegal checkpoint into Site 2. The soldier reluctantly handed over my change and we hopped back onto the motorbikes and headed for the camp.

As we drove in, I saw the look of elation and relief on the guides' faces. We had hardly stopped, when we were surrounded by people all smiling and patting us on our backs. It always amazed me how fast news spread in this camp. Everyone seemed to know we had been into Cambodia and were congratulating us on our efforts. They always loved to hear a story about Thai soldiers being deceived, as they had a real fear and hatred of them, and rightly so. The men brought out a bottle of beer and we all drank to our adventure and successful mission into Cambodia.

CHAPTER 10

It was August 1991, and the war was still raging over the border. Phoeuy came to see me at the office to tell me that his sister, Sophuat's eleven-year old son, Ly, had been injured by a rocket while tending cattle near their village in Cambodia. He was now in KID hospital, his mother with him. Phoeuy asked if I would go there to check on Ly's condition and report back to his father, who was anxiously waiting in Site 2, for news. I promised to go the following day.

On arrival at KID hospital, I found my way to the ward where the boy had been taken. As I came through the doorway, Sophuat ran to meet me, wrapping her arms around me, sobbing as she pointed to her little son. Between her sobs, she told me that the doctors had been forced to amputate Ly's left arm as it was damaged so badly. He was covered in bandages, and lying on a hard wooden bed, suffering serious injuries to his shoulder, throat, ear, chest, fingers and legs; obviously in a lot of pain, though not uttering a sound. Other beds in this ward held men, women and children, all suffering terrible injuries as the result of landmines, hand grenades, rockets and shells. It was a sad sight. I could not help but think how beneficial it would be, if the manufacturers of these formidable devices could be brought to a place like this to see the frightful suffering they caused. Surely, then, they would think twice before continuing with the production of these deadly weapons

Sophuat told me that Ly and his younger brother were out in the fields tending the family's cattle, when a rocket exploded next to them. Ly received the full blast; the younger child escaped injury altogether. His young brother ran home to get help. The badly injured child was bleeding profusely from his multiple wounds by the time his mother and father found him. They summoned a motorbike taxi and with Ly in her arms, Sophuat made the three-hour journey on the back of the motorbike to the border, from where they were transported by ambulance to KID hospital.

Now it would be my unenviable task to tell Ly's father about the loss of his son's arm. I made my way back to the new arrival area in Site 2, to locate Ly's family, who had arrived the night before. I found his father, breaking the news that Ly was alive and recovering, but that doctors could not save his arm. His expression went from joy to despair, bursting into tears when he heard news of the amputation. To lose a limb is a terrible disadvantage for a Cambodian, as people who are not 'whole', are scorned in their society, finding it almost impossible to secure employment or find a wife or husband. Nothing would console the father after hearing this sad news, so I promised to return the following day after I had visited his son in KID again.

Ly was to stay in hospital for weeks, where he received skin grafts on his neck, finger and arm stump, before being sent to rejoin his family, now living permanently in Site 2. Phoeuy's sister, Soki, who had lost a one-year-old daughter in the shelling, had also moved with her family to Site 2, all now living in the new arrival quarters. Once on the way to recovery, Ly was enrolled at the camp primary school. He was thrilled to be attending classes for the first time in his life, proudly showing me his schoolwork each time I visited. Back home in his village, where people were very poor, children were put to work in the fields and never given the opportunity of an education, so this was a great bonus for Ly and his two younger brothers and they were making the most of it.

A Forced Marriage and an Exorcism

A very agitated Phoeuy was waiting for me in COERR office, when I returned after spending three days in Bangkok. He had been away working in another camp, only to find on his return that his younger siblings, Khun and Khin were missing from his house. Neighbours told him that three women had come two days earlier and taken them away, saying they had been sold to a soldier.

A KPNLF soldier, Sathya, had approached Sopheap a few weeks before, for permission to marry Khun. His request was refused, as Sopheap knew he had a criminal record and was very violent. Sathya, angry about this refusal, returned with a gun, with which he threatened Sopheap. After consultation with Khun, who was adamant she did not want to marry this man, the request was again refused. Khun then moved to live with Phoeuy, where she felt safer. Now, Phoeuy was certain that this was the person who had taken his sister and brother. If it was Sathya who had abducted them, Phouey was certain he would take them to the army camp of Ban Trakeoun, where he was stationed, about twenty kilometres from the camp. He begged for my help in finding them. I called Joe Hegenuar on the radio, requesting help in locating the whereabouts of the missing two. He met, with Phoeuy, who told him of his suspicions regarding Sathya, and their possible abduction by him. Joe rounded up some photos of Khun and Khin and sent them to Ban Trakeoun, with a request for authorities to trace the missing two.

By this time Phoeuy, Sopheap and family were frantic with worry. No news had come through by late afternoon when I left the camp.

Phoeuy was waiting at the office when I arrived next morning, still with no news as to their whereabouts. We headed for the UN building, where Joe radioed through to the military camp. After a number of calls, the news came through that Khun and Khin had been located in Ban Trakoeun. Phoeuy's worst fears being realized, when he found that they were with Sathya. After consultation with military authorities, an order was lodged for their immediate return to Site 2.

Next morning I was greeted by Sopheap with the news that Khun, accompanied by Sathya, had returned the night before. He then informed me that they would be married that day. I couldn't believe my ears! How could this happen? He could see my dismay, as he went on to tell me why the family had approved the marriage.

Khmer custom decrees that if a girl spends the night with a man, even if it's against her will, she must marry him, as her chances of marriage after that are very slim. I told Sopheap that I would like to talk to Khun, to establish if she agreed with this plan or if she was being pressured into the marriage. I then informed Joe of the latest development. He agreed to come with me to talk to Khun and Sathya. At the house, Khun emerged looking very unhappy, so I invited her to come for a drive to see if we could sort something out. I had brought along a female interpreter, while Joe stayed to discuss matters with the family and Sathya.

I drove up to the reservoir where it was quiet and peaceful at this time of the day, stopping in a deserted part where we could talk. I asked Khun if she really wanted to go into this marriage or did she feel obliged to go through with it. She told me that she was not being forced but that she had agreed to marry Sathya. When I asked if she was happy about it, she burst into tears, telling me she was not but was frightened for the safety of her family, if she refused. I stressed the fact that she did not have to go ahead with the marriage, that UNBRO could offer protection to her and the family if she decided against it. However, she had resigned herself to this course, saying it was Khmer custom and she must abide by it. I could see that there was no point in pursuing the matter further, as she had made up her mind. We returned to the house where Joe was consulting with the family, but with the same result. It had been decided by all concerned the marriage would take place at three that afternoon.

I asked Sopheap about the wedding plans. He told me they had made arrangements for a celebrant to conduct the ceremony, but because they had no money, there would be no further celebration. Cambodian weddings are usually big affairs, the bride outfitted in an elaborate costume, with bridesmaids, intricate hairdos and loads of jewellery and a big feast to follow. There was to be none of this for Khun. She looked very miserable. I really felt sorry for her, so I decided to do my best to add some joy to her wedding day.

Phoeuy and I headed for the market, where we bought fruit, rice, meat, vegetables, cakes and drinks for members of her family, who would be the only guests present. This was delivered to the house, where the ladies busied themselves preparing dishes for the reception. Next, I arranged for the fine arts band to be present to brighten up the proceedings with some music, after which, we bought streamers and flowers to decorate the room. At least, it would look a little like a wedding celebration now.

Just before two o'clock, as Phoeuy and I headed for Sathya's house for the ceremony, we were met on the road by the bride and groom-to-be and family members. We stopped to find out why they were headed in the opposite direction. We were told Sopheap's fifteen-month-old daughter was having fits, saying they were brought on by bad feelings about the wedding, causing spirits to move into her body. They were taking the bridal couple back to Sopheap's house to appease the spirits!

They still had quite a distance to go, so I offered them a lift and they all clambered in. No sooner were we underway, than the car horn started blaring. I tried everything to stop it, but to no avail, I just had to keep driving with the loud horn blasting continuously. I could not help but think how ludicrous the situation was. Here I was, driving through the camp with a car full of people, including the prospective bride and groom, horn blaring, en route to an exorcism ceremony to cast out bad spirits. As we drove along, people were stopping in their tracks to see what all the noise was about. By now, I had resigned myself to the fact that it was impossible to silence the horn, saying to Phoeuy: "It looks like the spirits have got into the car too!" He enjoyed the joke and all the attention we were arousing along the way.

We finally reached Sopheap's house, where I dropped the family off and continued on, with the horn still blaring, to the COERR Technical School. As I drove into the courtyard, all staff and students came running out of the buildings to see what was going on; all expecting something drastic had happened. Luckily for me, our Burmese engineer, Kusoe, was there. He opened the bonnet and within minutes had disconnected the wires and stopped the racket.

The exorcism ceremony was underway when I arrived back at the house. I was greeted by the sight of family members holding candles and chanting, all gathered around the child, lying on the floor. I could see that she had a very high fever and I realized that the 'fit' she suffered was more than likely convulsions, caused by the fever. I advised them to get her straight into a cold bath to reduce the temperature.

They just looked at me, shaking their heads and saying, "This is a Khmer thing, you are a foreigner, you not understand." In other words, let us do it our way, which they did, anyway!

Surprisingly, she did recover quite quickly, even accompanying her parents to the marriage service, prompting me to think that maybe there was something in their 'pagan' ceremonies.

We headed back to Phoeuy's house, where the wedding ceremony was to be performed. Khun had no elaborate wedding outfit, just a white blouse and coloured sarong. She was looking very sad. I took her aside and asked again if she was quite sure she still wanted to proceed with the marriage. She replied that she would go ahead with it.

Khun insisted that I sit next to her during the ceremony, which was conducted by an old man from the temple. It was a simple service lasting only one hour, unlike most Cambodian weddings that go over two days. The couple sat on a mat on the floor, one each side of the celebrant, Khun holding tightly to my hand while the service was performed. When it was over, family members sprayed perfume over the couple to keep away bad spirits, fine cords were tied around their wrists as a blessing from the family, for a long and happy marriage, and many children. Still Khun had not smiled.

With the band playing in the background, the ladies busied themselves bringing out the food, placing the plates on the mat, while family members set themselves down to join in the wedding 'feast' - soup, chicken, beef and vegetable dishes with rice, followed by cakes, fresh fruit and soft drinks. I could not join them for the meal, for it was time for me to leave the camp.

Over the next week, I visited Khun every day to see how she was coping, finding her very unhappy but determined to make the best of it. Not long after, she moved to live in Ban Trakeoun military camp with Sathya and I lost touch with her and so did her family.

Each morning on arrival in camp, I would make my way, together with David, Leanne and Stephen, to a restaurant near our office for coffee. Stephen, a coffee addict, who considered himself somewhat of a connoisseur, rated Cambodian coffee as the best he had tasted. Coffee grains were spooned into a cloth container suspended from a wire hoop. It was then placed on the cup and hot water poured over. Spoonfuls of condensed milk were then added, finishing off with loads of sugar, unless we stopped them first. Their coffee was very bitter and made very strong, too strong for me, so I always needed a supply of hot water to weaken it. The staff soon came to learn each person's tastes, serving their coffee accordingly. Crusty bread rolls, made in the Vietnamese camp nearby, were brought in on request. This small respite was always enjoyed before we started work for the day.

Phoeuy's wife had now given birth to a little girl. With this added responsibility, Phoeuy decided he would have to find some work that would pay. He made the decision to become a guide, taking people from the camp to villages inside Cambodia and bringing others back. Attired in soldier's clothes for protection, he would guide the groups along these dangerous paths for a small fee.

He was returning along a track through the forest on one mission, bringing a group of people to the camp, when they were fired on by KPNLF soldiers. They all ran as the bullets whizzed around them, one bullet going right through Phoeuy's shirt missing his body by inches. An older man, travelling with his thirteen-year-old daughter was hit and wounded. The little girl begged Phoeuy to help. He picked up the injured man, carrying him in his arms the three kilometres back to Site 2. By the time he reached the hospital, the man was already dead, his little daughter overcome with grief.

On another of these journeys, KPNLF soldiers had captured a group of around twenty Vietnamese men, women and children, heading for the camp. The soldiers demanded money, becoming very angry when told they had none. The people begged to be allowed to proceed to the camp, from where they promised to send a request for money, to relatives in the USA. They refused; instead, sending two of their own soldiers into the camp. They approached a Khmer-speaking French priest, asking for a large amount of money for the release of these prisoners. The priest told them that he did not have that much money. When they realized their efforts had failed, the soldiers returned to where the Vietnamese people were being held captive in the forest, lined them up and cut their throats.

Phoeuy witnessed this from behind bushes, where he had taken refuge when he heard the commotion. I asked him why he did not report these killings when he returned to the camp.

He answered, "I was too frightened. It is safer to say nothing, or they would come and get me too."

Many terrible things were happening at this time. Witnessing this massacre was enough for Phoeuy, this work had now become too dangerous and he decided to look for safer employment.

He applied for a job as a bodyguard for Son Sann, the leader of the KPNLF, and was accepted to take part in the training, undergoing rigorous drilling for this job over the next few months. He was bitterly disappointed when omitted from the final selection, as this would have given him a full-time job on his return to Cambodia. He would just have to look for something else.

Quest for a Magic Rock

I had just arrived back in camp after being home in Australia for a month and as usual, one of my first undertakings on return was to visit Phoeuy and his family. I made my way to his house only to find it deserted. Neighbours told me that Phoeuy had gone away and Phally had taken the baby, returning to live with her parents. This did not sound right to me. I went on to see Phoeuy's friend, Rith, who said that Phoeuy had a problem and was on the run inside Cambodia. My first thoughts were, 'What's new! Here we go again!'

I asked about the problem and was told that a handicapped guy, Sath, had asked Phoeuy to go into Cambodia to do some business for him. I knew Sath and did not trust him. A very powerful military man, he always carried a gun in the camp, making everyone fearful of him. The mission on which he had sent Phoeuy, was to locate a 'magic' rock.

Cambodians are very superstitious people and really believe there are these special rocks, which hold extraordinary powers. Their belief is that these precious rocks have the ability to stop electricity, bring wealth, everlasting good health, allow people to fly, in addition to possessing many other amazing powers. Because of these so-called powers they are exceptionally expensive and much sought after. Phoeuy had agreed to make the dangerous journey into Cambodia to locate one of these rocks for Sath, who had promised him a 500 baht, a lot of money for camp people, if he could find one of these items and bring it back to the camp.

Later I heard the following story:

Phoeuy set off across the border into Cambodia on his hunt for one of these rare specimens. After making many enquiries, he heard that one could be found in a small village about thirty kilometres inside the border, so he headed there to check it out. He was taken by villagers to meet the owner of this rock. The man told him that he did have a magic rock, proceeding to give him a detailed description, but telling Phoeuy that it was unavailable for viewing. However, if he did want to purchase it, he could return with the asking fee of US$10,000, after which, he could examine the goods before making the final decision.

From the description given, it certainly sounded like the real thing to Phoeuy, so he hastened back to report his find. Sath was really pleased that one of these prized stones had been found so easily, as they were reportedly so rare. He was quite impressed after hearing a description of the find, sure that this was the magic rock he wanted. He told Phoeuy that the rock was being purchased for some Cambodians in the USA and he would have to consult with them before the decision was made to buy.

Sath contacted Phoeuy two weeks later asking him to go ahead, check out the rock and if it was the genuine thing, to purchase it on his behalf. He handed over a bundle containing $10,000 in US currency. Phoeuy gingerly accepted this package, never having handled more than a few dollars before, he was overwhelmed with the responsibility placed on his shoulders. He wrapped the money in bundles, distributing them through his backpack, in pockets, money belt and even some in his shoes, lest he be apprehended along the way.

Not long after he left, he became suspicious about this money, as it was all in new $100 notes, so he decided to test them out. He presented a note to a moneychanger in the nearest market, asking for it to be converted into baht. The man was very wary when he saw this large note being tendered by a Cambodian, holding it up to the light and checking it thoroughly before handing it back. He then shook his head, refusing to have anything to do with it, saying it was counterfeit money. This placed Phoeuy in a difficult position; What would he do now? Should he go ahead with the purchase with the fake money or return to Site 2 without the magic rock? He thought about it awhile, but the lure of the promised fee was too strong and he decided to go ahead with the mission.

His first task when arriving at the village later that day, was to request an inspection of the magic rock before his decision was made. He was told the rock was held at another place where he would meet the people who would allow him to view the rare item, but not until the next day.

Next morning, he was approached by two armed men, who took him to where a group of people were waiting in the forest. By now he was quite frightened. One of the men was holding a package wrapped in a krama, which he unwound; inside was a plastic bag, which he also removed, revealing a stone about the size of a small orange. There was nothing to distinguish this rock from any others in the area, but for a slight bluish tinge. Cambodian belief was that if the rock was 'magic', it would drip water and that it would stay wet. Phoeuy took the rock from the seller and held it in his hand. He could see that it was wet, small drops of water falling from it onto the ground.

After turning it over in his hand a few times and examining the rock all over, he decided that it looked like the real thing to him. The agreement was made for the purchase of this item for the asking fee of $10,000. Phoeuy, very nervous by this time, handed over the bundle of money, breaking into a cold sweat as the man counted the notes. The man flipped through them once, then again, to make sure they were all there, but not examining the notes closely, much to Phoeuy's relief. After reassuring himself that the count was correct, the man accepted the money, causing Phoeuy to relax a little before the magic rock was handed over to complete the transaction.

Phoeuy placed the rock in the plastic bag, wrapped it in a krama, then put it carefully into his backpack before setting off. He knew he would have to move fast, putting as much distance as possible between himself and the sellers before they found they had been duped and came looking for him. He kept off the main tracks, taking little known paths that would eventually lead him to the border.

During the journey he constantly checked the precious rock to see if it remained wet. Each time he looked, he was relieved to find it still damp - it certainly was the real thing. He was really pleased to arrive in the camp without mishap, late in the afternoon.

He went straight to Sath's house, proudly handing over the package. Sath's face broke into a smile as he opened the parcel, revealing the much sought after magic stone, really happy to have this priceless piece in his possession. He took it out of the wrapping, turned it over in his hands, looked at it carefully, then his face darkened.

"This stone is dry, it not the real one," he roared.

Phoeuy quickly retorted, "It must be, it was wet when I checked it this morning."

By now, Sath was in a violent rage. He shouted, "You keep the real one for yourself. I want my money back, now."

Phoeuy tried to convince him that he had not kept the magic stone, but to no avail. Sath was enraged. Phoeuy had another look at the stone, realizing that he had also been deceived, as it was bone-dry. Sath pulled out his gun and held it to Phoeuy's head

"Don't kill me! I will get your money back," Phoeuy cried out.

By now Phoeuy was very frightened, telling Sath that he would raise the money and bring it to him.

That night he fled into Cambodia, knowing full well that he could never raise that amount of money. When Sath realized that Phoeuy was gone, giving him no chance of retrieving his money, he was very angry, spreading the word around the camp that he would kill him.

After hearing this story, I went to visit Phally at her parent's house.

She was very frightened that Sath would come for her and the family. I decided to go over and talk to him myself. I had known Sath since I first came to Site 2 and he was always very friendly towards me. When I came to his house, he came out with a big smile, greeting me like a long-lost friend, that was, until I stated my reason for coming. He flew into a rage when I mentioned Phoeuy's name. I tried to reason with him, saying that Phoeuy had gone to get the rock in all good faith, and it was not his fault that he had been deceived into believing the rock was magic.

I felt so stupid talking about this 'magic' rock and was glad none of my friends could see me or hear this conversation. They would all think that I had finally gone 'troppo' after being in the heat too long!

Sath was very angry, and nothing I said would calm him. He said that he had to answer to the Cambodians in America, who had sent the money to buy the magic rock and who were now demanding the return of their money. Already, he told me, his prized motorbike had been taken. I finally took my leave, having achieved nothing.

About a month later, I paid a visit to Sopheap's house and was amazed to see Phoeuy there. I couldn't believe that he had come back to Site 2, after the trouble he was in.

I said, "Don't you know that your life is in danger."

He scoffed at that, saying, "He can't do anything to me. I am not frightened of him."

I warned him to be very careful, as Sath had many contacts who would report his presence in the camp. He just laughed.

Over the next few weeks, I did not see Phoeuy though I tried to contact him, it seemed like he had the sense to lie low for awhile. Even his wife was unaware of his whereabouts.

I arrived in the office a short time later, to find a young man waiting to see me. He told me that he worked at the prison and had been asked to give a letter to 'Mother Margot'. He handed over a folded piece of paper, which I opened straight away. It was a letter from Phoeuy. On reading it, I was dismayed to learn he had been arrested and was now in Dong Rek prison, and was asking for me to come there. I went straight over.

The policeman on duty was one of the young men I knew from the boarding school, and he allowed me in to see Phoeuy, although it was not visiting time. He directed me to a bamboo building in the compound. I waited while the padlock was unfastened before stepping through a low doorway into the prison cell. When my eyes adjusted to the dark interior, I saw that the hunched over figure sitting on the dirt floor, was a sad and dejected Phoeuy. He told me that he was walking up the street near his house the day before, when three policemen arrested him, the charge being the theft of US$10,000. He was very frightened, as he knew that Sath had many contacts in the justice system.

His wife did not know he had been arrested, so Phoeuy wrote her a note asking me to deliver it. After spending twenty minutes with him, trying to lift his spirits but to no avail, I left, promising to do my best to help. I made my way to their house. Phally came running out when she saw me, happy that I had come for a visit. I made an attempt to tell her the news in my struggling Khmer, but she did not understand, laughing at my attempts, until I handed her the letter. She read it, then burst into tears, sobbing uncontrollably. Her sister, who was with her, read the note and joined in, too. I tried to console them but it was impossible.

When Phally finally regained control, she gathered together a hammock and mosquito net, as well as some food, and we made our way back to the prison. Seeing Phoeuy there in the cell brought on more tears, both of them pleading for my help to gain his release. I promised to do my best, but had to admit to them that it would be very difficult, now that it was in the hands of the police.

After leaving the prison, I made my way to Sath's house, appealing to him to drop the charges. He was adamant that Phoeuy had stolen the money and would have to suffer the consequences. No way would he consider dropping charges.

Next, I headed for Sopheap's house to tell him the bad news. He was very upset to hear about his brother's arrest, also appealing for my help. I went to see the head of the police to request assistance, only to be told that the matter was now out of his hands, as a charge of fraud had already been laid. The worst news was that Phoeuy had been transferred to the new prison that morning. I knew that it would be a lot more difficult to get him out of there. I headed there to see if I could contact him. I was still under orders from Barry not to enter the prison, but I decided to give it a go anyway, as I wanted to see my friend. The guards were happy to allow my visit, obviously unaware of the ban, but I was told I would have to sign the visiting book I scrawled an unrecognizable signature, all the time hoping Barry would not check it, then I was led inside.

Phoeuy, with eighteen other prisoners, was in a big holding cell, at the end of the hallway that the other cells faced. He told me he was very worried about his situation, asking me to talk to Ken, who worked with the justice committees and police, to see if there was anything he could do. I promised to do that. Many prisoners, who knew me, were calling out, happy to see me. They came up to the bars to tell me this was worse than the old prison, now visiting hours had been cut, and they were always hungry.

One of the wives had complained to the human rights group about the limited rations they were receiving. This made the prison authorities very angry, and they immediately put a ban on families bringing in extra food. That night, I appealed to Ken for help regarding Phoeuy's dilemma. He promised to speak to the justice people, with the possibility that he may secure Phoeuy's acquittal through lack of evidence, but of course, this would take time. I also spoke to Joe, in UNBRO protection, who could not get him out, but promised to assist with early repatriation for Phoeuy and family, for safety reasons, if he was freed.

Visiting for prisoners' families was every second Friday, so I would wait out the front with other visitors, a bag of food in my hand, until it was my turn to go in.

Once inside, the prisoner was called and I would take my place, sitting on the cement floor for the ten-minute visit. After a few weeks inside the prison, Phoeuy was looking thin and his skin had taken on a pasty hue. He was very depressed and he looked terrible.

Two months had gone by and we seemed no closer to securing his release, when I received this letter, which Phoeuy had smuggled out:

Dear Mother,

How are you and for me is not good. My feeling is not good, feeling badly. Mother I tell you once more if I have no money, 5,000 baht I cannot get out from the prison. You cannot help and take me out of the prison with no money. Mother I don't beg you. This is I borrow you. I will pay you back when I go to Cambodia. If Mr Huk (Head of the justice committee and a good friend of Sath) comes back from Phnom Penh I cannot come out of the prison. You and Ken cannot help me because this is the role of Khmer court. You know they went to my house and beg my wife money. Mother I say and honest to you I cannot get out and I cannot stay in prison. I will kill myself in prison. If I was die please you take care my wife and my daughter for me. My wife she cry every day she very sad. I speak true and don't lie you. "We can find for that money but we cannot find the life". If you help me please you give to my wife in this week. If next week Mr Huk will come back to Site two.

Sincerely yours,

Phoeuy

I was really worried after I read this letter, but what could I do?

The so-called 'justice' committee would secure Phoeuy's release for a price. So much for all the training about honesty and justice they had received in the IPA - they would still do what they wanted, if it meant a monetary reward. This was justice in Site 2!

I decided that I would have to get my friend out of the prison before he killed himself, so I went to see my friend Vuth. I asked him if he could go quietly to speak to a justice committee member to find out what could be done, without divulging that a foreigner was involved. Vuth and Phally made an appointment to meet with this committee a few days later. They were told that Phoeuy's release would be approved by the committee, for the price of 5,000 baht. It looked like I would have to participate in this corruption if there was any chance of Phoeuy's release before Sath's influential friend, Mr Huk returned.

I set about raising the money. Tim and Ken both came forward with donations and I soon had the money together. Vuth arranged to meet with the committee to pay the bribe and organize Phoeuy's release. At this meeting, the money was handed over, with the promise that his release would take place over the next day or so.

The next day, Sunday, I made my way into the camp to see what was happening. I went straight over to Phally's house and was surprised to find Phoeuy already there; he'd been released at nine o'clock that morning. His face was beaming, as he threw himself into my arms, thanking me for my help, repeating over and over how happy he was to be free.

A conference took place with Phoeuy, myself, and family members, to discuss further plans. The outcome being that it would be best for him to leave the camp immediately. It would be too dangerous for him to stay in Site 2, knowing Sath would be furious when he heard about Phoeuy's release. I decided to spirit him out of the camp in my car. Being a Sunday and a holiday, the guards were usually more relaxed, but it could still be a risky exercise; although, I was becoming quite experienced in this field! Phoeuy packed his bag and said his goodbyes to Phally and other family members, who all gathered at the front of their hut waving, as we headed for the gate and hopefully Tapraya.

We stopped at the checkpoint at the main gate, for me to sign out. One of the soldiers came over and looked in, saying to Phoeuy in Thai, "Who do you work for?"

I sat, fearful that he would be discovered. Phoeuy kept his cool, answering, "I work for COERR."

The soldier looked searchingly at Phoeuy before stepping back and waving us on. We took off with sighs of relief. It did not bear thinking about the consequences if I had been caught taking an escaped prisoner out of the camp.

We still had to get through two more checkpoints but luckily there were no problems, though it was a huge relief when we finally arrived in Tapraya. Ken got quite a shock when I turned up with Phoeuy in tow, agreeing to allow him to stay in our house until I could get him to the border.

That night, Phoeuy told us of many terrible things happening in the prison; beatings, attempted suicides, lack of food and the crooked justice committee. He told me that almost every week, someone attempted suicide by hanging. All the prisoners would bang their hands against the bars and yell, until the prison officers came and cut the prisoner down.

Barry would come through with the prison chief on regular tours of inspection. He did not speak Khmer, so the prison chief would translate. One prisoner called, "Mr Barry, please tell me why they keep me here like this; I have done nothing."

Another man shouted, "Mr Barry we not getting enough rice, we are always hungry. Can you help us?"

The translation came back to Barry quite differently, the chief saying, "Don't listen to these men, they are crazy."

Phoeuy, the only English speaking prisoner, was afraid to intervene because of repercussions. Barry continued on his rounds quite satisfied that all was well.

Phoeuy stayed in my house while I went into the camp next morning. My first job there was to let Vuth know that all was well and I had Phoeuy in Tapraya. The problem would be how to get him into Cambodia, where he would be safe from Sath.

There was a degree of unrest in the camp at this time, with crowds of people milling outside the UNBRO offices demanding more money from UN, on repatriation. From the UN offices a crowd of agitators proceeded on to the repatriation staging area, gathering more people along the way, numbering thousands by the time they reached there. Rumours had been circulating that Vietnamese returnees would receive more than Cambodians on repatriation. Reported comparisons of this monetary assistance were incorrect and despite repeated attempts, the demonstrators refused to have discussions with UN officials.

Demonstrators forced Joe and Vuth to the top of one of the water tankers, holding them hostage there for hours in the hot sun. Eventually they were freed and the crowd dispersed, but not before threatening more demonstrations the following day. True to their word, the protesters gathered outside the UN offices next morning. Cambodian camp leaders tried to calm them down, urging them to co-operate with UNHCR, but to no avail. The situation was turning nasty, so the UN closed the camp.

Now that COERR workers had been banned entry, Viseth stood guard over our office in the camp, staying close to the radio and relaying the latest developments to us in Tapraya. We heard that around 80,000 demonstrators had stormed the DPPU offices, beating up police and threatening to attack any Cambodians working for the foreigners. Viseth was becoming very frightened as the mob drew closer. Already they had stormed the prison, releasing all the inmates, prisoners only stopping long enough to beat up their guards before making their escape. Now the rioters were fanning out all over the camp, looting and destroying everything in their path. As Viseth radioed with this latest news to us in Tapraya, he could hear them coming up the road towards the office. He was told to leave immediately and make his way to the fence, from where an agency vehicle would pick him up, as his life could be in danger.

Water supplies to the camp were cut off when protesters stoned the water trucks, and food rations were also halted. There was speculation that the events were the result of the work of agitators from outside the camp, with a view to disrupting the UN repatriation plan, but this could not be substantiated.

The camp was closed to us for a week. When we were finally allowed back in, food and water rations had been restored, but it was a sorry sight that met our eyes. All public buildings, offices, warehouses and workshops had been damaged and looted. In COERR office, all furniture, typewriters, computers, generators and stores were gone. My cupboard, where I kept supplies of clothes, fine arts equipment, musical instruments and many other goods, was bare.

The demonstration and subsequent riots had achieved nothing, but the cost of the loss and damage was very high, affecting the poor of the camp most of all. It was a long time before there was a semblance of order again. Most stolen goods and equipment were never replaced, as repatriation was imminent and agencies could see no advantage in spending the thousands of dollars it would cost to restock.

Phoeuy was still at my house in Tapraya when the news came through that the prison had been stormed and all prisoners released. My first reaction when I heard the news was, 'Oh no! I have just paid a 5,000-baht bribe to the crooked justice committee for nothing!'

The camp was still closed to us next day, so this would be a good opportunity to assist Phoeuy's escape across the border into Cambodia. Liz agreed to come too, so the three of us set off for Aranyaprathet next morning. We headed to Khim Khim's for breakfast, Liz and I walking in first, with Phoeuy following close behind. The first person I saw was Barry, sitting at a table facing us as we entered. Hoping to distract his attention from Phoeuy, I asked about his recent car accident and as he put his head down to show me his scars, Phoeuy took off. Barry would have been livid if he had known I was harbouring one of his prisoners and right here under his nose!

After this fright, we were happy to leave the town and head for Poipet. The Khmer market is about two hundred metres inside the border, with Cambodian traders illegally making their way back and forth along small tracks through the forest, most of the day. This was the path we planned to take, as it would be impossible to attempt to make it through the official checkpoint. Landmines were a big problem here, as many were laid in the heavy undergrowth surrounding the tracks, but safe if you kept strictly to the paths. Rolls of razor wire were spread along the border on the Thai side, with soldiers on guard at various points. Traders using the paths had flattened the razor wire so they could cross, sneaking in and out when the soldiers were otherwise occupied.

Liz and I disguised ourselves as best we could, with kramas over our heads and straw hats on top of these, carrying packs like the traders. Phoeuy carted his backpack containing all his belongings.

It surprised us that there were no soldiers on guard when we reached the trader's path, but as it was still quite early, we guessed that we must have arrived before they went on duty. We climbed over the razor wire, made our way down the ditch and onto the track. We were congratulating ourselves on our success when we heard a voice behind shouting, and heavy footsteps running after us. We didn't look around, just kept walking fast. I slipped some money to Phoeuy and told him to leave us and he hurried off. I had hoped for a better farewell, as I realized that I may never see him again, but it was not to be. A voice behind was shouting for us to stop, but we pretended not to hear. An angry Thai soldier finally caught up with Liz and I, berating us in Thai. We pretended that we didn't understand.

He was shouting, "Foreigners have no right to cross the border without passes and don't think you can fool me by dressing as Khmer."

We just played dumb.

Three more soldiers came running up and the first guy sent them off after Phoeuy. He was now out of sight and we assumed he would be well on his way by now. However, that was not the case, as we were to hear later from Phoeuy. He told us that when he turned the corner he started to run. After awhile, when he thought he was safe he sat down to rest. That was when the Thai soldiers found him. They grabbed him by the shirt but he shrugged his way out of it, at the same time hurling his backpack at them, then ran for his life into the bush, discarding his thongs as he went. Cambodian people in the vicinity, screamed out for him to stop as there were landmines everywhere, but Phoeuy kept going, too afraid of being caught and ending up in prison again. He told us he ran for a long way but was not followed, as the soldiers were too afraid to venture in. He hid until dark, then found his way to the market, arriving in only a pair of jeans. People there were amazed to see him return unharmed, as the word had spread that he was last seen running into the minefield. They welcomed him back, giving him food, shelter and clothes. He stayed there for two nights not knowing what to do next as he had lost everything. His most distressing loss being his half-brother's address in Phnom Penh, as he had planned to find his way there to meet up with him.

While this was going on, Liz and I were still being harangued by the angry Thai soldier. After ten minutes of shouting, he let us go with a warning never to make this attempt again! I never did heed this warning, making this trip many more times.

It was not long before Barry heard about my payment of the bribe for Phoeuy's release. He was furious, so I made sure to keep out of his way. After the prison was stormed and all inmates were freed by the rioters, he calmed down, pacified by the fact that I had paid out a 5,000-baht bribe for nothing. We were on talking terms again!

A week later, on returning home from work, I opened the front door and there was Phoeuy waiting for me. I couldn't believe my eyes. I was angry that he had returned after all our efforts to get him back to Cambodia. It was then he told the story of his escape. He said he had returned, as he had lost everything and wanted to get a message to his wife to let her know what had happened; also he needed money to find his way to Phnom Penh. I told him he would have to make it back on his own this time, as I could not risk a border crossing again so soon.

He did make it back, where he waited in the Cambodian town of Battambang for his wife and daughter to return.

Remo approached me one day, with the news that he was going to join Seng in Bangkok. He had received a message from Seng who had a job working on the boats and was earning good money, prompting Remo to make this decision. Another good reason for his leaving was that he had been banned by the family from any contact with his girlfriend, with whom he was very much in love. A 'rich' man in the camp had been chosen for her and the wedding would take place very soon. Remo was brokenhearted and planned to leave the camp before the marriage took place. I could understand his reason, but this would be a risky venture. I reminded him it would be more difficult for him as an illegal in Thailand, as he did not speak the language like Seng, who was fluent. However, he was determined to go, and set about plans to leave.

Over the next few weeks, I heard nothing from either Remo or Seng, so could only hope that Remo had made it and was not in Suan Plu prison. I kept in regular contact with Seng's wife. On one of these visits, she came out excitedly waving a letter she had just received from her husband. I was pleased to learn that Remo was now with him and also had a job on the boats, giving his address in Klong Toey, the slum area of Bangkok. I was planning a trip to Bangkok, so promised Seng's wife I would make an attempt to locate them.

Not long after I arrived in Bangkok, I made my way to Klong Toey, a squalid, rat-infested slum close to the docks. Buildings of all descriptions, but mostly ramshackle huts made of abandoned pieces of wood and iron were built in every conceivable space. Plank walkways built on stilts separated the groups of buildings, while cats, dogs and rats scavenged through the piles of rubbish and food scraps thrown beneath. There was no privacy here, all houses opening onto busy thoroughfares.

I had the numbers of Seng's house and block but it was difficult to locate, for there seemed to be no order in the numbering. I made several enquiries but was met with blank stares; nobody wanted to talk, not trusting a foreigner. After wandering around for an hour, I finally stumbled on the address I had been given. The Thai lady, who appeared, admitted that she knew Seng but was very suspicious of me, questioning my reason for contacting him. After explaining to her that he was a friend of mine, and showing his wife's letter, she relented and led me to his quarters. She knocked on the door, which was opened a crack with an eye peering through, before it was flung open and Seng rushed out calling, "Mother Margot," and throwing himself into my arms, followed closely be Remo. Now satisfied, the landlady left us.

Seng invited me in, where I met his roommates, all of them Cambodians. There were two from Site B camp near Surin and two from Site 2. These six men lived in this tiny room about two metres square, big cracks between the floor boards, no furniture and for which they paid

$10 a week each; easy money for the Thai landlord. They told me they were working long hours in the freezer room on the boats, earning $100 a month. This was huge money for these men, who had never had a pay packet in their lives. However, they told me that they were in constant fear of discovery and subsequent arrest, as periodic raids by Thai police were held to seek out illegal immigrants.

I took Seng and Remo into the city, where they had their first look at a department store, staring wide-eyed at everything. They enjoyed looking around at the displays, having their first ride on an elevator and lunching in a cafeteria. They told me they planned to stay another few months, save some money, then head back to the camp. I left them a few hours later, taking with me letters they had written for friends and family back in Site 2 together with money for Seng's wife.

They both returned to the camp only a few weeks later, after Thai police had swooped on Klong Toey, arresting many illegals. Luckily, they had both been working night shift on the boats and received warning about the raid. They did not return to their lodgings, making their way straight to the border and back into Site 2 under cover of darkness.

Some of the poorest and most maligned people in the camp were the wives and families of prisoners. It was a tough life for these women, with no income and no man to protect them.

When I was running the prison visiting service, wives would often approach me asking for messages to be given to their husbands or for my help in some way. Now that I had been banned from entering the new prison, I decided to assist these women. I sent Chenda to the prison on visiting day, to ask the wives waiting outside, if they would come to a meeting I planned to hold the following day. I approached Kalyan, president of the Cambodian Women's Peace Group, to talk to these women about their rights and advise them of services available. She was only too happy to do this.

Ten women, all with small children, turned up the following day at the meeting place. I introduced Kalyan, saying we had invited them to a friendly meeting to find their major needs but mainly to let them know that someone cared about them. Kalyan then spoke, telling them that they should not feel inferior because their husbands were in prison, and now that they were the head of the household, they had to be strong. One young woman sat with tears with streaming down her face.

By the time we adjourned for tea and biscuits, she had stopped crying, telling us that she felt so much happier now and would tell other wives to come to the meeting the following week. Her views were echoed by the others, who told us that they had felt so isolated, especially with neighbours giving them a hard time because their husbands were imprisoned.

At the next meeting, more women turned up. Kalyan again spoke to them with words of encouragement, then, after a chat over tea and biscuits, they were treated to a video show held in a nearby classroom. By now, the women were starting to relax and enjoy themselves.

Word soon spread and before long more than thirty women were attending our weekly sessions. They were all very poor, with old ragged clothes and shoes, their self-esteem very low, as it had taken such a beating since their husbands had been behind bars. I realized that before we went much further, they would need to build up their self-worth.

A Japanese aid agency had just set up a school where women were taught hairdressing and cooking. I invited a friend, Marg Moon, who worked for this organization, to come along and explain to the group about the classes, with the suggestion that some of them may care to enrol for the next course.

Marg attended our next meeting, explaining about the courses and offering to take them around the centre, so they could observe at first hand the opportunities available. Having small children would be no deterrent they were told, as the centre provided a childminding service for students. They were all keen to go on this tour, but worried about their shabby appearance. I promised to find some appropriate clothes for them before the day.

The following week they all turned up, happily wearing their new blouses and sarongs I had acquired from the Family Service Centre. They were enthralled with everything as we went through the workshops, watching with interest as the students gave haircuts, shampoos, facials, manicures and pedicures. Then they sat in on a cooking class, where the students were busy cooking many enticing dishes, relishing the tasting session at the end.

An invitation issued by the teacher, for anyone interested in becoming models for the hairdressing students, was snapped up by most of the group, who happily volunteered to come back at a later date for this treat. This was a real bonus for these women, who would never have been able to indulge in this luxury. By the next meeting, three of the ladies had already taken advantage of this offer and were proudly sporting their new hairdos. This inspired the remaining ladies to book in for their hair treatment also. There is no doubt about it, women everywhere, like to look nice and a new hairdo can work wonders. This, together with their new clothes, caused a big boost in their self-esteem and already there was a marked improvement in the level of their confidence. As a result of the tour, ten of the women enrolled as students in the cooking classes, another five in the beauty course.

Meanwhile, regular meetings were being held, a different activity being introduced each week. They were a video show, afternoon tea in the restaurant, a trip to the reservoir and a drive around the camp, all new and interesting pursuits for them and they were delighted to join in these activities.

Now that repatriation was close, the women voiced concerns for their prisoner husbands. Their questions being: Where would the prisoners be taken to? When would they leave the camp? How will we find them? I was not sure what arrangements were in hand for this, so I invited Joe to talk to the group. Joe explained to them that prisoners would be among the last people to leave the camp, those with only a short time left to serve, being set free; long-serving inmates to be transferred to prisons inside Cambodia, where they would complete the remainder of their sentence. Families of prisoners could request permission from UNHCR to defer their repatriation, so they could leave at the same time. This set their minds at rest, as it had been a matter of great concern for the wives.

I could see what a difference the hairdos had made for the ladies, so I planned to take them on a day trip to Aranyaprathet. Marg promised to accompany us. It was still very difficult to be granted this permission from DPPU, but I was fortunate to be successful again. By now, I had learnt a few tricks about the approach to use when making an application and it usually worked. A bit of praise about the work they were doing helped a lot, as well as stating a good reason for the excursion. I always managed to come up with appropriate and, sometimes, unusual grounds for this.

The time of this outing coincided with the first day of the camp demonstrations and although there was quite some unrest, it was still possible to enter the camp. Police had to clear a passage through the crowd of demonstrators, as I came in to pick up the ladies. I had included Phoeuy's wife, Phally, as he was in my house in Tapraya at this time, having just left prison. I planned to drop Phally and the baby off in Tapraya, where they could spend the day together with Phoeuy, before he made his way back to Cambodia. The prisoner's wives had arranged baby sitters for the day, so it would be a girls' day out.

The women, all dressed in their best, were full of excitement when Marg and I arrived in the van to pick them up. There was much chatter as we drove along the road through villages, past KID and into Aranyaprathet. Our first stop here being the beauty parlour where they were treated to Thai-style hairdos. They emerged looking great, all thrilled with their new look. Next on the agenda was the ornate local pagoda, followed by a tour through the town, taking in the shops and markets. The women had no money to spend but this did not appear to worry them. All were chatting merrily and exclaiming at the sight of all the goods available, everything new and interesting for them, after being cut off from the outside world for years.

After an hour spent wandering through the shops and streets, we headed back to the van for the next part of the outing, which would be at the reservoir not far from Tapraya. Everyone was hot and sticky by the time we arrived at this waterhole, so it was straight into sarongs and into the cool clean water. They loved it, giggling and chattering as they splashed around, enjoying this new sense of freedom. Two of the ladies told me that this was their first swim ever.

When they had refreshed themselves, we sat down to a picnic lunch beside the water, the women then taking a short siesta break. All too soon, it was time to pack up and take off for the long drive back, stopping in Tapraya just long enough to pick up Phally, before heading on to the camp.

Not far from Site 2, we were flagged down by an agitated Joe, who told us that the situation in the camp was very bad and that we must not proceed, telling us that hundreds of demonstrators had marched on the DPPU offices, surrounding them and demanding their rights. All workers, including UN staff, had left the camp. Marg and I talked it over then decided that we must continue on, as the women all had small children at home and needed to be with them. Joe was not happy about our decision, warning us that we must go in at our own risk, but we went anyway.

There were no soldiers on guard duty at the gates as we drove through, but we could hear the shouting from demonstrators in the background. We had not gone far, when our progress was halted by a screaming, baton-wielding group surrounding the car. They checked us out, then, realizing there were only women on board, they waved us on. The crowd parted, making way for us to proceed but it was slow going. As soon as I found a clear space I stopped, beckoning to my passengers to alight and make their way home from there, then turned around and headed out without any trouble. It would be a few days before the demonstrators calmed down, order was restored and workers were allowed back into the camp.

The ladies turned up at the next meeting, full of talk about their excursion and telling us how much this rare outing had meant to them.

As I was soon to return home for a break, these meetings would cease for that time, so I suggested to the women that they meet at each other's houses for a cup of tea and chat once a week. Later, I learnt that these weekly meetings had proved highly successful, one of the women telling me that, "We just laughed and laughed." This was great for these people, who could barely raise a smile before.

Over the months I had been involved with this group, I could see an emerging confidence and a dramatic rise in self-esteem. It had taken such a small amount of time and little effort to make these changes, just the fact that they knew someone cared about them and they were not alone with their worries had made so much difference. It was gratifying to see the results.

Repatriation Looms

Talk of repatriation had been going on for a year or more, but now it was becoming a reality, due to the signing of the Peace Accord on October 23rd, 1991, in Paris, under the auspices of United Nations. Nineteen countries had signed this agreement committing themselves to 'promote and encourage respect for and observance of human rights and fundamental freedoms in Cambodia.' The accords were made to put an end to the twelve-year war, declaring that all factions - Government forces, ANS, KPNLF and KR - must disarm before democratic elections were to be held in approximately one and a half years from the signing.

Despite the signing of this treaty, it took some time for the camp people to believe that peace in their country was at last in sight. Only two years before, peace talks had failed at a Paris conference and they feared a repeat. However, it did not take long for the young people to get into the party spirit when camp administrations organized many celebrations to mark this historic event. Streets and buildings were decorated, parades held and dancing areas set up. Before long, the streets were full of revellers waving flags, dancing, laughing and cheering at the good news. Celebrations continued into the night and next day, when the reality of peace in Cambodia finally sunk in. It was great to move around the camp and see the joy of the people, when they realized that they would be heading home at last.

I was being kept very busy, still overseeing the fine arts groups, checking out and examining lifeguards, holding street children excursions and the prison family support group. The larger programmes of fine arts and Lifeguards were mostly run by their Cambodian leaders now, though, I was still required to bring in monthly supplies and oversee them.

As repatriation neared, it was decided to hold a combined dance and drama festival, giving all a chance to see this traditional art before the camp closed. A public performance would be held in the largest dance building in Dong Rek camp, as well as individual presentations in the respective dance centres. Invitations were issued to camp leaders and aid workers, for the main performance on opening day, at which, each group would contribute at least one item. The festival would last all week.

An Australian friend, Andrea, was visiting at that time, so I seconded her to train a team of girls as usherettes. On the big day, the girls presented themselves looking beautiful, all dressed in similar silk outfits with coloured scarves around their waists and flowers in their hair. They took their places at the door, to hand out programmes to the guests and pass them on to girls inside, who would usher them to their seats.

The festival turned out to be a huge success, attended by many camp leaders and foreigners working in the camp, who had not been afforded the opportunity of watching traditional dance and drama performed before. Short dramas were especially written for the festival and each dance group chose to perform their own favourite dance. Presentations on all facets of Cambodian traditional dance and drama were held, showing cha-am, mohory theatre, yike theatre, mime, basak, classical and folk dance. The crowds loved it.

After the main performance on the first day, each centre entertained people in their section for the rest of the week, with daily presentations drawing huge audiences.

This festival provided a memorable finale for the fine arts programme. Groups would still continue with performances, but we realized that soon, as repatriation got under way, dancers and actors would be lost to the programme as they returned to their country.

Pen Chenda, my good friend and translator, came to tell me that he planned to leave for Phnom Penh, where he would look for work, deciding it would be better to go early, rather than wait for repatriation when jobs could be more difficult to find.

The international group sent into Cambodia to monitor the elections, UNTAC (United Nations Transition Authority of Cambodia), planned to hold examinations in the camp for English speakers, the successful applicants to be employed as translators in Cambodia. Being assured of employment on return would set many minds at rest, as this was a big worry for camp people.

As these tests would soon be held, Chenda decided to wait and take part in the them before making his way over the border. He would go alone, leaving his wife and six children to be repatriated at a later date by UNHCR.

The examinations were held and many camp people were successful. According to UNTAC officials, who held the examination, Site 2 people, taught by English speakers, were far ahead of their counterparts in Cambodia. Successful applicants were rated in three categories: good, average and basic - receiving cards indicating their level. Translators would be paid according to the level achieved.

Chenda passed with flying colours and received a level-one rating. Now, he would leave. I was very sad to see him go, as we had become good friends. I would also miss him as my translator and wondered if I would ever see him again. We promised to keep in touch.

January 1992. As the time for the first repatriation drew near, camp people were getting very nervous. Would they be accepted by the people who had stayed behind? Where would they find employment? Where would they live? These were the questions they repeatedly asked.

Registration for repatriation was now complete. People had chosen the province to which they wished to return. UNHCR had given families a choice of the following options from which to choose:

(a) Receive building materials for a small house and land
(b) Receive implements and assistance to set up a business
(c) Receive $50 cash per adult and $25 per child

All returnees, no matter which option they chose, would receive a weekly ration similar to that provided in the camp, for twelve months after return. Most people chose to take the cash incentive, which was later to prove the best option. Land given to UNHCR for returnees was never good. Usually, it was far from the village, often under water in the wet season and many times when people went to claim their property, they were forced to pay for it by village leaders.

Plans were ready for UNHCR to return 40,000-50,000 people a month back to Cambodia, from all camps along the border. A staging area had been set up in Site 2 for the first part of the repatriation procedure. People chosen were to make their way there with their belongings, where they would be processed. They would stay the night in these quarters, before boarding buses bound for Cambodia early next morning. The date for the first group's repatriation was March 30, 1992.

Stephen and I made our way to the staging area, when we arrived in camp that day. The first group would be people choosing to return to Bantheay Meanchey, the closest province. By 7.30am the 527 returnees were sitting in the twelve buses, their luggage already stowed aboard, waiting nervously for their return home. We put our heads inside the door of each bus, wishing the occupants good luck on this, a very memorable occasion. UNHCR, together with DPPU officials, had planned an official send-off for the first group of returnees, choosing to hold this ceremony in the rice distribution field in Rithysen camp. Marquees had been set up, with the seats already occupied by invited dignitaries, camp leaders, heads of aid organizations, embassy representatives and more than a hundred journalists.

The people were quite confused when they arrived at the reception centre, as they thought they were on their way to Cambodia. This was a traumatic time for them and all they wanted was to get home, but first they had to sit while speeches were presented by Col. Suchinda, the Supreme Commander of the Thai Military, officers from UNHCR, camp leaders and other officials. Each family was presented with a gift from UNHCR and finally, after two hours, the ceremony was over and the people reboarded the buses for the long-awaited journey home.

While all this was going on I met a friend, Phil Blenkinsop, a photographer based in Bangkok, who was from my home town of Perth. He told me that the journalists had been invited to accompany the convoy on their return to Sisophon in Cambodia, and suggested that I join them on one of the press buses. After years of working with these people and hearing of their longing to return, I wanted to be there with them on this auspicious occasion. I decided to give it a try. I boarded one of the two buses full of journalists. No one seemed to be there to screen passengers or check credentials, so I made my way up to the back where I found a carton to sit on, for all seats were taken.

Repatriation buses took off and our vehicles followed. As they made their way out of the camp, the streets were packed with waving people. It seemed the whole population of Site 2 had turned out to wish them luck on their return home.

We drove along the road to Aranyaprathet, branching off to the border road, arriving there at midday. Everyone had to leave the buses here, to cross the border on foot, before reboarding for the final leg of the journey. The buses were held up for more than an hour at this border crossing, during which time I walked along, talking to the returnees. One of the fine arts guys was returning with his family and he invited me to join them for the remainder of the journey. I accepted his invitation, happy to have the opportunity to share in this experience with the returnees. It was not long before UNHCR officials checking all the buses, saw me with the people and ordered me off, saying no foreigners were permitted to travel with the Cambodians. I waited until the officials left then climbed back on again.

A French girl, Olivia, whom I knew from the camp, looked in and I invited her to join me, soon to be followed by a Japanese journalist. Just as the convoy was preparing to leave UNHCR officials made a final check of all buses. An officer saw the Japanese guy and ordered him off. Meanwhile, Olivia and I covered our heads and leant over so only our backs could be seen. We withstood this check and the buses took off.

It was great to be with the returnees and see their reactions as we sped along through small towns and villages. It was very emotional, as many were in tears at the sight of their country after all those years of exile. Along the way, there were banners flying with 'Welcome Home' printed in large letters, people lining the road, schoolchildren clapping and waving small Cambodian flags, many passing in gifts of fruit and bottles of water, each time we slowed down. Our bus was full of chatter and parents were busily pointing out coconut palms and mango trees, to their children; things they knew nothing about. There was great excitement when the children saw their first buffalo, screaming with delight, pointing and calling out to their parents. One woman saw someone she knew in one of the villages, joyfully calling out to her. The women were all talking nonstop, but the men were strangely quiet, just looking out, many with concerned looks on their faces, no doubt worrying about their acceptance, jobs, and future support of their families.

Two hours later, we arrived in Sisophon to a great reception. As we drove through the town there were thousands lining the streets, many looking anxiously at the faces in the buses hoping to find lost relatives. We left the town, driving for another five kilometres before arriving at the reception centre. Returnees would spend a week here, to have medical checks and more processing before being taken with their belongings by truck to their chosen destination.

However, before any of this could take place, the people had to endure more official ceremonies. Everyone was taken off the buses and made to stand in line while waiting for Prince Sihanouk to arrive. By now, the people were very tired, children fretting, babies crying and I could see that all they wanted to do was settle in.

The Thai Supreme Commander arrived and took his place on the podium. He was becoming very edgy whilst waiting for Prince Sihanouk, who was already one hour late. Eventually, we heard the sound of his helicopter in the distance. The landing pad was cleared of people, who all stood back but not far enough. They realized their error when the helicopter came in to land, the rotors blowing up clouds of red dust, completely enveloping those close by and covering waiting officials. This did not make the Supreme Commander any happier and he left, not waiting to greet the prince.

It was extremely hot, and everyone was very thirsty, but there was no drinking water available. The gathering had to endure another hour of speeches by Prince Sihanouk and Cambodian officials. It was now time for us to leave, as we must be over the border before it was closed for the night. As we were ushered back on to the press buses at 5pm, I looked back to see the returnees still sitting in the same place, looking absolutely exhausted after a traumatic and tiring day that began for them at 4am.

I felt myself to be very fortunate to have had this opportunity to share such a momentous occasion with the Cambodian people. From this day on, the repatriation buses were to leave Site 2, twice a week, filled with people making their journey home.

About this time, soon after workers arrived in the camp, a fire started in one of the huts in Ampil, close to the camp entrance. Fanned by strong winds, it was soon out of control, sweeping across almost the entire Ampil and San Ro camps, destroying everything in its path. The bamboo and thatch huts were no match for the intensity of the flames, which demolished them in a matter of seconds. At the height of the fire, flames were leaping five to six metres in the air, the heat unbearable. There was chaos, as screaming people fled, most with not enough time to grab anything. Nothing in the fire's path was saved; administration buildings, Teacher Training College, Technical School, education offices, coffee shops, Lifeguard Centre, KWA/MHTH, all suffered the same fate as did 1,700 homes. In the matter of an hour, more than 8,000 people were homeless and destitute. Camp administrations, the UN and aid organizations lost books, files, equipment and stores. Years of work was destroyed. Casualties from this conflagration were amazingly low, with reports of only one death and twenty people treated for minor burns.

When aid workers arrived the next day, devastation greeted them. The whole area where the fire had swept through was now a pile of grey ash with smoke still rising in places. Broken water barrels, charred books, and the remains of sewing machines and generators were everywhere. Some people wandering aimlessly while others picked through the ashes hoping to find something that had survived the inferno. It was a sad sight.

I rang the Australian Embassy in Bangkok to request assistance for the people left destitute by the fire. They were fantastic, immediately promising AUD$10,000 for the fire victims. Lud and I took the bus to Bangkok the following day, to pick up this welcome donation and purchase supplies. On arrival at the Embassy, we were greeted with the good news that they would now double the original offer for this worthy cause. The cheque for AUD$20,000 was made out to COERR, so after receiving it from embassy officials we made our way to that office. Then, in a COERR truck, we headed for Bobe market to purchase supplies of clothes for the fire victims.

The afternoon was spent choosing sarongs, T-shirts, men's pants and children's clothes, completely filling the back of the truck. These goods would be transported to the border next day. After consultation with COERR officials, we decided to spend the remaining money on cooking pots and jerry cans. These would be useful items, both in the camp and for when the people returned to Cambodia.

The ANZ women's group had also heard about the fire and boxes of donated clothes were waiting for us at the guesthouse when we returned from the market. The immediate response from the Australian people was fantastic.

A few days later, supplies were all in the camp and gifts of clothing, jerry cans and cooking pots were presented to fire victims. The recipients were most grateful for these donations, as nothing had survived the fire.

As I looked around at the desolate area that had previously housed a thriving community, I could not help but wonder when the misery would end for these people. It seemed that they would just survive one tragedy to be hit by another, time after time.

CHAPTER 11

Our journey for peace begins today and every day. Slowly, slowly, each step is a prayer, each step is a meditation, each step will build a bridge.

Maha Ghosananda

A peace walk (Dhamma Yietra) was being planned in Cambodia. Its purpose being, to take the spirit of peace into areas that had only known fighting for many years and to spread the word of peace to villagers along the way, through the demonstration of nonviolent behaviour, prayers and Buddhist teachings. The supreme patriarch monk of Cambodia would lead this walk. This monk, Maha Ghosananda, was known, loved and respected by all Cambodians, a man who directed his steps to helping his troubled compatriots search for peace after decades of war. When talking to his people, he would spread the peace message: Cambodia will only know peace when all Cambodians discover peace in their own hearts.

The walk was planned to start in the north-western town of Battambang, proceeding through rural communities to Pailin, the headquarters of the Khmer Rouge, continuing on, to finish one month later, at the temples of Angkor Wat in Siem Reap province, a distance of 430 kilometres. This arrival was planned to coincide with Vesak Puja, the highest holy day of Buddhism.

I intended to take part in this walk. Concerned for my safety, Tim, who was now working on a landmine awareness programme in Cambodia, tried to dissuade me from participating. However, when these efforts failed, he decided to join, as well, telling friends, "I will go along to look after my mother." How true this would prove to be!

Liz and Bob had both resigned from their jobs in the camp, forming a group, CPR (Coalition for Peace and Reconciliation) aimed at promoting peace in Cambodia, through nonviolent means, with their headquarters now in Phnom Penh. It was great to catch up with them in Battambang, where they were assisting with the organization of the Dhamma Yietra.

A week before starting time, I joined with many others in the pre-walk training, which included nonviolence, landmine awareness, first aid, short walks and instructions for participants. Walkers were advised to keep luggage to a minimum: mat, mosquito net and change of clothes. Although trucks would accompany the walk, to carry the bags, there would be times when vehicles could not get through and walkers would have their own packs and daily water supply to carry.

Prospective participants from all over the country assembled at Wat Bo Viel, the planned take-off point in Battambang. Cheered on by hundreds of wellwishers, the Dhamma Yietra took off at 7am, wending its way through the streets of Battambang town, before heading out on Route 10, towards Pailin. The walk created quite a spectacle, led as it was by Maha Ghosananda and 450 monks in their bright orange robes, followed by 150 nuns in white, a hundred or more lay people bringing up the rear.

Many, locals and foreigners, had joined in to support the walk to its first destination of Omal village, ten of these foreigners, planning to stay on to complete the full walk. The presence of foreigners in the entourage added stimulus to the walk, gave hope to villagers along the way and reassured them that there was concern for their country in the outside world.

The blazing sun did not deter the crowds, who lined the roads as we made our way towards Omal, this first part of the walk taking three hours. We arrived hot and tired, found a shady spot and sprawled out on the rocky ground, happy for the respite. In no time, we were surrounded by hundreds of curious villagers; men, women and children gathered around to look, staying to watch us eat, observing our every move. We did not realize then that we would experience this unwanted attention right through. Lunch was followed by a rest period, before setting off again at 2pm, the hottest time of the day, for the eight-kilometre walk to Wat Phnom Sampo, where we would spend the first night. By now, local supporters had departed to return to Battambang.

The walk always followed the same format with the monks leading, followed by nuns, with lay people bringing up the rear. This meant we were last in, making it difficult to find a suitable place to sleep, where the ground was free of rocks and where we could find somewhere to hang our mosquito nets. At this first overnight stop, we were fortunate to find a grassed area about two hundred metres from the pagoda, where the ten foreign walkers assembled. Four Americans - Liz, Bob, Patty, Kevin; two Australians - Tim and myself; two Thais – Daa and Fang; one Indian – Ashoke; one Malaysian - Sam, made up this group. There were no trees, so we found some long sticks that we pounded into the hard ground with rocks, stringing our mosquito nets from these and making sure it was all set up before darkness fell, as there was no lighting here.

Water for bathing was always a problem, with so many people arriving at the village pagodas. We bathed outside, clad in a sarong, and as the walk progressed, we experienced many different ways of performing this task. We would wash, using water from a bucket, barrel or well, or if we were lucky, in dams or rivers, the latter to be shared with local buffalo, cows and dogs. Sometimes, kindly villagers would invite us into their yard to share their meagre water supply.

All food for walkers was supplied by villagers. This was a mammoth task, but no matter what time we arrived or how small the village, within a short time of the call being broadcast over the speakers, local people would start arriving with their offerings of food for the walkers. In the poorer villages, it would often be watery cabbage soup, peanuts or mangoes, in bigger towns, chicken or fish dishes, but nobody ever went hungry. The generosity of these villagers was astounding.

The walk would start at five o'clock each morning, the walkers awakened by the loud ringing of the temple bells at 4.30am. The first couple of times, it took me a while to wash, get dressed and pack up in that time and I had to hurry to catch up with the group. However, it was not long before I learnt to organize things the night before, so that I could make the end of the line before they took off. We would walk for about three hours before it became too hot, stopping for breakfast either on the side of the road or in a village pagoda, then continue walking, always arriving at our destination before 11am so the monks could eat their last meal of the day before midday.

Toilets had been one of my main worries before embarking on this journey, as I knew that these amenities were not provided in villages, nor in most pagodas. However, this did not prove to be a huge problem, as feared. Although we were drinking litres of water, it was all being sweated out. We learnt to find somewhere to squat after dark and if you did come across a monk doing the same, or vice versa, you discreetly moved on; after a few days, none of this really mattered. Getting dressed in the midst of seven hundred or more people was a worry at first but I soon became adept at holding a sarong up under my chin, while I dressed beneath.

As we made our way out of the pagodas each morning, hundreds of people would be lining the roads with their buckets of water, decorated with flowers and candles, palms joined together in greeting, waiting patiently to receive their water blessing from the monks. Even in remote areas, word spread from village to village and scores of people turned out to hear the words of peace and receive their blessing. As we neared the war zone, soldiers on their knees, with their guns lying beside them, were waiting. One soldier, beseeched Maha Ghosananda to bless his gun, so the bullets might miss their intended targets, saying, "I pray that I will not kill anyone. I pray for an end to this war."

After three days walking, we heard the sounds of battle in the distance as we approached the village of Ban Ampil. We passed many people on the road, running from the fighting. Warnings not to step off the road were given to all walkers, as we were now in landmine territory. Young men, trained in landmine awareness, were now scouting ahead, reconnoitring for mines or booby traps, which could have been planted on the road the night before.

Everyone was tired after walking for days, blisters appearing, bandaged feet and swollen ankles but no one was giving up. The physical demands of the walk only served to remind us of the purpose of the journey. When I spoke to one of the monks, saying my feet were very sore, his answer was: "The pain in your feet brings you closer to the pain of Cambodia. Suffering can alleviate suffering."

As we came closer to the war zone, a broadcast over the Khmer Rouge radio station was heard telling their people that the walk, which was approaching, was 'Just another army, but without guns!' We wondered what our reception would be.

Many villagers had already evacuated Ban Ampil when we arrived on the fourth day, so the meal was very sparse, consisting of rice, peanuts and watery soup. We didn't care, as we were never hungry when we arrived, always so tired that all we wanted to do was crash. However, it was impossible to get away from prying eyes and this was getting at everybody. People would arrive, form a circle around the foreigners, never saying a word and just stare, it was very unnerving.

Now that we had left the larger towns, the water available for bathing and washing bodies and clothes was brown and smelly. Bottled drinking water was still being brought in each day by truck but we were warned that soon the roads would disappear and we would have to drink the local stuff, using purifying tablets.

The pagoda where we were to stay overnight was surrounded by landmines, keeping Tim and his assistants busy fencing off and posting warning signs, which featured skull and crossbones with 'DANGER MINES' in both Khmer and English. Within the first hour of our arrival, there were five landmine explosions close by and as we settled down for the night, the sounds of battle could be heard raging not far away.

We spent an uneasy night, having to contend with ants and insects, as well as the steady boom, boom, of the guns, which remained audible through until morning. It would be daylight before we could venture on to the road now, due to the possibility of landmines or booby traps. When we took off, more warnings were given for everyone to stay in the middle of the road, but still some of the young monks thought it macho to step into the fields when we stopped for a rest. Tanks and government troops now shared the road with us, all heading in the same direction.

The walk continued on to Kilo 38, usually a bustling village but now a ghost town, as all villagers had fled the fighting. Walkers paused here for prayers and meditation, as shells continued to fly over our heads towards Khmer Rouge territory. We could feel the ground shake under our feet as they landed. Government soldiers and tanks were now returning from the front, their commander telling our leaders that they were retreating and advising the walkers to do the same. We were told the Khmer Rouge were advancing and would soon be in this village. Organizers of the walk held a meeting, the outcome of which was the decision to return to Ban Ampil. This was disappointing for the walkers, as the aim of the walk was to continue into Khmer Rouge territory to spread the word of peace, after all, that was what the walk was all about! However, we had to follow instructions.

We reluctantly turned to retrace our steps. Confusion ensued, as some of the young monks panicked, catching whatever transport was available, motorbikes, carts or trucks, to take them back to Ban Ampil, while the remaining walkers trudged along in searing heat, the sounds of battle loud in our ears.

Our return triggered off panic in Ban Ampil and within a short time all remaining villagers were evacuating on oxcarts, motorbikes, bicycles and on foot, families with all their belongings including chickens, pigs and cows. We learnt later that the villagers had decided that if the monks returned, then things must be serious, leaving them no option but to evacuate. Little did we know we were soon to join them!

We settled back into the pagoda and were just setting up our sleeping gear for the night, when we were told that we must also withdraw, as the situation was worsening, so we packed up and joined the refugees. By this time, the road was full, darkness had fallen and it was difficult to keep our footing on the potholed surface while carrying our heavy backpacks. It was an eerie feeling, shuffling along the road in the dark with hundreds of refugees, the only sounds the scraping of many feet and the steady beat of the Japanese monk's drum at the head of the column, everyone deep in their own thoughts of survival. After three hours, we arrived back at the pagoda where we had been two nights before, all exhausted after a long and stressful day. We found somewhere to hang our mosquito nets and crashed.

The decision had now been made to revert to another route, which would take us along paths so narrow that we must walk in single file. This would stretch the walk out to more than two kilometres long. Backpacks containing sleeping gear, clothes and water for two days would now have to be carried, as trucks could no longer get through.

We headed off on this new route two days later, our last stop being at a deserted army outpost, where we sat in the blazing sun to eat our lunch before venturing on to the track, now deep into tree-less landmine territory. It was Liz's 31st birthday.

After ninety minute's walking, some of the older monks and nuns had stopped to rest on the track, causing a split in the ranks, but the foreigners stayed together, continuing on. Rockets were flying over our heads and exploding on the other side, giving us some indication of what lay ahead.

A group of government soldiers came out of their camp, gathering on the side of the track to watch the procession. Two of their number joined in to guide the walkers along the safe path, after one of the monks had asked for their help. We had only gone about two hundred metres with these two extra walkers, when Khmer Rouge soldiers on the opposite side of the track caught sight of soldiers among the walkers and opened fire. This was when we were caught in the crossfire and all hit the ground.

The battle raged on over our heads for what seemed an age, before there was a lull in the fighting. Monks next to us got to their feet and ran back towards where others were sheltering about ten metres away. I turned to Tim lying next to me, asking, "What shall we do?" By this time, more people were running back, so we decided to join them, crouching as we ran. We had only gone a few metres when gunfire broke out and we all hit the ground again. This, we found later, was when people were hit.

After the gunfire died down, we joined a group of walkers sheltering under a tree, all unsure of what to do next, the nuns praying loudly. It was not long before Khmer Rouge soldiers came along, telling us to resume walking. We all rose to our feet and began to move forward hesitantly. Not far along the track, we came on one of our walkers, who had been wounded in the shoulder. He was crying out in pain as medics treated him.

Further on, an old man from the pagoda was sitting on the side of the track holding his injured leg, from which blood was pouring, a serene look on his face, though he must have been in considerable pain.

As Tim, the official photographer, stopped to take a photo, an irate KR soldier came running up and grabbed the camera, another seized the back of my shirt and started pushing and pulling me along the path, shouting in anger as he did so. I had hold of Tim's arm as I was dragged about a hundred metres along the track, on the way, passing the body of the monk lying beside the path. When the soldiers saw this, they became very distressed, screaming out: "We've killed a monk, we've killed a monk!" - this being the worst deed a Buddhist can commit.

We were pushed to the ground, our bags confiscated, while one of the soldiers gestured towards my money belt. I went to open it, which made him very angry and he hit me across the face, knocking my sunglasses off, then grabbed the belt and dragged me towards him. Tim told them to wait while he came around to unbuckle it, before handing it over, whispering to me as he did so to stay calm and avoid direct eye contact.

By this time, Liz, Kevin, Patty and Daa, had also been captured. When he saw that Patty was upset, Tim called out to her, "Just do as they tell you."

The soldier closest to him raised the butt of his gun over Tim's head in a threatening manner but fortunately did not use it. They threw Daa, who had long hair tied back in a ponytail, to the ground, grabbed the krama round his neck, forcing back his head and spitting the words 'Yuon, yuon' in his face.

Tim and I both called out, "He's Thai, he's Thai," knowing they would kill him if they considered him Vietnamese. They left him alone.

Meanwhile, the rest of the walkers were passing fast, eyes glued to the ground, though I did see some of them sneaking glances across at us. When told by the soldiers to follow them into the forest, we looked at each other in dismay, knowing we were in landmine territory. But we had no choice, so, flanked by eight armed KR soldiers, we were led off. I could not help but think of the three foreigners, one Australian woman and a British man and woman, who had been taken by the KR a matter of weeks before, with no clue as to their whereabouts. We were to find out later that they had already been slain by their captors, their bodies found a few weeks later.

Now, recalling the landmine training, I tried to walk in the footsteps of the soldier in front, but he was walking too fast, so I gave up, trusting he knew the area well.

The soldiers were asking us: "Have you heard of the Khmer Rouge? Are you afraid?"

Liz replied in Khmer that we are not afraid of the KR but we are frightened of landmines.

They set a fast pace and we had to follow. They were urging us to go faster, which was difficult, as the ground was uneven and we were very tired. We were led through head high elephant grass, the sharp blades cutting arms and legs, our clothes sticking to our backs as we pushed on under the hot sun, unsure where we were being taken.

Tim's bag had been handed back to him when they stole the others, obviously too worn out for them to consider. Inside was a dangerous looking machete, to be used for prodding for landmines. I was concerned, as we didn't know what lay ahead, whispering to Tim to get rid of it. As we walked, he slid it out, dropping it into a clump of grass beside the track where it bounced on its end and fell back next to the path. Luckily, no one saw it.

After twenty minutes of fast walking we met up with other KR soldiers. By this time, we were very thirsty. They gave us water to drink from our bottles they had confiscated and after a short rest, we took off again. We had to trust that they knew the area, though we were concerned when the leading soldier started off on one of the many paths, only to be stopped by another calling out, "No, no, not that way there are landmines there!"

As we made our way further into the forest, rockets were still flying over our heads and we had to hit the ground a number of times. Not sure if we would make it out, I took this opportunity of whispering, "Tim, I love you, I'm sorry I got you into this."

He was great, his arm around me helping me along, even though he was limping himself. I was afraid that this attention may antagonize the soldiers and told him so. Tim turned to the soldiers, telling them, "This is my mother and I am looking after her." This prompted a distinct change in their attitude towards us, the soldiers then becoming quite friendly, asking the usual Cambodian questions: "How old are you? How many children do you have?"

We had now reached a clearing in the forest, the soldiers concerned about our white shirts, saying that we could easily be seen by the enemy and demanding that we take them off. Kevin assured them that we were as white underneath, so after a short consultation they allowed us to cover the shirts with our kramas.

The leading soldiers stopped a few times to see if we were being followed, once in the middle of an open area where they shushed us, indicating they had heard something. Their hearing must have been very acute, as we had not heard a thing. They were whispering amongst themselves, saying, "Is it us, or is it them?" A discussion ensued then one of them called out loudly, "Oy!"

We waited for the bullets! Luckily, the answer came back, "It's us!" More soldiers emerged from the bushes and joined us, now our captors numbered fifteen.

We were told that they were taking us to their base on the Thai border, about three hours walk, where the Thais had built a good road for them. Around this time there had been much conjecture about the Thai Military assisting the Khmer Rouge, hotly denied by the Thais, but now confirmed by these soldiers.

Another hour's walking brought us to a clump of trees where more soldiers were sheltering. Their commander, was busy talking on his radio, saying he had six foreigners with whom he was unable to communicate. A soldier accompanying us was quick to intervene, telling him not to worry as Liz spoke Khmer fluently. On hearing this, he relaxed.

First, he spoke to Daa in Thai, apologizing profusely because he, a Thai, had been taken, saying, "You are our brothers and neighbours, you understand us!" Then he turned to us, wanting to know what the foreigners were doing here. Liz was able to explain about the Dhamma Yietra, its purpose and about the leader, Maha Ghosananda. The commander already knew of this monk and related the work he had done in the border refugee camps. He said that the Khmer Rouge want foreigners in Cambodia to remain neutral and non-partisan, to understand that all Cambodians, including the Khmer Rouge, want peace, but they intended to keep fighting until their country was liberated from the puppet Vietnamese government. He spoke to us for more than an hour, during which time, he asked that we not say bad things about them to the press, apologizing for the killing of the monk and requesting that apologies be given to Maha Ghosananda for the disruption to the Dhamma Yietra.

While this was going on, soldiers were busy going through our bags under another tree, sharing out the loot. The commander said he was sorry that we had been robbed but that the soldiers with our belongings were far away by now, then asked us each in turn, what we had lost, writing it down. I guess, so he could share in it later! After more apologies and assurances that they want peace too, he told us we were free to go, but advised us not to go to Bavel, the town where the walk was headed, as the Khmer Rouge were set to take that town.

Liz asked for an escort to guide us through the minefields, but he refused, pointing out which track to take. We looked in dismay at the direction he had indicated, realizing how difficult this would be, as there were many small paths crisscrossing each other. It was now the middle of the afternoon and very hot. We were given two litres of water and sent on our way.

The track we followed was very uneven, making it difficult to keep on our feet and to make it worse, rockets were still flying over our heads and exploding nearby. Tim was limping along on his sore leg and I was so tired I found it hard to keep up, but we had to maintain a fast pace in an endeavour to make it out before dark.

It was an hour before we stumbled on the path the walkers had taken, identifiable by the litter. Only that morning, we had reprimanded the walkers for discarding empty water bottles and papers along the way, but now we were pleased that these signs were there, giving us an indication that we were now on the right track. We turned left, hoping we were heading in the direction which would lead us to the walkers. After twenty minutes staggering along this path, we caught sight of a local man coming towards us. It was a relief to meet up with another person, indicating that we could not be too far from a village. The villager told us that he had come with an oxcart earlier, to pick up the dead and wounded peace walkers, but had dropped his watch and had now come back to retrieve it. What luck for us, as we now knew we were on the right track! He told us that there were some walkers about two kilometres ahead. It turned out to be five.

All the water had gone by now and we were exhausted and terribly thirsty. Ahead of us, we spotted water lying in a rice field, giving us renewed energy at the thought of a welcoming drink. Unfortunately, this water had been lying there for some time and was covered in green slime. I did not care, falling down on my knees in it, soaking my head, hat and krama. I even filled my water bottle with this stinking water after filtering it through my krama, and adding a purifying tablet. I had to wait ten minutes before having a swill; it tasted beautiful! The others would not try it, preferring to wait. This was when I made a vow that I would never go anywhere without water again!

We pushed on, finally coming upon some monks and nuns resting under a tree. It was great to catch up with people from the walk before continuing. Another kilometre along the track, more walkers had settled at a waterhole. By this time my clothes were filthy and I could hardly lift one foot after another. The nuns were great, pouring water over me, clothes and all, massaging my legs, while Tim massaged my feet. This short respite rejuvenated us and we took off again, determined to reach Bavel before nightfall. We had been walking another fifteen minutes, when motorbikes appeared searching out stragglers. I climbed aboard, thankful to be off my feet at last. Word had spread around the town that the foreigners had been taken by the Khmer Rouge, which to them, meant a death sentence, so as we made our way through the streets and people realized we had survived, we received a tumultuous welcome.

Another great reception awaited us at the pagoda, where we were soon surrounded by walkers happy to see us alive and well, Sam and Fang running up to give us big hugs. Nuns gathered around to massage my legs and bring food. It was great to be back again, though we were distressed to learn that a nun, as well as the monk, had been killed and five people wounded in the fighting.

Local villagers came over to offer us sleeping quarters for the night. We gratefully accepted, as it would be good to get away on our own after such an exhausting and stressful day. Liz would certainly have a birthday to remember!

We settled down on the floor, where quilts had been placed for us to sleep on. Sleep came fast, as we were all so tired, but we had a rude awakening at 5am by very heavy shelling close by. My first thought was, 'Oh no, I'm not ready for this!'

True to their word, the Khmer Rouge were attacking the town. We crawled out and flattened ourselves on the ground under the house. A lull in the fighting a short time later, gave us the opportunity to hurry over to the temple where many frightened people were taking shelter. The Khmer Rouge were unsuccessful in their efforts to take the town of Bavel and after another hour they gave up and all was quiet again.

That morning a memorial service was held for the two dead. It was a very touching ceremony with many of the monks in tears, Maha Ghosananda making the statement: "We will continue the Dhamma Yietra. This violence is indeed why we are walking. It is regrettable, but it is also the reason to continue, to diffuse war with loving peace and compassion, so we may achieve peace and reconciliation."

A guard of honour was formed by the 450 monks stretching out along each side of the road as the cars containing the two bodies set out on the sad journey back to Battambang.

One of the nuns, embodying the spirit of the Dhamma Yietra, said, "I am not angry. I forgive the Khmer Rouge. If we go on seeking revenge each time, it will never end. We are tired of the war and violence, that is why we are walking, to cultivate peace and nonviolence in our hearts and country, so we must continue the walk. The alternative is accepting the bloodshed and then the violence and destruction will never stop."

The Dhamma Yietra pressed on; the number of walkers had swelled to almost double its original size, everyone more determined than ever to complete the walk. It progressed through areas that had known nothing but war for the past ten years, the people living in constant fear and anxiety, yet still turning out to receive their water blessing and hear the words of peace. Many of these were displaced persons, who were forced to flee their homes numerous times and were now living out in the fields.

Two weeks later, the Dhamma Yietra walked quietly into Siem Reap town, continuing on to the temples of Angkor Wat to hold a commemoration ceremony to mark the end of this epic march for peace, Maha Ghosananda reiterating that peace could only come slowly, "Step by step, like breathing in and breathing out, like walking, like the way we built this monument."

This walk was to be one of the many I participated in over the years, each one with different experiences, but none as dramatic as this one.

A Final Get-Together

In Site 2, repatriation was well under way, many camp people now back in their country, a number of programmes had closed down and many aid workers were leaving, some to return home, others to work in Cambodia. Ken and I decided to bring together as many camp workers as possible, both past and present, for a big party to top all others; a fitting finale to our years of working here. We put our heads together to plan something quite different for this occasion.

We decided to stage this reunion on October 23rd, the first anniversary of the signing of the peace treaty and to hold it on the island of Koh Daich, in the Mekhong River, in Cambodia. This was the home of a former camp resident, Samnang, who had often talked about this beautiful island, inviting us to visit if ever we made it to Cambodia. Samnang had now returned and was delighted when he heard we intended to hold our celebration there. Invitations were sent out to ex-workers all over the world to attend this reunion.

It was now possible to obtain visas and enter Cambodia from the Thai border, so Ken, Kim (a new worker from Canada) and myself, took advantage of this and made our way over the border a week before the party. Arriving early would give us the opportunity to see the city, catch up with camp friends who had returned, and make arrangements before guests arrived.

By now, acceptances had been received from as far afield as France, USA, Australia, Scotland and Bangladesh, from people delighted at the prospect of meeting up with old friends and workmates.

It was a great thrill for me to make this long awaited trip, and finally have the chance to see for myself the city of Phnom Penh, about which I had heard so much from my Cambodian friends. On arrival in the city, we hired motorbike 'taxis', which took us along wide boulevards lined with huge frangipani trees. The road was filled with trucks, cars, motorbikes, cyclos and bicycles, horns blaring and bells ringing, as our bike riders kept up a fast pace, weaving in and out of the traffic completely ignoring all road rules; if there were any! I was to become accustomed to this but at this time, it was pretty scary and I just shut my eyes, hoping for the best.

There was a strong French influence here, with the wide boulevards and French colonial villas, many dilapidated, crumbling and occupied by squatters. Others were restored to their former glory and housing rich Cambodians or foreign workers. It was certainly a city of contrasts, from the restored mansions to the broken down buildings and slums of the back streets, the footpaths full of beggars, street kids and whole families living there. We found our way to the COERR office where we would stay whilst in Cambodia.

Later, we ventured out to explore Phnom Penh by night. It was a great surprise; now the dull and dirty streets we had seen earlier were a blaze of colour with neon signs flashing, strings of bright lights adorning buildings and crowds of people filling the footpaths and roads. We were surprised at the number of eating places in this city featuring foreign food, with a choice of French, Thai, Italian, Chinese, Korean, Indian and even pizzas. We had a great meal at a Chinese restaurant, leaving there at eight-thirty to find the streets almost deserted. We learned that Cambodians headed home early, making their own unofficial curfew, claiming the streets too dangerous at night. This did not seem to deter the foreigners, large numbers of whom could be seen enjoying themselves in restaurants, nightclubs, bars and dance halls.

The following morning I headed off to find my Cambodian friends. Chenda's family had now returned, so I planned to locate them first. I made my way to the office of the religious organization for which Chenda worked and from there I was directed to his house a short distance away. The whole family came running out, shouting with delight when they saw me, never expecting to see me in Phnom Penh. It was great to catch up with them. I informed Chenda of the tentative plans for the party and he and his wife kindly offered their assistance. This would be a big advantage, as they knew their way around the city by now and were adept at bargaining for the best prices.

I had Remo's address, so I found my way to his house where I received another great welcome, going on to Seng's place for another reunion. It was good to meet up with these good friends, away from the barbed wire confines of Site 2, now free in their own country. Seng and Remo took me on a guided tour of their city, covering the palace, museum, library, government buildings and parks. It was a happy day.

Ex-workers were now arriving from overseas and from the Cambodian provinces, all delighted to catch up with old friends and looking forward to the big celebration. By the time the party day dawned, everything was under control, thanks to the tireless efforts of Chenda and his family. They had bought all the food from the market, taking it to the island by boat early in the morning, where arrangements had been made for locals to prepare an evening meal for us.

Five o'clock was rendezvous time at the 'Cambodiana', a big hotel on the river in Phnom Penh. Thirty-seven people turned up, resulting in plenty of noise, talk and laughter. We had to coax everyone away at 7pm, leading them to the big wooden flat-bottomed boat that had been hired to take us to the island. Our great Cambodian friends were waiting, having already loaded the drinks, ice and luggage aboard. As the boat took off on the one-hour trip, we popped the first bottle of champagne.

A fantastic sight met our eyes on arrival at Koh Daich. About 600 people lined the shore - almost the whole population of the island. Kim and I had gone over earlier in the week to seek permission for the party and make arrangements. The word had soon spread of our party plans and impending arrival. A pathway lit with candles in paper bags had been cleared for us and as we made our way through, people on all sides were welcoming us. It was a touching reception.

As we made our way through the crowds, the head monk came forward to greet us. He formally welcomed us to their island, awarding us the freedom of his pagoda and grounds, for as long as we stayed. A great meal awaited us at the temple. There was local fish wrapped in banana leaves and cooked over the fire, chicken curry, vegetable dishes with rice, followed by fresh, island fruit. A big crowd stayed to watch us eat, waiting around to see what was next in store.

After dinner, a place was cleared for dancing and the music turned on. The watchers stood goggle-eyed, as the French people treated them to an exhibition of jiving. Cambodian dance music was also played and attempts made to include onlookers in the local dance, the romvong, but they were too shy, just being happy to stand and watch the foreigners' antics. It was 2am before the music and dancing finally finished and revellers retired to sleep on the pagoda floor, under their mosquito nets. As a treat for the young local people, we had hired a television set and video player with a number of popular videos, which kept them up all night watching the same movies over and over.

Crowds were still milling around in the morning. Samnang was not on the island but his wife came over to take us on a tour. It was a beautiful island, very clean, with banana, coconut and mango trees growing wild all over, the fruit there for the picking. All islanders were involved in the silk weaving industry; ladies could be seen sitting at their looms outside their houses, weaving magical designs. As we made our way around, we were greeted with big smiles of welcome from the locals and many invitations to join them in their homes.

Soon it was time to take our leave, as the boat had arrived for the return journey. About a hundred people made their way to the water's edge to farewell us, waving and inviting us back as the boat took off. It had been an enjoyable event, made more memorable by the great welcome from the island people.

. Now everyone was asking, "Where will the next party be held?"

A Disastrous Boat Trip

We had decided to leave the country a different way, by taking a boat up the river and into the big Tonle Sap lake to Siem Reap, home of the fabled temples of Angkor Wat. From there we would make our way over the border and back to Tapraya.

There were ten of us, who took off on this big wooden vessel, carrying about a hundred passengers, the decks covered in cargo. What a mistake! The one-day, one-night trip, turned into a four-day, three-night nightmare! Because we were expecting a short trip, we took only enough food and water for that length of time but this soon ran out. Luckily, Cambodians aboard knew that time means nothing in this country and had come prepared with plenty of supplies they willingly shared with us.

Before we left the docks in Phnom Penh, a huge iron barge, full of bricks, had been lashed to the side of our craft, causing our boat to proceed at a snail's pace. By the second day we had only covered 70 of the 350 kilometres. After enduring two days of this slow progress, we decided to get off, but by then we were a long way from land, making disembarking impossible. Tonle Sap Lake is like a huge inland sea; once out in the middle, you cannot even see the shores. For one full day and two nights, the two craft were tied up to mangrove trees in the middle of the lake, as the wind was too strong to continue. As the waves grew in size, the boats started crashing together causing the side of our boat to cave in under pressure. All the men on board were called to help, holding the barge back with their feet to prevent it causing more damage. Finally, by the third day, when the storm had not abated, they decided to cut the iron boat loose before our boat fell apart altogether.

Without this encumbrance, we zoomed along for half a day, before anchoring near land for the night. No sooner had darkness fallen than shelling starting close by. All lights were extinguished and passengers warned to be quiet as the battle raged. We survived the night, though everyone was very frightened and no one slept. We continued on to Siem Reap next morning, relieved to finally make it and step onto land again after a nightmare trip. By now, it was too late to visit Angkor Wat, as we had to return to work, so we hired taxis to take us to the border, arriving back home late that night. We had looked for a 'different' way to return and this had certainly been it.

One good thing emerged from our long journey. Ken and Agnes rekindled their romance, making plans for their future together.

1992. Ken had resigned from his job in Site 2, planning to return to the USA before going on to work in Cambodia. He and Agnes planned to marry in France, in a few months time, before they returned to live in Phnom Penh. It was sad when the time came to say goodbye to my housemate, good friend and confidante, over the last five years, never knowing if I would catch up with him again. I knew I would miss his company, good humour and friendship. I travelled up to Bangkok with him, before seeing him off at the airport, then made the long trip back to Tapraya on my own.

By now, almost half the camp population had been moved back to Cambodia, including many of my friends. The lifeguard programme had ceased to exist due to the cessation of worker rations, but the fine arts programme was still functional, though on a smaller scale. Many of the street children had returned and several of our foreign workers were leaving. I realized that my usefulness here was at an end and it was time for me to move on, too. It was with regret that I made the decision to leave at the end of the year, a couple of months away.

I was kept busy over this time finalizing programmes, balancing books, writing reports and saying farewell to my Cambodian friends, who remained. By now, the camp was only a shell of its former self. Where, previously, huts had been tightly packed together, now were many vacant spots, a pile of ashes the only sign that a family home had once stood in this place. The outskirts of the camp were now empty of huts, as remaining families were gradually moved in closer for safety reasons. The main market, previously the hub of the camp, was reduced to a few stalls, where trading still carried on but without its former hustle and bustle. Essential services such as hospitals, administration offices, dental services, mother/child health centres and family services, still remained and would until the end but only with skeleton staff.

I did not want any fanfare when I left, making sure I had said all my goodbyes well in advance, as I knew the final day would be an emotional one for me. As I drove out of the camp, I thought of my time working there and the changes I had seen over the years. Memories were both good and bad. It was reassuring, to see the vast improvement in the nutritional standards, from the earlier days, when many children were suffering malnutrition, to the much better standard of health at this time. Education was a big plus, with many teachers receiving excellent training before graduating from the TTC. Classes in public administration and law had prepared many students for the business field and nurses and medics had received top class training from qualified staff. Engineering students had learnt the basics, to prepare them for entry to university and many people were leaving the camp fluent in French and English languages. Employment should not be too much of a problem on return, for those who had taken advantage of free education available in Site 2.

On the negative side, I could see that because the camps were in operation for so long, it built up a dependency on handouts, which would be difficult for many people to come to terms with, when they returned. There were those, who had come as teenagers, now married and returning with a family, never having had to support themselves. A vast majority of camp people would return to the rural areas with no knowledge of farming, the mainstay in those regions. Many children, who had the opportunity of attending school in the camp, would be denied this advantage when they returned. Education was not free in Cambodia, though purported to be so, underpaid teachers demanding a weekly fee from students. Then there was the ever-present fear that they may not be accepted. People who had stayed in Cambodia regarded the returnees as traitors, for leaving their country in time of trouble; they resented all the benefits afforded camp people, while they struggled for an existence at home. All these things made people fearful for what they faced on return.

Life would not be easy for them.

It was good to be back home but I felt drained. For the first three weeks, I just shut myself away, hoping this would give me time to adapt. It was difficult to adjust to this life again, where everyone was intent on their own little world. Just to walk into the supermarket and choose food, having to make decisions between all the new types and brands, was difficult. To see the aisles full of pet food and witness the money people spent on these items, made me wince when I thought of the camp fare of mainly rice and tinned fish. It was difficult not to question why our lives here are so privileged, how we can just go around the corner to shop for a choice of food, go to the doctor, play sports, go to the beach or a park. Why we have freedom and democracy, when people in other parts of the world are denied these basic rights. Why two thirds of the world's people live in or below subsistence level, while we have plenty.

I soon found that nobody was really interested in listening to what was happening in other parts of the world. I guess, the attitude was, 'If its bad I don't want to know about it.' This was the hardest thing for me to face. However, I did not dwell on this aspect, as I knew I would have to readjust to this life.

A month before I left the camp, I had submitted a proposal for a human rights programme to be set up in Cambodia, so I would have to wait to see if this was approved, meantime I tried my best to settle back into Western life.

My thoughts would often drift back to the years I had spent working in the camp. How fortunate I had been to have this opportunity and how my life had been enriched by the experience; the memories of these years etched forever on my mind, knowing that after working with these courageous and resilient people, my life would never be the same. I felt privileged to have shared in their lives, listened to their stories, their hopes, fears and plans for the future. Our main job as camp workers, had been to provide hope for these people living in such desperate circumstances, to build on their hopes for the future and to encourage existing hopes, sometimes giving hope when there was none. I could only trust that some of these hopes and dreams would materialize on return to their country, that in some way, I had contributed as much to their lives as I knew I had gained from them.

As I sit here writing, the memories come flooding back. There were surely more good times than bad, because they are the ones that spring to mind when I recall those years. It is hard to write an end, because really there is no end to this story. An end to the camp, yes, but the former residents will go back to their cities, towns, villages and rice fields and their struggles will go on, because life is not easy for Cambodians. They will have to face ongoing civil war, political turmoil, landmine danger, unemployment and many other hardships, but having already perceived the courage of these people, I feel certain they will struggle through, because Cambodian people are true survivors.